THE ESSENCE OF THE BRONTËS

Muriel Spark was born in Edinburgh in 1918 and was raised and educated there. After some married years living in Africa, she returned to England, where she edited *Poetry Review* from 1947 to 1949 and published her first volume of poems, *The Fanfarlo: and Other Verse*, in 1952. In the early 1960s she worked in New York, eventually making her home in Italy. Her many novels include *Memento Mori* (1959), *The Prime of Miss Jean Brodie* (1961), *The Girls of Slender Means* (1963), *The Abbess of Crewe* (1974), *A Far Cry from Kensington* (1988) and *The Finishing School* (2004). Her short stories were collected in 1967, 1985 and 2001, and her *Collected Poems I* appeared in 1967. Dame Muriel was made Commandeur des Arts et des Lettres (France) in 1996 and awarded her DBE in 1993. She died in Italy on 13th April 2006, at the age of 88.

Also by Muriel Spark from Carcanet Press

Curriculum Vitae
All the Poems
Mary Shelley
The Golden Fleece: Essays

The Essence of the Brontës

A Compilation with Essays

Muriel Spark

Carcanet

First published in the United Kingdom in 1993 by Peter Owen Publishers

This edition first published in the United Kingdom in 2014 by
Carcanet Press Limited
Alliance House
Cross Street
Manchester M2 7AQ

www.carcanet.co.uk

A CIP catalogue record for this book is available from the British Library

ISBN 978 1 84777 246 6

The publisher acknowledges financial assistance from Arts Council England

Printed and bound in England by SRP Ltd, Exeter

Contents

Acknowledgements

Many of the Brontë letters first appeared in Mrs Gaskell's *Life of Charlotte Brontë* (1857). Others are taken from the text of *The Brontës: Their Lives, Friendships and Correspondence* (vols. 1–4 of *The Shakespeare Head Brontë*) edited by T.J. Wise and J.A. Symington (1932) (rep. Basil Blackwell 1980). For permission to reprint these letters, grateful acknowledgements are due to Messrs Basil Blackwell, Oxford.

The letters selected have been printed in full except in a few cases where irrelevant text has been omitted; in such cases the omissions have been indicated.

For valuable assistance concerning the text of these letters the editor is deeply indebted to the late Mr H.K. Grant, Hon. Librarian of the Poetry Society.

The text for 'Emily Brontë: Her Life' is taken from *Emily Brontë: Her Life and Work*, Muriel Spark and Derek Stanford, London, 1953, and New York, 1966.

Selections from Emily Brontë's poetry first appeared in *Selected Poems of Emily Brontë*, edited by Muriel Spark, London, 1952.

The 'Bookstand' piece was originally broadcast by the BBC on 16 April 1961. 'My Favourite Villain' was originally broadcast on the BBC Light Programme 'Woman's Hour', 12 October 1960.

For permission to use the amended variation on the text of Emily Brontë's poems, acknowledgements are due to C.W. Hatfield's *Complete Poems of Emily Brontë* and the publishers of that work, Columbia University Press and Oxford University Press.

Introduction
Muriel Spark and the Brontës

Boyd Tonkin

In 1976, by then long resident in Italy, Muriel Spark resumed a correspondence with her old friend Hugo Manning. One letter from Rome thanks him for the gift of a book about the Brontës. For the fêted and garlanded writer, now in her late fifties and 14 novels into a career that would comprise 22 in all as well as short stories, drama and autobiography, the book brought back memories. It sent her to a time when she had nothing and had, so far, done almost nothing of the work that she truly valued. To Manning, a poet, journalist and fellow spiritual seeker whom she had known and liked in her penniless Kensington bedsit years of the early 1950s, she recalled 'my days of Brontë study', along with 'all the poverty, adventure and hope that went with them'.

That mellow reminiscence conjures up the picture of striving apprentice author learning from the Haworth sisters in a spirit of humility, emulation and admiration. True, for three or four years after 1949, the Brontës' lives and works became something of an obsession for Spark. Among the four siblings, it was the author of *Wuthering Heights* who most directly engaged her. A BBC television script from 1961 confesses that 'For many years I was intensely occupied by Emily Brontë – almost haunted'. Already a divorced mother, but separated from her son Robin (who lived with her parents in Edinburgh), Spark had bounced around shabby post-war London from room to room and job to job – most notably, as the secretary of the Poetry Society and editor of its journal *Poetry Review*. Tethered to this shambolic and penurious Bohemia, she dreamed of the proud autonomy that would allow her to flourish as a woman and an artist. No wonder the sibyls of the West Riding appealed.

Her first book, published in 1951, was *Child of Light*, a 'reassessment' of Mary Wollstonecraft Shelley still strikingly modern in its perceptive rescue of the author of *Frankenstein* from the shadow of her husband and parents. By the time of its appearance, however, the Brontës had taken charge. Spark's plan for a joint biography to partner a new edition of Anne's works came to nothing. Still, from that project she salvaged an edition of the family's letters, published in 1954. She also edited an edition of Emily's verse (1952) and then, partly in collaboration with poet and critic Derek Stanford, her lover, collaborator, fellow-adventurer and (for a while) soulmate, produced a wider critical-biographical study (1953). These were fringe productions, researched and edited on a shoestring by aspirational young literati under the patronage of shiftless rogues and mavericks. The phrase 'labour of love' does indeed apply. But, as with Spark's co-dependent link to the erratic and exasperating Stanford, other emotions came into play as well.

Turn to what she wrote about the Brontë sisters, and – as so often with Spark – every presumption will be overthrown. (She did have some sympathy to spare for drifting and bibulous brother Branwell, so like the London literary barflies she knew, but says little about him except to note that 'his great misfortune was that he was a man' – and thus exempt from his sisters' elevating struggle.) Page by waspish, probing page, she does not hail a trio of role models or genuflect before a family of sainted path-finders. Quite the opposite. Spark tends to take the Brontë greatness as read, save for a warm appreciation of the 'traditional aspects' of Emily's verse against the unjustified neglect of 'anthologists'.

Instead, she fires at the Yorkshire heroines a sceptical salvo of reservations, qualifications, caveats and critiques. From her impatience with Charlotte as a bossy 'impresario' who turned her family into catchpenny melodrama, and her disgust with Emily's 'perverted martyrdom', through to her verdict, as late as 1992, that poor overlooked Anne was in the end 'not good enough', a querulous, suspicious or even downright hostile note recurs. Spark may love the Brontës and their work, but that does not mean she likes them very much.

What is going on here? A sentimental or conventional reader might expect the hero-worship due to stalwart godmothers in art from a successor who indirectly took the profit from their pains. Yet Spark – never in any way sentimental or conventional – sees flaws, marks limits and scolds follies at every turn. Many of her assessments read not so much like a cool appraisal as a family quarrel, bitter and intimate. She may deplore the Brontës' posthumous encirclement by soppy 'legend' and unfounded speculation. Yet Spark herself reaches the point where she can say about Emily that 'if she had not died of consumption, she would have died mentally deranged'. This, we feel, is strictly personal.

So Spark's involvement with the Brontës as critic, editor and fragmentary biographer does not take the form of simple homage or tribute. It serves instead as an exorcism or perhaps an inoculation. She has to get the sisters out of her system, if necessary by ingesting as much of their unquiet spirit as will protect her against future attacks. In the essay on the Brontës as teachers – impossible to read now without thinking of Miss Jean Brodie, whose *Prime* would arrive in 1961 – Spark writes that 'genius, if thwarted, resolves itself in an infinite capacity for inflicting trouble, or at least finding fault'. That 'thwarting' and its rancorous side-effects seemed to dog her at this period. As Martin Stannard's exemplary biography of Spark puts it, 'In her art and life she demanded acknowledgement while receiving little in either sphere. She was not breaking through as a major poet and Stanford was hesitant about marriage.' In her early thirties, stalled on more than one front, the fledgling poet, not-yet-novelist and woman of letters found in the Brontës both a deeply tempting path through hardship to glorious achievement – and the wrong road for her. She inflicted trouble and found fault with them, the better to define her own best route.

This intimate dispute had tangled roots. On Spark as both poet and critic, the rebooted classicism associated with T.S. Eliot in his post-war pomp cast a sort of spell. Already separate in outlook and aesthetics, she had via the Poetry Society and its ramshackle hangers-on had quite enough of the surreal balderdash of the 'Neo-Romantic' movement. Her pen was from the first, as Auden wrote of Christopher Isherwood's, 'strict and adult'. In her visit to Haworth churchyard for the BBC she would remark – in cooler, more balanced terms than the lonely striver of a decade previously could muster – on the gulf between Emily's dedication to 'primitive forces of life and death' and her own fictional art of ironic, analytic miniaturism, developing like 'cells in a honeycomb'.

The great erotic rhapsodies in *Jane Eyre* and *Wuthering Heights* would not so much leave her cold as chill her with the risks of a self-effacing surrender. For Charlotte, as she notes with no sign of any approval, 'the submission of a strong personality to one even stronger signified love on the highest level'. So much for Mr Rochester. As for Heathcliff, in a *Woman's Hour* broadcast in 1960 about her 'Favourite Villain', she calls him a 'real Prince of Darkness' and – crucially – 'a kind of moral hypnotist'. Only by these critical acts of exorcism, we sense, did Spark believe that she could snap out of the Brontë hypnosis. She had both to face down her tempters, and transform or convert them.

Hence the somewhat eccentric discussion of *Wuthering Heights*. Spark deems Emily a 'natural celibate' in search of a 'mystical union' and a woman who 'does not appear to have needed any object of amorous and sexual attention'. Many readers of Emily's novel, a work devoured and adored since 1848 by young readers who crave a life that revolves around 'amorous and sexual attention', will be baffled by this judgment. It is certainly not a self-portrait of the author who wrote it. When Spark writes that 'it is a generally observed fact that Emily's men and women appear to be "sexless"', the jaws of Cathy and Heathcliff's devotees will hit the floor. But such a wayward judgment might contain a glimpse of what Spark then hoped she could, or should, become.

Spark views Emily as a mystic without a vocation, indeed a nun *manquée*, who in the absence of true faith 'became her own Absolute' and sacrificed her life to this blasphemous self-image. However strained the reading, Spark stuck by it. In *Curriculum Vitae*, her selective memoir from 1992, she calls the Emily essay 'my most closely reasoned piece of non-fictional prose'. To her, Emily in effect committed suicide through self-neglect and so yielded up her own life and gift on the altar of Romantic narcissism, since Romanticism always drives its acolytes towards the 'test of action'. So ends the 'impassioned super-woman', not a mighty self-fashioner but a frail consumptive on the windswept winter moor who shuns doctors and refuses medicine. And yet, 'In an earlier age, Emily Brontë would most possibly have thrived in a convent'.

Here's the nub: Spark's 'haunting' by the sisters coincides with her gradual transition from unbelief to Christian faith. Spark had never felt close to the creed of her Jewish forebears. Yet by 1949 she could tell Stanford that 'I shall set out on a pilgrimage… searching for Faith'. As warnings, rivals, tempters, the Brontë clan and their archetypal pantheism served as stages along that path. If Nature and Imagination were their gods, the gods had failed. Step by step, she sought an ecclesiastical rock rather than a moorland cairn. As she shuttled between the bedsits of Kensington, she also began to frequent its churches: first Anglican, from 1952, and then Roman Catholic. She was confirmed into the Church of England in 1953 but a year later had already moved along to Rome. For a while after her reception into the Church, she even thought of becoming a nun.

Her Brontë immersion accompanied the crises and journeys that would re-make the jobbing literary aspirant into a lifelong, and deeply original, novelist. Her pilgrimage to faith met other obstacles. Slowly, painfully, she broke with Stanford. Over-use of Dexedrine – a kind of amphetamine – plunged her briefly into paranoid delusions in which T.S. Eliot played a bizarrely prominent part. But by 1952 she had won the *Observer*'s Christmas short-story competition (out of 7,000 entries) for 'The Seraph and the Zambesi', which draws on the natural wonders she had seen in Southern Rhodesia during her ill-fated marriage. It is, as Stannard writes, 'a surreal Nativity story, but it is also about her own rebirth'. Her introduction to the Brontë letters picks out the 'element of storm' as a key to the sisters' art, with 'some cataclysmic event of nature' put to work as the 'sympathetic manifestation of some inner, personal tempest'. This is just how Spark's own career in fiction gets under way, but – a defining proviso – with a supernatural agent imported to lift the scene beyond merely human dread or desire. By then, approaching 34, Spark had outlived Emily and Anne Brontë, if not yet Charlotte. Now her angelic 'seraph' rises above the thunderous cataract. Heathcliff, of course, must haunt the moorland rocks forever.

At this stage Spark seems to yearn, seraph-like, to rise high above the ferment. To do so she must both imbibe and become immune to the Brontës, a 'tribe' so near to her and yet so far. Her presentation of them strenuously keeps its distance from identification or idolatry, precisely because both attitudes might come so readily. Charlotte, as instigator and manager of the Brontë family myth, comes under criticism for the relentless self-dramatisation which makes mountains out of molehills and a spectacle out of 'every triviality of her daily existence'. Emily, meanwhile, suffers from 'aloofness and unsociability', not to mention the 'misanthropic turn of mind' disclosed by her love for animals.

Perhaps the lady doth protest too much. The Brontës, after all, offered Spark a mirror or a reflecting pool that might have swallowed her whole. Look at the letters that she selected, and at many points they read almost like a displaced manifesto for their editor. After her double bereavement, with Emily and Anne gone, Charlotte writes that 'The faculty of imagination lifted me up when I was sinking… its active exercise has kept my head above water since'. Defiantly, she proclaims to G.H. Lewes that 'Out of obscurity I came, to obscurity I can easily return', and that 'I cannot, when I write, think always of myself and of what is most elegant and charming in femininity'. She also tells Lewes that 'I wished critics would judge me as an *author*, not as a woman'. As for the despised governess's celebrated apologia in *Jane Eyre*, it would have struck as resonant a chord with Spark at this time as with any other reader. 'Do you think, because I am poor, obscure, plain and little, I am soulless and heartless? You think wrong! I have as much soul as you – and full as much heart!'

Yeats wrote, in the year of Muriel Spark's birth, that 'We make out of the quarrel with others, rhetoric, but of the quarrel with ourselves, poetry.' Her beef with the Brontës represents a quarrel with herself. Out of it came a 'vocation' at least as intense as theirs but, in her terms, less self-consuming and self-worshipping. In later years, when the intimate threat posed by the sisters had passed, an underlying affinity comes back into plain sight. Spark's renewed connection with Hugo Manning helped to plant the seed for the semi-autobiographical novel *Loitering with Intent* (1981). Its novelist heroine Fleur Talbot suffers less confusion, isolation and near-despair than her creator. Fleur does, however, espouse a view of fiction as a quest to realise a myth of the self that sounds almost Brontëan. For her, 'Without a mythology, a novel is nothing. The true novelist, one who understands the work as a continuous poem, is a myth-maker'. At such moments Spark surely stands beside and behind her heroine rather than passing judgment in hindsight on a deceived younger self.

In 1988, with *A Far Cry from Kensington*, Spark returned to her apprentice years. In that novel, her reconciliation with the sisters feels more complete. Its heroine Nancy Hawkins at one point slips into an explicitly Brontë-esque state of alienation and hallucination on a London bus. 'I felt like Lucy Snowe in "Villette",' she reports, 'who walked, solitary in Brussels on a summer night, among the festival crowds'. By this time the muse of comedy – classical, balanced, ironic comedy – has long prevailed for Spark. The delusions, the fixations, of youth arouse sympathy but carry no risk. No longer seducers, tempters or antagonists, the Brontës can serve as odd, beloved friends again.

Foreword

More than most authors, especially those of the nineteenth century, the Brontës were aware of themselves as personalities. They fully understood the dramatic properties of their position. Charlotte, the spokeswoman of the tribe, never failed to present a picture of dramatized loneliness and scenic effects when writing about her family. It was as if she knew that their family situation and their talents placed them on a stage from where they could hypnotize their own generation and, even more, posterity. Their lives, even apart from their writings, formed a work of art. Haworth Parsonage overlooked the graveyard. Life bordered on death. Three lonely girls, a morose widowed father and a frantic brother, in the first half of the nineteenth century, was a perfect scenario.

In this book I have put together my own writings on the Brontës together with a selection of family letters and a selection of Emily's poems.

Charlotte's letters have been chosen with the express intention of presenting a 'Brontë autobiography'. I found, when I first chose these letters for my book, *The Brontë Letters* (1954), that they lent themselves to a dramatic story-telling arrangement. Charlotte put the family personality into these letters, most of which were addressed to her friend, Ellen Nussey.

In 1857, only two years after Charlotte's death, Mrs Gaskell's *Life of Charlotte Brontë* was read as avidly as any of Charlotte's novels. The Brontë story itself had started to become a national phenomenon.

After the second edition of my *Brontë Letters* was published I received a charming and strange letter which seemed to confirm my conviction that Charlotte as impresario had by the 1860's already succeeded in vividly promoting not only the Brontë works, but their lives, their melancholy, their tragedies, as a romantic representation.

Dec. 11th 1967.

Dear Muriel Spark,
Your book 'The Brontë Letters' has just come my way, & I have been much interested in it.
My Mother, Mrs. Dean, née Elizabeth Berridge, who died in 1933 at the age of 81, was at school in Yorkshire, & she told me that Ellen Nussey came several times & read Charlotte Brontë's letters to the pupils. It is interesting to think that perhaps some of the letters in your book may have been read to my Mother by the recipient.
I am now in my eightieth year, & I thank you for the pleasure you have given me.

Yours sincerely,
Dorothy D. Dean

It is always moving to have contact with someone who has had contact with history. But apart from that, I was, and still am, intrigued by this renewed evidence that Ellen Nussey was well aware of the gripping narrative value of the Brontë situation. The plays and films were to follow.

In compiling the present book I have decided to omit all my writings exclusively on Anne Brontë. In the 1950s I published articles on the poems of Anne Brontë and on Anne's novels, *Agnes Grey* and *The Tenant of Wildfell Hall*, but I do not now agree with my former opinion of Anne Brontë's value as a writer. I think her works are not good enough to be considered in any serious context of the nineteenth century novel or that there exists any literary basis for comparison with the brilliant creative works of Charlotte and Emily. But Anne had a distinctive personality. She is presented here as Charlotte presents her, a pale shadow, a girl saddened by loneliness and ill health, somewhat morosely religious. She was a writer who could 'pen' a story well enough; she was the literary equivalent of a decent water-colourist, as so many maidens were in those days.

I published a selection of Emily Brontë's poems in 1952 with an introductory essay which I want to perpetuate. The selection was made on the basis of what I considered to be Emily's best poems, but here again I sense a personal projection of the author's spiritual life-force which is more condensed and direct, less diffused and spread out amongst different characters, than one finds in *Wuthering Heights*.

Like many artists, Emily, and also to a decided extent Charlotte, had a social-behavioural problem. In them, it took the form of melancholy silence. We know that during their perod of adult-education in Brussels, they were invited to visit English homes, but the hostesses simply could not get any form of responsiveness out of them. It seems almost that they were in love with their loneliness, their northern melancholy. All the more, heart and soul, did they pour forth their feelings in the written page.

Death, that struck when I was most confiding
In my certain Faith of Joy to be

Emily's lovely lines, whatever their ostensible intention – her poems were characterized frequently in the Gondal-myth sequences – have surely a sound of her own authentic spiritual experience.

I have entitled this book *The Essence of the Brontës*, for the essence is what I intend to convey in the words of Charlotte and Emily Brontë themselves as well as in my own.

S. Giovanni in Oliveto
December 1992

Muriel Spark

Illustrations

1

The Brontës as Teachers

The Brontë 'Gun Group', drawing by Branwell Brontë
(*left to right* Emily, Charlotte, Branwell, Anne)
(*by courtesy of Walter Scott*)

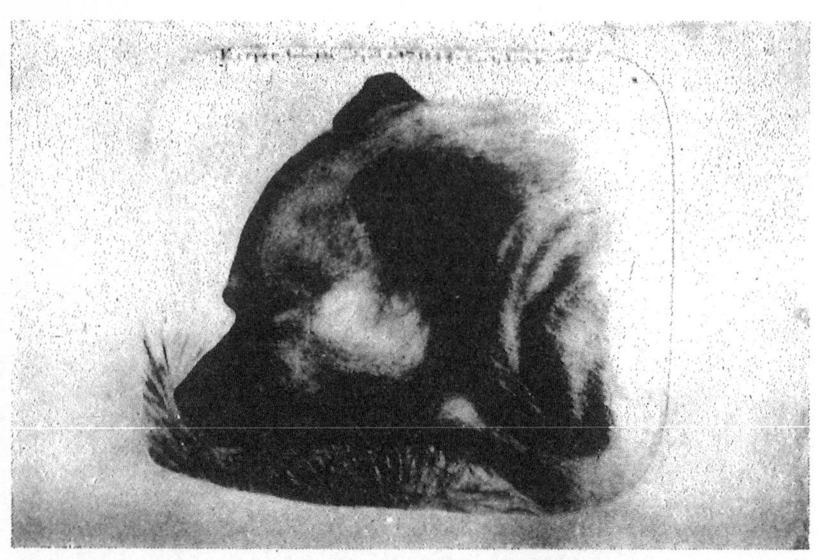

Original watercolour of her dog, Keeper, by Emily Brontë
(*by courtesy of the Brontë Society*)

The Brontës as Teachers

The general feeling about the incursion into teaching of Charlotte, Branwell, Emily and Anne Brontë is that it was little short of martyrdom. The letters of Charlotte, the diaries of Anne, the novels of both, abound with evidence that the experience of being teachers was an agony to all four. Nothing, we are given to understand, could be worse than to be a private governess, a tutor or a school teacher to such pupils as came the Brontës' way; nothing worse than to be employed by such people as engaged the Brontës.

I am in sympathy with the view that their enforced choice of careers was a pity, (except that it provided marvellous material for fiction) and rejoice with everyone else that at least three of them discovered their true vocation in time to write their unique, unconformable books. But were the Brontës mere lambs among wolves when they set forth to teach? I suggest that if anything could equal the misfortune of their lot as teachers it was the lot of the respective pupils and employers of Charlotte, Branwell, Emily and Anne.

Charlotte was the first to teach. Having practised for a while on her sisters she left Haworth Parsonage in 1835 to become a resident mistress at Roe Head school where previously she had been a pupil. Her formal education had covered little more than two years' schooling supplemented by home tuition from her maiden aunt. When, just turned nineteen, she became a mistress at Roe Head, her main qualification as an instructor of the young was a protected upbringing; this was, after all, judged to be the highest qualification a girl could produce. The headmistress (that Miss Wooler who remained a lifelong friend to Charlotte) began by treating her as a friend. Charlotte stayed with Miss Wooler for over two years, but according to her letters and diaries she was miserable most of the time, as she well might be. Here is one of her diary entries:

> All this day I have been in a dream, half miserable, half ecstatic . . . I had been toiling for nearly an hour with Miss Lister, Miss Marriot, and Ellen Cook, striving to teach them the distinction between an article and a substantive. The parsing lesson was completed; a dead silence had succeeded it in the schoolroom, and I sat sinking from irritation and weariness into a kind of lethargy. The thought came over me: Am I to spend all the best part of my life in this wretched bondage, forcibly suppressing my rage at the idleness, the apathy, and the hyperbolical and most asinine stupidity of these fat-headed oafs, and of compulsion assuming an air of kindness, patience and assiduity? Must I from day to day sit chained to this chair, prisoned within these four bare walls, while these glorious summer suns are burning in heaven and the year is revolving in its richest glow? Stung to the heart with this reflection I started up and mechanically walked to the window. A sweet August morning was smiling without . . . I felt as if I could have written gloriously . . . If I had had time to indulge it I felt that the vague suggestion of that moment would have settled down into some narrative better at least than anything I ever produced before. But just then a dolt came up with a lesson.

Now, all this did violence to Charlotte, who wanted to write, not teach. But what we are concerned with here is the effect of her frustration on the Misses Lister, Marriot and Cook, not to mention the unfortunate 'dolt' who interrupted Charlotte's reverie. Were they all so unlike normal children, were they all such 'fat-headed oafs' that they failed to sense Miss Brontë's contempt and fury? One cannot help feeling that they gained less from Charlotte's instruction than she expended upon it by way of 'suppressing my rage'.

But poor Charlotte was to fare worse. She presented herself in 1839 as governess to the children of a Mrs Sidgwick who, poor soul, did not dream she was about to harbour an eminent Victorian. Charlotte immediately transferred her dislike of the job to Mrs Sidgwick and her children, though she was not averse to Mr Sidgwick. Charlotte's complaints were many and bitter: Mrs Sidgwick never left her a free moment to enjoy the spacious grounds and neighbouring countryside; Mrs Sidgwick would not allow the children, 'riotous, perverse, unmanageable cubs', to be corrected (a charge which Charlotte was to bring against her next employer and Anne against hers, somewhat contrary to notions of middle-class rearing of children in the 19th century); Mrs Sidgwick took Charlotte to task for sulking, whereupon Charlotte wept; Mrs Sidgwick expected Charlotte to love the children; and, final indignity, Mrs Sidgwick 'overwhelms me with oceans of needlework, yards of cambric to hem, muslin nightcaps to make, and, above all things, dolls to dress'.

It sounds quite drastic. Certainly the patent misery of the new governess must have seemed so to Mrs Sidgwick who, from other accounts, is said to have been an amiable woman. No doubt she loaded on the needlework with a view to keeping Charlotte from brooding, to give her something to occupy her mind, for it is remarkable how often in those days melancholy was equated with vacancy of purpose and cheerfulness with a full life. Still, we cannot blame Mrs Sidgwick for being an average mediocre nonentity; she never claimed to be other. If anything was to blame it was the system which included needlework among other semi-domestic tasks in the normal duties of a governess. Unless we look upon Charlotte as a famous author, which we are not doing at the moment, the sewing was no real outrage. And whether it was any more degrading, any greater a bore, than is the supervision of conducted tours and school lunches to the present-day teaching profession, is a question.

This record of Charlotte's brief sojourn with the Sidgwicks would be incomplete without the testimony of one of the Sidgwick pupils in later years, after Charlotte's distaste for his family had been made public by Mrs Gaskell. He declared that 'if Miss Brontë was desired to accompany them to Church – 'Oh, Miss Brontë, do run up and put on your things, we want to start' – she was plunged in dudgeon because she was being treated like a hireling. If, in consequence, she was not invited to accompany them, she was infinitely depressed because she was treated as an outcast and a friendless dependant.' Since most of the Brontë victims were inarticulate, locked forever in the pillories of the Brontë letters and novels, I find this brief protest rather touching, coming from the otherwise mute and admittedly inglorious Sidgwick child.

As this was a temporary post Charlotte only had to endure it for less than three months. Before she left, one of the little Sidgwicks threw a Bible at her. He later became a clergyman.

Next comes Mrs White. Charlotte soon discovered that 'she does not scruple to give way to anger in a very coarse, unladylike manner'. Charlotte preferred Mr White, in spite of her conviction that 'his extraction is very low'. Meanwhile, she said, she was trying hard to like Mrs White. This effort was fruitful, notwithstanding Mrs White's bad grammar of which Charlotte was critical, and the fact that Charlotte feared her to be an exciseman's daughter. In the end, Mrs White won over the parson's daughter, who came to admit that she was intrigued by the 'fat baby', and called her pupils 'well-disposed' though of course, 'indulged'.

Behold now Charlotte in her last teaching post. The *Pensionnat Héger* in Brussels is the scene, and Charlotte, having gone there to study French and German, has now become an English mistress in this school for young ladies. Her employer, Mme Héger, has grown rather suspicious of the English teacher and spies upon her; Charlotte apparently cannot think why. She prefers M. Héger. The schoolgirls are 'selfish, animal and inferior'. And we are further delightfully informed that 'their principles are rotten to the core'. Charlotte's colleagues hate each other, and she them. So her letters go on. One of her fellow mistresses, worse than the rest, acts as a spy for Mme Héger, is false, is contemptible, is Catholic. In fact they are all Catholic, and in fact, as Charlotte writes to Branwell, 'the people here are no go whatsoever'.

As the months proceed, Charlotte is giving English lessons to M. Héger, who seems well satisfied with her work and gives her presents of books occasionally. Charlotte declares that his goodness towards her compensates for the "deprivations and humiliations' which are her lot, but on which she is not explicit.

But presently M. Héger takes to avoiding Charlotte, having first lectured her on the subject of 'universal *Bienveillance*'. She, however, is no universalist; her *bienveillance* is focused on the object of her master whom she observes is 'wonderfully influenced' by his wife. With curious logic Charlotte now finds she can 'no longer trust' Mme Héger, and driven back to Haworth by that lady's suspicions, proceeds to confirm them by writing a series of impassioned letters to M. Héger until he implores her to stop.

Let us now look at the teaching career of Branwell Brontë. At the age of twenty he joined the staff of a local school from which he retreated within six months. The small boys made fun of his red hair. After fortifying his dignity with a long interval of writing, painting, hard drinking and opium eating, he became tutor, in 1840, to the children of a Mr and Mrs Postlethwaite. Branwell's view of his job can best be savoured from his own account of it written to one of his former drinking cronies:

> If you saw me now you would not know me, and you would laugh to hear the character the people give me . . . Well, what am I? That is, what do they think I am? – a most sober, abstemious, patient, mild-hearted, virtuous, gentlemanly philosopher, the picture of good works, the treasure-house of righteous thoughts. Cards are shuffled under the tablecloth, glasses are thrust into the cupboard, if I enter the room. I take neither spirit, wine, nor malt liquors. I dress in black, and smile like a saint or martyr. Every lady says, 'What a good young gentleman is the Postlethwaites' tutor.' This is a fact, as I am a living soul, and right comfortably do I laugh at them; but in this humour do I mean them to continue.

Branwell ends by saying that as he writes one of the Postlethwaite daughters is sitting close by. . . . 'She little thinks the Devil is as near her. . . .'

Branwell's attitude to these folk, whatever else it amounts to, does make a welcome contrast with that expressed by his sisters in similar circumstances. The sons of the family he describes as 'fine spirited lads' – these being, no doubt, merely Charlotte's 'riotous, perverse, unmanageable cubs' in a lighter aspect. And Branwell depicts Mr Postlethwaite as 'of a right hearty, generous disposition' and his wife as 'a quiet, silent, amiable woman.' But within a few months Branwell's restless ambitions tore him from the Postlethwaites to visit Hartley Coleridge, and thence back to Haworth.

His next and last post as tutor came three years later. Anne introduced him into the household where she was employed as a governess. He was to teach the son of the house. His employer, Mr Robinson, was an aging invalid; Mrs Robinson was much younger. Branwell preferred Mrs Robinson. 'This lady', he wrote later, '(though her husband detested me) showed me a degree of kindness which, when I was deeply grieved one day at her husband's conduct, ripened into declarations of more than ordinary feeling.' It took Mr Robinson two and a half years to confirm his suspicions, whereupon he wrote to Branwell, then on holiday, 'intimating' as Charlotte reported, 'that he had discovered his proceedings . . . and charging him on pain of exposure to break off instantly and forever all communication with every member of his family'. Branwell insisted that Mrs Robinson returned his passion. Years afterwards, when Brontë biography began its voluminous course, she took occasion to deny it.

Anne's post with the Robinsons was her second. The youngest Brontë proved the most patient of the four, and though by no means devoid of talent and the will to write, endured her teaching career for a longer period than the others. However, in proportion as she exercised restraint, so did her novels reveal exactly what she had restrained in the way of spleen. At the age of nineteen Anne took charge of the two eldest children of a Mrs Ingham. Before long, Charlotte was busy passing on Anne's news: her pupils were 'desperate little dunces', 'excessively indulged', 'violent' and 'modern'. Anne left this family after eighteen months' attempt to cope with them; she was somewhat the worse for the experience.

Anne was twenty-one when she went to the Robinsons. Charlotte, who exaggerated most things, gave out that Anne was 'a patient, persecuted stranger' amongst 'grossly insolent, proud and tyrannical' people. Direct evidence from Anne has not survived beyond two diary fragments, the first of which commits her no further than 'I dislike the situation and wish to change it for another'. (Her novels provide the usual terrible children.) She remained four years, during which time her pupils had become very fond of her. In fact, the Robinson girls continued to visit and write to Anne, long after she had left the family and her brother had been dismissed in disgrace from it. Anne's only other direct comment on the job refers to her earlier dislike of it: 'I was wishing to leave it then, and if I had known that I had four years longer to stay, how wretched I should have been; but during my stay I have had some very unpleasant and undreamt-of experience of human nature'. This last lament is taken to refer to Branwell's intrigue with Mrs Robinson and can be found precisely stated in *The Tenant of Wildfell Hall*.

Emily, like her sisters, was nineteen when she set off to be a teacher of Law Hill School and it seems fairly certain that Emily was still nineteen when she did the sensible thing and returned. All we know of her stay at Law Hill is that she wrote a letter which, according to Charlotte, 'gives an appalling account of her duties – hard labour from six in the morning until near eleven at night, with only one half-hour exercise between. This is slavery'. 'I fear', Charlotte adds, 'she will never stand it'. Emily did not stand it. But the curious thing is, that during this period Emily's poetic output was higher than at any other time, which seems to indicate that she was not entirely starved of leisure.

Emily did not long endure her job as a music-teacher at the

Héger establishment. When she was called back to Haworth with Charlotte on the death of her aunt, Emily showed no desire to return with her sister to Brussels. Much has been made of the fact that M. Héger expressed approval of Emily (after she was dead and famous) declaring, somewhat ambiguously I have always thought, that she should have been a navigator. He also gave the opinions that she might have been a great historian and she should have been a man. Nowhere does he say that she should have been a music-teacher. And at the time, M. Héger felt moved only to inform Emily's father, 'She was losing whatever remained of her ignorance, and also of what was worse – timidity'.

For the three sisters it was torture while it lasted; for Branwell, fun while it lasted. Their frail constitutions were damaged and much of their creative energy dissipated in the uncongenial schoolroom. They did their best to earn a living in the only way open to them. But from the point of view which it has been my purpose to adopt, it might also be thought that genius, if thwarted, resolves itself in an infinite capacity for inflicting trouble, or at least for finding fault. It is demanding too much of genius to ask it to keep its personality out of anything; even the lesser talent can seldom do so.

Branwell's conduct was unprofessional, to say the least. Charlotte was not, to say the least, proof against those states of mind which the most protected upbringing will not protect. Anne's reaction was to hoard her resentment. Emily's way, by far the most successful, was to get out of the predicament with all speed (and note: she shows no obsession in her work with the governess theme). The Brontës, however, gained ample revenge for all injustices real or imagined.

So one might, therefore, without compunction enquire whether their employers – the Sidgwicks and Inghams and Whites – did in fact fail in their duty to their employees; or were they merely unfortunate in crossing the Brontës' path? I should say that if their sense of duty were wanting, it was to their children. And along with this thought comes the realization, supported from other sources besides the Brontës, that the wealthy middle class of England during the last century were willing to hand over their children to any young woman who came out of a clergyman's home, neurotic or ailing as she might be.

The Brontës once planned to start a school of their own. The project, as mercifully for others as for themselves, came to nothing. Branwell's wasted life gave a warning signal to his sisters, and miraculously they asserted their creative powers.

I have not depended on their novels to support this essay, since I believe that fiction is a suspect witness (and if it is not stranger than truth, it ought to be). But, of course, unmistakable versions of Brontë pupils and employers are to be found in the novels of Charlotte and Anne.

Perhaps the lesson to be drawn, for any writer with the necessary will of iron, who lacks only the opportunity to write, is that he should prove himself no good at anything else.

M.S.

2

Letters of the Brontës

edited and introduced by Muriel Spark

Introduction

The letters of famous people can be placed into two categories: there is the type of letter which becomes itself a valuable contribution to literature through its wit, style or wisdom; another kind is that whose main importance lies in the provision of a background to its author's life. Especially in the correspondence of great writers and poets, these two factors are very often combined; the letters of Coleridge and of Keats, for example, are at once works of literary delight and what are popularly known as human documents; while those of Jane Austen, written with the object of imparting domestic news in the most amusing possible manner, offer both an outline of the outward events of her life and a vehicle for her particular brand of irony.

Yet it very often happens that a writer's capacity for prose expression of a high order is jealously preserved for creative or critical work intended for publication; the letters of such writers fall mainly into the second category, that of biographical material. Forever open to the sentimentalizing of the curio-hunter and relic-worshipper, or to the theorizing of biographers, it is to this category that the Brontë letters, for the most part, belong. That is not to imply that the correspondence of this remarkable family is devoid of grace, humour and perspicacity, for it contains all these attributes. The distinction is a general one, and in making it I would like to distinguish also between an essential and a superficial employment of such biographical data. For where outstanding figures of literature are concerned, surely the greatest benefit to be derived from a study of their lives is that which penetrates the operation of the creative mind, interpreting the spirit which motivated it. Questions of environment and parentage, of those intimate details concerning love affairs, clothing, even diet, with which Brontë biography in particular abounds – all are secondary considerations if not focused on the existence of *Jane Eyre, Villette, Wuthering Heights* or *The Tenant of Wildfell Hall.* I have used the word 'secondary' rather than 'irrelevant' in this context since biographical material of the Brontës may be considered exceptional in one respect: the story of this family presents a dramatic entity and a progressive panorama, equal in range and emotional power to any of their own novels. It is not difficult, therefore, to understand why new Brontë biographies appear frequently, nor why theories, some in varying degrees of wildness, have been constructed round the thousand-odd Brontë letters in existence.

The dramatic side of the story having been recognized at an early date, it was inevitable perhaps that a protagonist should have been demanded; and natural, too, that Charlotte, whose letters form the great bulk of the family documents, should have become the leading character around whom her father, brother and sisters seem to move. Yet this assumption is really not justifiable. Most of the letters are Charlotte's, but from what they tell us of her family, of their struggles, attitudes, triumphs and sorrows, it seems the more apparent that each member of the household is an unusual personality, despite the discrepancy of their separate achievements. It is not until we come to examine these figures, both in isolation and in their correlation to each other, that we can perceive in Emily's aloofness and unsociability the qualities of profound poetic spirit; it is when we understand the frustrations and despair that Charlotte underwent, or the desires and foibles peculiar to her nature, that we discover the author of *Jane Eyre*; only in the domestic scene can we find the clue to Branwell's failure, and to the consistent disparagement of Anne's achievements by Charlotte.

In making the following selection, I have tried to choose those letters most salutary to the clear presentation of the Brontë story, unencumbered by the mass of correspondence devoted to events extraneous to the main course of their lives. If this drama has no single protagonist, it has a pronounced motif – one that recurs constantly throughout the Brontë lives and works. This motif is the element of storm: time and again the sisters described some cataclysmic event of nature as a sympathetic manifestation of some inner, personal tempest. The theme first occurs in the shipwreck reference by their mother, Maria Branwell, in one of her letters; its pagan presence was felt by their clergyman father when he wrote of his wife's death, '. . . another storm arose, more terrible than the former – one that shook every part of the mortal frame and often threatened it with dissolution. My dear wife was taken dangerously ill . . .', and again, 'One day, I remember it well; it was a gloomy day, a day of clouds and darkness, three of my little children were taken ill. . . .' The storm, whistling through the stone-flagged parsonage that overlooked the graveyard of Haworth, returned to sever the chestnut tree at Thornfield, in *Jane Eyre*; it fastened on the grim outline of Wuthering Heights and slammed the inimical doors of Wildfell Hall. Not one of the Brontës but faced its spirit and implications.

Patrick Brontë, one of ten children of an Irish farmer, made his way to Cambridge University with £7 in his pocket. There, by means of a grant partly endowed by William Wilberforce and a reduction of fees by his college, he was able to take a Bachelor of Arts degree, and in 1806 was ordained. After occupying several curacies he met Maria Branwell, a young Cornishwoman of a clerical family, whom he married in 1812, and it was the children of this obscure Irish and Cornish alliance who came to achieve lasting recognition by readers of English literature.

Throughout the family correspondence Patrick Brontë makes many appearances, although few of his own letters exist. Those that bear his signature show him to be forceful and egotistical, with that pathetic naïvety which appears in his offers of marriage to Mary Burder after his wife's death. It is known that he had eccentric habits, but these were means to his own self-expression; as far as the Haworth *ménage* was concerned, he behaved like a conventional Victorian paterfamilias. Whenever the question of domestic arrangements arose, whenever one or other of his children left home in pursuit of a career, and even in the matter of Charlotte's marriage, it was always 'Papa's' comfort that received the first consideration. Yet, for his time, he was not an unduly oppressive parent. He was immensely proud of his children's attainments; and Mrs Gaskell in her *Life of Charlotte Brontë* tells of his early recognition of the unusual qualities of their minds, and his attempts to elucidate them.

If the Brontë talent owed anything to the father, it was the fantastic strain of his Celtic blood; his attempts at authorship – some dismal poems and pious tales – show little but a will to write. There were, however, some elements in his nature which were clearly transmitted to his children, prominent amongst them being a propensity for scholarship. This appears both in Charlotte and in Branwell, although the latter lacked his father's and his sister's sustained determination to fulfil the uses of learning. But by far the richest inheritance the Brontë children received from their father was the symbol of storm. He was, like them, fascinated by the wildest forces of nature, the crude Yorkshire moorland surrounding Haworth providing a peculiarly sympathetic background. Patrick Brontë could scarcely resist giving vent to his obsession, even from the pulpit. The theme of one of his sermons was a local earthquake, and so delighted was he with his subject that he published the sermon, for sale at price sixpence; the earthquake provided him with the same theme for a poem entitled 'The Phenomenon: or An Account in Verse of the Extraordinary Disruption of a Bog which took place in the Moors of Haworth. . . .' This he also published and made available for twopence.

For a brief insight into Maria Branwell's character we depend almost entirely upon the few letters she wrote to Patrick Brontë before her marriage. It is evident that she enjoyed writing and took care with her prose: stiff though it is, her language shows discrimination; innately cautious, she rarely made a seemingly audacious statement without immediately qualifying it. But she was by no means feeble. 'For some years,' she wrote, 'I have been subject to no *control* whatever. . . . It is pleasant to be subject to those we love. . . .' In these sentences she defined the nature of love as it was later known to her daughter, Charlotte, who always portrayed the independent woman, above all things mistress of herself, in the heroines of her novels, with whom she more or less identified herself. But they always fell in love with their masters, and to Charlotte the submission of a strong personality to one even stronger signified love on its highest level. In her own experience, it was only before her own master at the Brussels *pensionnat* that she was rendered humble; she subjugated herself to no others of her acquaintance as she did in her letters to M. Héger. This, indeed, is one of the principal points of distinction between Charlotte's novels and those of her sisters, accounting largely for the popularity of her works immediately upon their appearance; it was a time when women were attempting to reconcile with their emotional needs, a desire for a greater degree of independence than their sex had enjoyed before; and Charlotte's stories defined a code acceptable alike to the male and female of her time. Although it was not until almost forty years after Maria Branwell's letters were written that Charlotte was to read them, it was the inheritance of her mother's doctrine that informed Charlotte's nature and mentality.

Six children were born to Maria and Patrick Brontë before they moved to the parsonage at Haworth, and there, just over a year later, the Brontë mother died painfully of cancer. Her place as housekeeper and guardian to the children was taken by her sister, known to the family as 'Aunt Branwell'; however cold the character of this lady seems to have been, the Brontë children may be considered to have benefited rather than suffered from her reserve. Although many words have been wept over the loveless childhood of the Brontës, it is very probable that maternal feelings in their aunt would have stifled their talents, finely attuned as they were to all emotional reverberations; as it was, the figurehead of Aunt Branwell presented to the young family the personification of authority, ungirt by the emotional tangle that often exists between mother and children. So long as they obeyed what household rules she laid down; so long as they attended to religious devotions; so long as they appeared healthy, Aunt Branwell did not interfere with them – their inner lives were their own to order as they pleased. Rarely were early-Victorian children allowed such liberty of thought and activity as were the Brontës. Paradoxically, there is every possibility that had their mother lived she would have humanized them to the extent of reducing their creative powers; while their personal sufferings might have been mitigated, their genius might in some measure have been muffled by her love.

Of the six children only four – Charlotte, Branwell, Emily and Anne – survived childhood. The two eldest, Maria and Elizabeth, were brought home from Cowan Bridge School to die within a month of each other – events which left a tortured impression on Charlotte. It was her eldest sister, and not Miss Branwell, who had replaced the mother-image in Charlotte's mind. She idolized Maria, and her rage against the school authorities, who had so seriously neglected the dying girl, was given full scope in the first chapters of *Jane Eyre*.

It would not be possible here to examine the Brontës' extraordinary childhood in detail, nor the prolific writings which attest to the range and vividness of their imaginations. The juvenile works of Charlotte and Branwell are voluminous. Prominent among these works is the saga of Angria – a legendary country of the children's invention which they populated with heroes, traitors and eccentrics of their own making. Emily and Anne later broke away from this literary alliance, forming the legend of Gondal, which was, if anything, even more imaginatively charged than that of Angria. The loves, treacheries, griefs and excesses of the exotic people of Gondal moved in the poetry of Emily and Anne to the time of their latest compositions. They kept up this game until Emily's death, and long after they were grown women we find references to Gondal in the few scraps of diary papers that remain to us by the hand of Emily and Anne. The only direct evidence that exists of the early activities of the two younger girls took the diary form, and, written when Emily and Anne were aged sixteen and fourteen respectively, the following fragment will show how natural a part of their daily lives the world of Gondal had become:

> I fed Rainbow, Diamond, Snowflake, Jasper pheasant (alias). This morning Branwell went down to Mr. Driver's and brought news that Sir Robert Peel was going to be invited to stand for Leeds. Anne and I have been peeling apples for Charlotte to make an apple pudding and for Aunt's. . . . Charlotte said she made puddings perfectly and she . . . of a quick but limted intellect. Taby said just now Come Anne pilloputate (i.e. pill a potato). Aunt has come into the kitchen just now and said Where are your feet Anne. Anne answered On the floor Aunt. Papa opened the parlour door and gave Branwell a letter saying Here Branwell read this and show it to your Aunt and Charlotte. The Gondals are discovering the interior of Gaaldine. Sally Mosley is washing in the back kitchen.
>
> It is past twelve o'clock Anne and I have not tided ourselves, done our bed work, or done our lessons and we want to go out to play We are going to have for dinner Boiled Beef, Turnips, potatoes and apple pudding. The kitchen is in a very untidy state Anne and I have not done our music exercise which consists of b major Taby said on my putting a pen in her face Ya pither pottering there instead of pilling a potate. I answered O Dear, O Dear, O Dear I will derectly With that I get up, take a knife and begin pilling. Finished pilling the potatoes. Papa is going to walk. Mr. Sunderland expected.
>
> Anne and I say I wonder what we shall be like and what we shall be and where we shall be, if all goes on well, in the year 1874 – in which year I shall be in my 57th year. Anne will be in her 55th year, Branwell will be going in his 58th year and

Charlotte in her 59th year. Hoping we shall all be well at that time We close our paper.

EMILY AND ANNE,
November the 24, 1834.

The story of the adult life of the four Brontës more or less tells itself in the following selection of their letters. It is the story in its original form, and so I shall not attempt to improve upon, nor anticipate it. I propose, therefore, to offer no more than an extended 'Dramatis Personae' – an outline of the types of character that speak and act in these letters.

Charlotte, whose correspondence is necessarily more largely represented than that of the others, altered her tone and style according to her correspondent. Her letters to Ellen Nussey, her friend from school days to the end of her life, show Charlotte's inner being only so far as she wished to reveal it, except for some early letters belonging to a particular phase in the relationship. To Ellen she gave few confidences and much gossip: to her father, she was respectful, conventional and patient; to Emily, gay and confiding; and to Branwell, she appears frank, sisterly, sometimes slangy. In her letters to eminent writers and literary friends, Charlotte made an effort to give the best of her intelligence while preserving a subtle appearance of modesty; to her discarded suitor, Henry Nussey, her tone was polite and patronizing; and to M. Héger, impetuous, passionate and distracted. But this polygonal shape of Charlotte's personality has led to much immoderate interpretation of it, and only by observing each facet of her personality as part of a whole and in due proportion can we form an integrated idea of this complex woman. We do find, however, that she was clearly the most energetic and ambitious of her family. It was she who put into motion the scheme that sent her to Brussels with Emily; it was Charlotte who arranged for the first publication by the three sisters – *Poems by Currer, Ellis and Acton Bell.*

But Charlotte, although practical, was no realist. She was given to dramatizing every triviality of her daily existence; in her novels she used every particle of experience that came her way, and with artistic justification viewed each casual encounter equally with her closest associates, with an eye, as it were, to business. All people who attracted her interest, all events that contacted her creative feelers, were reproduced or caricatured in her books. It is not to be supposed that Charlotte, while thus indulging her imagination, should neglect herself. We find, for example, that after her first meeting with Mrs Gaskell, the latter came away with a fairly heart-rending account of Charlotte's history,[1] not a little incommensurable with the facts. Tragic indeed as her life had been, Charlotte could not forbear to embellish the melancholy side of her existence; nor did she hesitate to distort the bleak actuality of the Brontë household, knowing that her tale intrigued to the full the popular novelist in Mrs Gaskell. And we may well applaud this aspect of Charlotte's mind, since it was the essence of her greatness.

A need for love was an important fact in Charlotte's personality. It found its first outlet when, at the age of twenty, she became a teacher in a girls' school. With an intelligence far above the average, and possessing few personal attractions, she was overcome by a series of dark moods that found expression in religious melancholy mingled with a sentimental attachment to Ellen Nussey. Teaching never suited Charlotte; she was, however, too proud and, at that time, too idealistic to seek the customary escape through marriage. The moral censorship of her ethos could not lead her to recognize the nature of her repressed youthful emotions, and in her temporary state of unbalance she turned to her closest friend outside her own family. The letters written to Ellen during 1836 are disturbed with Calvinistic doubts and torments, with impassioned appeals for comfort to Ellen, for whom she conceived a kind of spiritual love; and with fervent expressions of imagined guilt. This is not to suggest that these letters show a sinister peculiarity in Charlotte; but we should understand, I think, that the nervous stress of uncongenial surroundings, combined with the suppression of normal emotions and the complete absence of male company, was bound to cause an upheaval in a highly creative and sensitive mind. In Charlotte's case, she found relief in a harmless, if abnormal and morbid, correspondence with Ellen Nussey.

It will be observed that as soon as Charlotte entered into an exchange of letters with the Poet Laureate, Southey, however brief and unsatisfactory this may have been, her phase of anguish began to pass. So, too, she discovered a way of fulfilment after her rejection by M. Héger, when she set her mind immediately to the matter of compiling and publishing the sisters' poems.

Since the extant correspondence of the other members of the Brontë family is comparatively small, we might well ask to what

[1] Mrs Gaskell's letter to Catherine Winkworth, 25 August 1850.

extent their characters can be identified with Charlotte's pronouncements upon them. Of Emily she wrote with admiration, sometimes with bewilderment, and later with sincere, bitter grief. Even had we not *Wuthering Heights* and the eloquent, lyrical poetry of Emily before us, their author's monolithic and articulate personality would still appear implicit in Charlotte's letters. These letters after Emily's death reveal in what love and respect Charlotte held that stoical, isolated spirit. Yet, in the same way, Charlotte's references to Anne give the impression of underlying resentment. Scarcely could Charlotte utter a kind word about Anne's literary merit, but she qualified it with an ungenerous phrase; expressing solicitude for her youngest sister's welfare, she did not hesitate to enlarge upon her shortcomings, both in her letters about Anne and in the posthumous prefaces to her work. Were it not for the unassailable evidence of *The Tenant of Wildfell Hall* and Anne's small but quite distinguished poetic output, the youngest Brontë would scarcely seem worth noticing.

Emily had no time for inessentials; and letter-writing, woman-to-woman friendships, gossip and social functions were alike trivial to her. She thrived only in her native environment, that of the moors and her family circle; indeed, she was never happy away from home, being thought intractable and awkward by strangers. Because of the dearth of documents by the hand of Emily Brontë, it is around her that the wildest theories have been woven. All we can say definitely about her, however, is that she was a strange woman; but, then, *Wuthering Heights* is a strange novel, one that could never have been the product of an orthodox mind. The fondness for animals which we know she felt suggests that she was one of those reserved, uncommunicative beings who do not like to be questioned; in fact, someone who knew her reported that her strongest love was for animals, and it is true that her work contains evidence of a misanthropic turn of mind. Of human feelings, her most profound was certainly for Anne – a situation which, one is led to suspect, rankled a little with Charlotte. Emily and Anne formed the habit of writing periodical messages to each other, in the style of memoranda to be opened at four-yearly intervals. Four of these papers exist – two each by Emily and Anne; and so pertinent are they to the thoughts, ambitions and relationship of these two people that they have been included in this selection although they are not strictly in the epistolary form.

The proud independence of Emily's death, her inflexible refusal to accept consolation, are represented vividly in Charlotte's letters about her. Two years later Charlotte wrote in a preface to *Wuthering Heights* a passage that reveals the essence of her sister with a certitude surpassing all other biographical writings on Emily. 'In Emily's nature', she wrote, 'the extremes of vigour and simplicity seemed to meet.'

> Under an unsophisticated culture, inartificial tastes, and an unpretending outside lay a secret power and fire that might have informed the brain and kindled the veins of a hero; but she had no worldly wisdom; her powers were unadapted to the practical business of life: she would fail to defend her most manifest rights, to consult her most legitimate advantage. An interpreter ought always to have stood between her and the world. Her will was not very flexible, and it generally opposed her interest. Her temper was magnanimous, but warm and sudden; her spirit altogether unbending.

Charlotte felt her sister's death no less keenly than did Anne, who did not long outlive Emily.

As artists, Charlotte and Emily Brontë need no introduction; their works have been celebrated widely and have been the subject of some of the most eminent critical essays of the later nineteenth and twentieth centuries. It is not so with Anne. George Moore has referred to Anne Brontë as 'a sort of literary Cinderella', and, to be sure, her justified position in literature has persistently been ignored, much less defined. Two main causes can be said to have given rise to this circumstance: firstly, Anne's works were comparatively few, consisting of two novels and fifty-eight poems; she began to die in heart and body before she had consolidated her status as a writer; and she did not live to reproduce, in more resounding terms, that compelling, authentic note that nevertheless speaks in her work. But a more prominent reason for Anne's artistic eclipse is the attitude of Charlotte, her first and, as it might seem, her most authoritative critic. It should perhaps be said, in fairness to Charlotte, that had it not been for her practical endeavours, her initiative in approaching publishers, and her determination that the Brontë sisters should leave their mark on English letters, we might never have heard of any of them. It cannot be denied, though, that whenever Charlotte wrote of Anne's work, she appears to have felt it almost a moral duty to depict Anne as a gentle, devout, obedient young woman, whose creative works amounted to no more than modest accomplishments. Charlotte was a fairly acute critic in her mature years, and that she did not lack taste is proved by her early recognition of Emily's superior poetic talent. Yet she took it upon herself to choose the flattest and most commonplace of Anne's poems to present to the public as the best of her youngest sister's work. And these are introduced with the following pronouncement, justified only by Charlotte's own unrepresentative selection:

> I find mournful evidence that religious feeling had been to her but too much like what it was to Cowper – I mean, of course, in a far milder form. Without rendering her a prey to those horrors that defy concealment, it subdued her mood and bearing to a perpetual pensiveness.

The Tenant of Wildfell Hall is not a great novel. It is, however, an important work – one that showed Anne Brontë to be free of much humbug that cluttered even Charlotte's work. It takes a stand against accepted social tenets; it questions the tacit matrimonial principles of the age. Anne handled problems of drunkenness, depravity and spiritual coarseness with the unflinching candour that marked the work of later realist writers; she knew how to develop her characters. Of this novel Charlotte felt it necessary to tell the world, 'The choice of subject was an entire mistake. Nothing less congruous than the writer's nature could be conceived. The motives which dictated this choice were pure, but I think, slightly morbid.' Anne herself, it should be said, had apologetically declared this novel to have been written out of a sense of duty, and as a warning to others. And although one might incline to believe that Anne was seriously justifying her work of art in the eyes of herself and her critics, it can hardly be thought that Charlotte was deluded; had she taken an impartial view of *Wildfell Hall* she must have discovered its merits.

Charlotte's pronouncements seem curiously to have established, for most subsequent assessors of Anne Brontë, an irrefutable dictate. Especially where her poems are concerned do we find a tendency to ignore, rather than to underestimate, her best poetic work. Anne's poetry has not the sweeping vigour of Emily's, but there is lyricism and originality of a high order in much of her verse, especially in her Gondal pieces. She was also a deft manipulator of the difficult ballad forms.

So far as can be judged from the Brontë letters, Anne made no outward attempt to resist Charlotte's attitude, nor is it to be supposed that Charlotte was a harsh sister to Anne – the obvious resentment took subtle shapes, possibly of a half-conscious nature. It might be said, too, that at the root of Charlotte's insidious deprecation, and the sly implications of the ever-repeated phrase, 'quiet, gentle Anne', there was possibly a benevolent motive, a misguided sense of protection: Charlotte had herself suffered from the moralistic carpings of critics, and may have felt compelled to portray Anne as a dull though virtuous woman who had unfortunately written an undesirable book.

Overshadowed as Anne must always be by her more gifted sisters, her writings none the less take no mean place in nineteenth-century literature, and in spite of her implied want of verve, it was Anne alone of the three sisters who persisted in her distasteful vocation as governess; for neither Emily nor Charlotte succeeded in their attempts at teaching.

The Brontë son did not fulfil his early promise; his great misfortune was that he was a man. If he had been constrained, as were his sisters, by the spirit of the times; if he had been compelled, for want of other outlet, to take up his pen or else burst, he might have been known today as rather more than the profligate brother of the Brontës. Although, as critics are never tired of pointing out, his youthful letters to *Blackwood's Magazine* are singularly lacking in tact, they reveal that degree of ambition and inner certainty that is necessary to the artist. Receiving no encouragement from *Blackwood's*, he tried Wordsworth with a challenging and courageous, if over-impetuous letter, and it is to that poet's discredit that he ignored Branwell's appeal, even though it is known that Wordsworth received the letter and imparted a distorted version of it to Southey.

Of Branwell's rakish career, little need be added to the story told in the letters. It should be explained, however, that the account Branwell gave of his stay at Thorp Green, where he was employed as tutor, became a subject of violent recrimination long after all the Brontë children were dead. The tale of Branwell's seduction by the mistress of the house was transmitted to Mrs Gaskell by Charlotte, who, with the rest of her family, faithfully believed all Branwell had told them. But when Mrs Gaskell recounted his version of the affair in her *Life of Charlotte Brontë*, the lady who was supposed to have led to Branwell's downfall demanded that a committee of investigation should be set up. She was an influential woman, and although it would have been difficult for the most impartial investigator to prove much either way at so late a date, her name was ostensibly cleared, and Mrs Gaskell inserted an apology in *The Times*. To this day it remains questionable whether Branwell's story was authentic, or if, as has been suggested, the whole sequence of events was a product of his opium-inflamed mind. Possibly the truth contains something of both solutions.

Branwell lacked his sisters' single-mindedness; his interests lay in too many directions for him to achieve competence in any one pursuit. For a time he took lessons in painting, but his ambition to enter the Royal Academy was never fulfilled. The organ, the flute, military bands, prize-fighting, the new railroads, poetry and translation were amongst the miscellaneous wonders that filled his thoughts and disintegrated his purpose. Indulged by his father, surrounded by proud, talented and self-sufficient sisters, he turned in bewilderment to his admiring cronies at 'The Black Bull', where his friends' brandy and his own talent were drained in the promotion of his eloquence.

Of his inconsistent and loosely contrived writings only his translations of Horace have any claim to recommendation, and these, first introduced by John Drinkwater, show the promise of a literary merit Branwell could not apply himself to attain.

I do not wish to panegyrize the Brontë letters as models of style. They are not, in fact, particularly elegant, but neither are they turgid nor harsh. None of the Brontës was capable of producing the vulgar altiloquence too often found in letters of the period. Their language is apposite if not rich; their mode of construction symmetrical if not adroit.

In Charlotte's correspondence with her publishers and other literary friends much sound criticism of the books she had read is to be found; and in the brief evidence we have of Anne as a letter-writer we see a felicity that might almost belong to the eighteenth century, coupled with no small ability in presenting an argument.

Circumscribed as was the daily existence in the Haworth parsonage, these letters do not make commonplace reading, but stand as testimony to the stringent odds, the personal anguish and storm, against which the Brontë genius strove and flourished.

Ponden Hall, 'Thrushcross Grange' in *Wuthering Heights*
(by courtesy of Walter Scott)

1

MARIA BRANWELL
TO THE REVD PATRICK BRONTË

Wood House Grove,
August 26th, 1812.

My Dear Friend,

This address is sufficient to convince you that I not only permit, but approve of yours to me – I do indeed consider you as my *friend*; yet, when I consider how short a time I have had the pleasure of knowing you, I start at my own rashness, my heart fails, and did I not think that you would be disappointed and grieved at it, I believe I should be ready to spare myself the task of writing. Do not think that I am so wavering as to repent of what I have already said. No, believe me, this will never be the case, unless you give me cause for it. You need not fear that you have been mistaken in my character. If I know anything of myself, I am incapable of making an ungenerous return to the smallest degree of your kindness, much less to you whose attentions and conduct have been so particularly obliging. I will frankly confess that your behaviour and what I have seen and heard of your character has excited my warmest esteem and regard, and be assured you shall never have cause to repent of any confidence you may think proper to place in me, and that it will always be my endeavour to deserve the good opinion which you have formed, although human weakness may in some instances cause me to fall short. In giving you these assurances I do not depend upon my own strength, but I look to Him who has been my unerring guide through life, and in Whose continued protection and assistance I confidently trust.

I thought on you much on Sunday, and feared you would not escape the rain. I hope you do not feel any bad effects from it? My cousin wrote you on Monday and expects this afternoon to be favoured with an answer. Your letter has caused me some foolish embarrassment, tho' in pity to my feelings they have been very sparing of their raillery.

I will now candidly answer your questions. The *politeness of others* can never make me forget your kind attentions, neither can I *walk our accustomed rounds* without thinking on you, and, why should I be ashamed to add, wishing for your presence. If you knew what were my feelings whilst writing this you would pity me. I wish to write the truth and give you satisfaction, yet fear to go too far, and exceed the bounds of propriety. But whatever I may say or write I will *never deceive* you, or *exceed the truth*. If you think I have not placed the *utmost confidence* in you, consider my situation, and ask yourself if I have not confided in you sufficiently, perhaps too much. I am very sorry that you will not have this till after to-morrow, but it was out of my power to write sooner. I rely on your goodness to pardon everything in this which may appear either too free or too stiff, and beg that you will consider me as a warm and faithful friend.

My uncle, aunt, and cousin unite in kind regards.

I must now conclude with again declaring myself to be yours sincerely,

Maria Branwell

2

MARIA BRANWELL
TO THE REVD PATRICK BRONTË

Wood House Grove,
November 18th, 1812.

My Dear Saucy Pat,

Now don't you think you deserve this epithet far more than I do that which you have given me? I really know not what to make of the beginning of your last; the winds, waves, and rocks almost stunned me. I thought you were giving me the account of some terrible dream, or that you had had a presentiment of the fate of my poor box, having no idea that your lively imagination could make so much of the slight reproof conveyed in my last. What will you say then when you get a *real downright scolding*? Since you shew such a readiness to atone for your offences, after receiving a mild rebuke, I am inclined to hope you will seldom deserve a severe one. I accept with pleasure your atonement, and send you a free and full forgiveness; but I cannot allow that your affection is more deeply rooted than mine. However, we will dispute no more about this, but rather embrace every opportunity to prove its sincerity and strength by acting, in every respect, as friends and fellow-pilgrims travelling the same road, actuated by the same motives and having in view the same end. I think, if our lives are spared twenty years hence, I shall then pray for you with the same, if not greater, fervour and delight that I do now.

I am pleased that you are so fully convinced of my candour, for to know that you suspected me of a deficiency in this virtue would grieve and mortify me beyond expression. I do not derive any merit from the possession of it, for in me it is constitutional. Yet I think where it is possessed it will rarely exist alone, and where it is wanted there is reason to doubt the existence of almost every other virtue. As to the other qualities which your partiality attributes to me, although I rejoice to know that I stand so high in your good opinion, yet I blush to think in how small a degree I possess them. But it shall be the pleasing study of my future life to gain such an increase of grace and wisdom as shall enable me to act up to your highest expectations and prove to you a helpmeet. I firmly believe the Almighty has set us apart for each other; may we, by earnest, frequent prayer and every possible exertion, endeavour to fulfil His will in all things. I do not, cannot, doubt your love, and here I freely declare I love you above all the world besides! I feel very, very grateful to the great Author of all our mercies for His unspeakable love and condescension towards us, and desire 'to shew forth my gratitude not only with my lips, but by my life and conversation'. I indulge a hope that our mutual prayers will be answered, and that our intimacy will tend much to promote our temporal and external interest.

I suppose you never expected to be much the richer for me, but I am sorry to inform you that I am still poorer than I thought myself. I mentioned having sent for my books, clothes, etc. On Saturday evening, about the time you were writing the description of your imaginary shipwreck, I was reading and feeling the effects of a real one, having then received a letter from my sister giving me an account of the vessel in which she had sent my box being stranded on the coast of Devonshire, in consequence of which the box was dashed to pieces with the violence of the sea and all my little property, with the exception of a very few articles, swallowed up in the mighty deep. If this should not prove the prelude to something worse I shall think little of it, as it is the first disastrous circumstance which has occurred since I left my home, and having been so highly favoured it would be highly ungrateful in me were I to suffer this to dwell much on my mind.

Mr. Morgan was here yesterday, indeed he only left this morning. He mentioned having written to invite you to Bierley on Sunday next, and if you complied with his request it is likely that we shall see you both here on Sunday evening. As we intend going to Leeds next week, we should be happy if you would accompany us on Monday or Tuesday. I mention this by desire of Miss F., who begs to be remembered affectionately to you. Notwithstanding Mr. F.'s complaints and threats, I doubt not but he will give you a cordial reception whenever you think fit to make your appearance at the Grove. Which you may likewise be assured of receiving from your ever truly affectionate –

Maria

Both the Dr. and his lady very much wish to know what kind of address we make use of in our letters to each other. I think they would scarcely hit on *this*!

3

PATRICK BRONTË
TO THE REVD JOHN BUCKWORTH

Near K., Yorkshire,
November 27th, 1821.

My Dear Sir,

I have just received yours of the 23rd inst., and it is like good news from a far country or the meeting of old friends after a long separation. Your kind letter breathes that good sense, that Christian spirit and brotherly tenderness, which I have ever considered as prominent features in your character, and which are well-suited to soothe and benefit a mind like mine, which at present stands much in need of comfort and instruction. As I well know that you, as well as a much esteemed friend of mine who is near you, will take an affectionate interest in my affairs, whether they be prosperous or adverse, I will proceed to give you a brief narrative of facts as they have succeeded one another in my little sphere for the last twelve months.

When I first came to this place, though the angry winds which had been previously excited were hushed, the troubled sea was still agitated, and the vessel required a cautious and steady hand at the helm. I have generally succeeded pretty well in seasons of difficulty;

but all the prudence and skill I could exercise would have availed me nothing had it not been for help *from above*. I looked to the *Lord* and He controlled the storm and levelled the waves and brought my vessel safe into the harbour. But no sooner was I there than another storm arose, more terrible than the former – one that shook every part of the mortal frame and often threatened it with dissolution. My dear wife was taken dangerously ill on the 29th of January last, and in a little more than seven months afterwards she died. During every week and almost every day of this long tedious interval I expected her final removal. For the first three months I was left nearly quite alone, unless you suppose my six little children and the nurse and servants to have been company. Had I been at D[ewsbury] I should not have wanted kind friends; had I been at H[artshead] I should have seen them and others occasionally; or had I been at T[hornton] a family there who were ever truly kind would have soothed my sorrows; but I was at H[aworth], a stranger in a strange land. It was under these circumstances, after every earthly prop was removed, that I was called on to bear the weight of the greatest load of sorrows that ever pressed upon me. One day, I remember it well; it was a gloomy day, a day of clouds and darkness, three of my little children were taken ill of a scarlet fever; and, the day after, the remaining three were in the same condition. Just at that time death seemed to have laid its hand on my dear wife in a manner which threatened her speedy dissolution. She was cold and silent and seemed hardly to notice what was passing around her. This awful season, however, was not of long duration. My little children had a favourable turn, and at length got well; and the force of my wife's disease somewhat abated. A few weeks afterwards her sister, Miss Branwell, arrived, and afforded great comfort to my mind, which had been the case ever since, by sharing my labours and sorrows, and behaving as an affectionate mother to my children. At the earliest opportunity I called in a different medical gentleman to visit the beloved sufferer, but all their skill was in vain. Death pursued her unrelentingly. Her constitution was enfeebled, and her frame wasted daily; and after above seven months of more agonizing pain than I ever saw anyone endure she fell asleep in Jesus, and her soul took its flight to the mansions of glory. During many years she had walked with God, but the great enemy, envying her life of holiness, often disturbed her mind in the last conflict. Still, in general she had peace and joy in believing, and died, if not triumphantly, at least calmly and with a holy yet humble confidence that Christ was her Saviour and heaven her eternal Home.

P.B.

4

PATRICK BRONTË TO MARY BURDER

[*July 28th, 1823.*]

Dear Madam,

The circumstance of Mrs. Burder not answering my letter for so long a time gave me considerable uneasiness; however, I am much obliged to her for answering it at last. Owing to a letter which I received from Miss Sarah, and to my not receiving any answer to two letters which I wrote subsequently to that, I have thought for *years* past that it was highly probable you were married, or at all events, you wished to hear nothing of me, or from me, and determined that I should learn nothing of you. This not unfrequently gave me pain, but there was no remedy, and I endeavoured to resign, to what appeared to me to be the will of God.

I experienced a very agreeable sensation in my heart, at this moment, on reflecting that you are *still* single, and am so selfish as to wish you to remain so, even if you would never allow me to see you. *You* were the *first* whose hand I solicited, and no doubt I was the *first* to whom *you promised to give that hand.*

However much you may dislike me now, I am sure you once loved me with an unaffected innocent love, and I feel confident that after all which you have seen and heard you cannot doubt my love for you. This is a long interval of time and may have effected many changes. It has made me look something older. But, I trust I have gained more than I have lost, I hope I may venture to say I am wiser and better. I have found this world to be but vanity, and I trust I may aver that my heart's desire is to be found in the ways of divine Wisdom, and in her paths, which are pleasantness and peace. My dear Madam, I earnestly desire to know how it is in these respects with you. I wish, I ardently wish your *best* interests in *both* the worlds. Perhaps you have not had much trouble since I saw you, nor such experience as would unfold to your view in well-defined shapes the unsatisfactory nature of all earthly considerations. However, I trust you possess in your soul a sweet peace and serenity arising from communion with the Holy Spirit, and a well-grounded hope of eternal felicity. Though I have had much bitter sorrow in consequence of the sickness and death of my dear Wife, yet I have ample cause to praise God for his numberless mercies. I have a *small* but *sweet* little family that often soothe my heart and afford me pleasure by their endearing little ways, and I have what I consider a competency of the good things of this life. I am *now settled* in a part of the country *for life* where I have many friends, and it has pleased God in many respects to give me favour in the eyes of the people, and to prosper me in my ministerial labours. I want but *one* addition to my comforts, and then I think I should wish for no more on this side eternity. I want to see a dearly Beloved Friend, kind as I *once* saw her, and as *much* disposed to promote my happiness. If I have ever given her any pain I only wish for an opportunity to make her ample amends, by every attention and kindness. Should that very dear Friend doubt respecting the veracity of any of my statements, I would beg leave to give her the most satisfactory reference, I would beg leave to refer her to the Rev. John Buckworth, Vicar of Dewsbury, near Leeds, who is an excellent and respectable man, well known both as an *Author* and an able Minister of the Gospel to the religious world.

My dear Madam, all that I have to request at present is that you will be so good as to answer this letter as soon as convenient, and tell me candidly whether you and Mrs. Burder would have any objection to seeing me at Finchingfield Park as an *Old Friend*. If you would allow me to call there in a friendly manner, as soon as I could get a supply for my church and could leave home I would set off for the South. Should you object to my stopping at Finchingfield Park overnight I would stop at one of the Inns in Braintree – as most likely my old friends in that town are either dead or gone. Should you and Mrs. Burder kindly consent to see me as an old friend, it might be necessary for me before I left home to write *another* letter in order that I might know when you would be at home. I cannot tell how *you* may feel on reading this, but I must say *my* ancient love is rekindled, and I have a *longing* desire to see you. Be so kind to give my best respects to Mrs. Burder, to Miss Sarah, your brothers, and the *Little Baby*. And *whatever* you resolve upon, believe me to be yours *Most Sincerely*,

P. Brontë

5

MARY BURDER TO PATRICK BRONTË

Finchingfield Park,
August 8th, 1823.

Reverend Sir,

As you must reasonably suppose, a letter from you presented to me on the 4th inst. naturally produced sensations of surprise and agitation. You have thought proper after a lapse of fifteen years and after various changes in circumstances again to address me, with what motives I cannot well define. The subject you have introduced, so long ago buried in silence and until now almost forgotten, cannot, I should think, produce in your mind anything like satisfactory reflection. From a recent perusal of many letters of yours bearing date eighteen hundred and eight, nine and ten addressed to myself and my dear departed Aunt, many circumstances are brought with peculiar force afresh to my recollection. With my present feelings I cannot forbear in justice to myself making some observations which may possibly appear severe – of their justice I am convinced. This review, Sir, excites in my bosom increased gratitude and thankfulness to that wise, that indulgent, Providence which then watched over me for good and withheld me from forming in very early life an indissoluble engagement with one whom I cannot think was altogether clear of duplicity. A union with you under then existing circumstances must have embittered my future days and would, I have no doubt, been productive of reflections upon me as unkind and distressing as events have proved they would have been unfounded and unjust. Happily for me I have not been the ascribed cause of hindering your promotion, of preventing any brilliant alliance, nor have those great and affluent friends that you used to write and speak of withheld their patronage on my account, young, inexperienced, unsuspecting, and ignorant as I was of what I had a right to look forward to.

Many communications were received from you in humble silence which ought rather to have met with contempt and indignation ever considering the sacredness of a promise. Your confidence I have never betrayed, strange as was the disclosure you once made unto me; whether those ardent professions of devoted lasting attachment were sincere is now to me a matter of little consequence. 'What I have seen and heard' certainly leads me to conclude very differently. With these my present views of past occurrences is it possible, think you, that I or my dear Parent could give you a cordial welcome to the Park as an *old friend*? Indeed, I must give a *decided* negative to the desired visit. I know of no ties of friendship *ever* existing between us which the last eleven or twelve years have not severed or at least placed an insuperable bar to any revival. My present condition, upon which you are pleased to remark, has hitherto been the state of my choice and to me a state of much happiness and comfort, tho' I have not been exempted from some severe trials. Blessed with the kindest and most indulgent of friends in a beloved Parent, Sister, and Brother, with a handsome competency which affords me the capability of gratifying the best feelings of my heart, teased with no domestic cares and anxieties and without anyone to control or oppose me, I have felt no willingness to risk in a change so many enjoyments in my possession. Truly I may say, 'My Cup overfloweth', yet it is ever my desire to bear mind that mutability is inscribed on all earthly possession. 'This is not my rest', and I humbly trust that I have been led to place all my hopes of present and future happiness upon a surer foundation, upon that tried foundation stone which God has laid in Zion. Within these last twelve months I have suffered a severe and protracted affliction from typhus fever. For twenty-eight weeks I was unable to leave my bedroom, and in that time was brought to the confines of an eternal world. I have indeed been brought low, but the Lord has helped me. He has been better to me than my fears, has delivered my soul from death, my eyes from tears, and my feet from falling, and I trust the grateful language of my heart is, 'What shall I render unto the Lord for all his benefits?' The life so manifestly redeemed from the grave I desire to devote more unreservedly than I have ever yet done to His service.

With the tear of unavailing sorrow still ready to start at the recollection of the loss of that beloved relative whom we have been call'd to mourn since you and I last saw each other, I can truly sympathize with you and the poor little innocents in your bereavement. The Lord can supply all your and their need. It gives me pleasure always to hear the work of the Lord prospering. May He enable you to be as faithful, as zealous, and as successful a labourer in His vineyard as was one of your predecessors, the good old Mr. Grimshaw, who occupied the pulpit at Haworth more than half a century ago, then will your consolations be neither few nor small. Cherishing no feeling of resentment or animosity, I remain, Revd. Sir, sincerely your Well Wisher,

Mary D. Burder

6

PATRICK BRONTË TO MRS. FRANKS

Haworth, near Bradford,
Yorkshire,
April 28th, 1831.

Dear Madam,

Having heard of your kind attention to Charlotte,[1] I have taken the liberty of writing to thank both Mr. Franks and you for this, and to assure you that we have not forgotten, in our little family, your other various acts of kindness. Charlotte would be highly gratified. She still remembered having seen you at Kipping, and has often heard us speak of you, whilst we took a retrospective view of Good Old Times. I have just received a letter from our mutual friend, Miss Outhwaite, which has given me some uneasiness. It appears that some whose opinions I highly value greatly misunderstand my motives, in being an advocate for temperate reform, both in Church and State. I am in all respects *now* what I *was* when I lived in Thornton – in regard to all political considerations. A warmer or truer friend to Church and State does not breathe the vital air. But, after many years' mature deliberation, I am fully convinced that, unless the *real* friends of our excellent institution come forward and advocate the cause of temperate reform, the inveterate enemies will avail themselves of the opportunity which this circumstance would give them, and will work on the popular feeling – already but too much excited – so as to cause, in all probability, general insurrectionary movements, and bring about a revolution. We see what has been lately done in France. We know that the Duke of Wellington's declaration against reform was the principal cause of the removal of him and the other ministers from power. And there is now another instance before our eyes of the impolicy of this perverseness. The anti-reformers have imprudently thrown the ministers into a minority, and consequently Parliament is dissolved by the King in person, and in all probability another Parliament will soon be returned, which may be less particular than the other, and perhaps go too far in the way of reformation.

Both, then, because I think moderate or temperate reform is wanted – and that this would satisfy all wise and reasonable people

[1] Charlotte boarded at Miss Wooler's school at Roe Head, in the neighbourhood of her father's friend, from January, 1831, until May, 1832.

and weaken the hands of our real enemies, and preserve the Church and State from ruin – I am an advocate for the Bill, which has just been thrown out of Parliament. It is with me merely an affair of conscience and judgment, and sooner than violate the dictates of either of these, I would run the hazard of poverty, imprisonment, and death. My friends – or some of them at least – may differ from me as to the *line of conduct* which ought to be followed, but our *motives* and our good *wishes* towards Church and State are the same.

But to come nearer home. I have for nearly a year past been in but a very delicate state of health. I had an inflammation in my lungs last summer and was in immediate and great danger for several weeks. For the six months last past I have been weak in body and my spirits have often been low. I was for about a month unable to take the church duty. I now perform it, though with considerable difficulty. I am certainly a little better, yet I fear I shall never fully recover. I sometimes think that I shall fall into a decline. But I am in the Lord's hands, and hope that He will at the last give me a happy issue out of all my troubles and take me for ever into His heavenly kingdom. We have been much concerned to hear from time to time that you have not been quite so strong as usual. It is our earnest wish and prayer that the Lord may support and comfort you and spare you long and in mercy to your husband and your children. I have only once been at Kipping since I last saw you and Mrs. Firth there. The family were kind to me, but I missed my old friends and I could not feel comfortable, and I soon departed, intending never to call again. Miss Branwell still continues with me and kindly superintends my little family, and they all join with me in the kindest and most respectful regards. When you write to, or see, Mrs. Firth, be so kind as to remember us all to her in the most respectful and affectionate manner. Be so good also to thank Mr. Franks in our name for his kind attention to Charlotte, and believe me to be, dear madam, very respectfully and truly yours,

P. Brontë

7

CHARLOTTE BRONTË
TO BRANWELL BRONTË

Roe Head,
May 17th, 1831.

Dear Branwell,

As usual I address my weekly letter to you, because to you I find the most to say. I feel exceedingly anxious to know how and in what state you arrived at home after your long and (I should think) very fatiguing journey. I could perceive when you arrived at Roe Head that you were very much tired, though you refused to acknowledge it. After you were gone, many questions and subjects of conversation recurred to me which I had intended to mention to you, but quite forgot them in the agitation which I felt at the totally unexpected pleasure of seeing you. Lately I had begun to think that I had lost all the interest which I used formerly to take in politics, but the extreme pleasure I felt at the news of the Reform Bill's being thrown out by the House of Lords, and of the expulsion or resignation of Earl Grey, etc., etc., convinced me that I have not as yet lost *all* my penchant for politics. I am extremely glad that aunt has consented to take in *Fraser's Magazine*, for though I know from your description of its general content it will be rather uninteresting when compared with *Blackwood*, still it will be better than remaining the whole year without being able to obtain a sight of any periodical publication whatever; and such would assuredly be our case, as in the little wild, moorland village where we reside, there would be no possibility of borrowing or obtaining a work of that description from a circulating library. I hope with you that the present delightful weather may contribute to the perfect restoration of our dear papa's health, and that it may give aunt pleasant reminiscences of the salubrious climate of her native place.

With love to all, – Believe me, dear Branwell, to remain your affectionate sister,

Charlotte

8

CHARLOTTE BRONTË TO ELLEN NUSSEY

Haworth,
January 1st, 1833.

Dear Ellen,

I believe we agreed to correspond once a month; that space of time has now elapsed since I received your last interesting letter, and I now therefore hasten to reply. Accept my congratulations on the arrival of the 'New Year', every succeeding day of which will, I trust, find you wiser and better in the true sense of those much-used words. The first day of January always presents to my mind a train of very solemn and important reflections, and a question more easily asked than answered, frequently occurs, viz.: How have I improved the past year, and with what good intentions do I view the dawn of its successor? These, my dearest Ellen, are weighty considerations which (young as we are) neither you nor I can too deeply or too seriously ponder. I am sorry your two great diffidences, arising, I think, from the want of sufficient confidence in your own capabilities, prevented you from writing to me in French, as I think the attempt would have materially contributed to your improvement in that language. You very kindly caution me against being tempted by the fondness of my sisters to consider myself of too much importance, and then in a parenthesis you beg me not to be offended. O! Ellen, do you think I could be offended by any good advice you may give me? No, I thank you heartily, and love you, if possible, better for it. I had a letter about a fortnight ago from Miss Taylor, in which she mentions the birth of Mrs. Clapham's little boy, and likewise tells me you had not been at Roe Head for upwards of a month, but does not assign any reason for your absence. I hope it does not arise from ill-health. I am glad you like *Kenilworth*; it is certainly a splendid production, more resembling a Romance than a Novel, and in my opinion one of the most interesting works that ever emanated from the great Sir Walter's pen. I was exceedingly amused at the characteristic and naïve manner in which you expressed your detestation of Varney's character, so much so, indeed, that I could not forbear laughing aloud when I perused that part of your letter; he is certainly the personification of consummate villainy, and in the delineation of his dark and profoundly artful mind, Scott exhibits a wonderful knowledge of human nature, as well as surprising skill in embodying his perceptions so as to enable others to become participators in that knowledge. Excuse the want of *news* in this very barren epistle, for I really have none to communicate. Emily and Anne beg to be kindly remembered to you. Give my best love to your mother and sisters, and as it is very late permit me to conclude with the assurance of my unchanged, unchanging, and unchangeable affection for you. – Adieu, my sweetest Ellen; I am, ever yours,

Charlotte

9

CHARLOTTE BRONTË TO ELLEN NUSSEY

Haworth,
June 19th, 1834.

My *own* dear Ellen,

I may rightfully and truly call you so *now* you *have* returned, or are returning from London, from the great city which to me is almost apocryphal as Babylon or Nineveh, or ancient Rome. You are withdrawing from the world (as it is called) and bringing with you, if your letters enable me to form a correct judgment, a heart as unsophisticated, as natural, as true, as that you carried there. I am slow, *very* slow to believe the protestations of another. I know my own sentiments because I can read my own mind, but the minds of the rest of men and women kind are to me as sealed volumes, hieroglyphical, which I cannot easily either unseal or decipher. Yet time, careful study, long acquaintance, overcome most difficulties; and in your case I think they have succeeded well in bringing to light and construing that hidden language, whose turnings, windings, inconsistencies, and obscurities, so frequently baffle the researches of the honest observer of human nature. How many after having, as they thought, discovered the word friend in the mental volume, have afterwards found they should have read *false* friend! I have long seen 'friend' in your mind, in your words, in your actions, but *now* distinctly visible, and clearly written in characters that cannot be distrusted, I discern *true* friend! I am really grateful for your mindfulness of so obscure a person as myself, and I hope the pleasure is not altogether selfish; I trust it is partly derived from the consciousness that my friend's character is of a higher, a more steadfast order than I was once perfectly aware of. Few girls would have done as you have done – would have beheld the glare and glitter and dazzling display of London, with dispositions so unchanged, hearts so uncontaminated. I see no affectation in your letter, no trifling, no frivolous contempt of plain, and weak admiration of showy persons and things. I do not say this in flattery – but in genuine sincerity. Put such an one as A.W. in the same situation, and mark what a mighty difference there would be in the result! I say no more; remember me kindly to your excellent sisters, accept the good wishes of my Papa, Aunt, Sisters, and Brother, and continue to spare a corner of your warm, affectionate heart for your *true* and *grateful* friend,

Charlotte Brontë

10

CHARLOTTE BRONTË TO ELLEN NUSSEY

Haworth,
July 4th, 1834.

Dear Ellen,

You will be tired of paying the postage of my letters, but necessity must plead my excuse for their frequent recurrence. I *must* thank you for your very handsome present. The bonnet is pretty, neat, and simple, as like the giver as possible; it brought Ellen Nussey, with her fair quiet face, brown eyes, and dark hair, full to my remembrance. I wish I could find some other way to thank you for your kindness than words. The load of obligation under which you lay me is positively overwhelming, and I make no return. In your last you tell me to tell you of your faults and cease flattering you. Now, really, Ellen, how can you be so foolish! I won't tell you of your faults, because I don't know them. What a creature would that be, who, after receiving an affectionate and kind letter from a beloved friend, should sit down and write a catalogue of defects by way of answer! Imagine me doing so, and then consider what epithets you would bestow upon me – conceited, dogmatical, hypocritcal, little humbug, I should think would be the mildest. Why, child! I've neither time nor inclination to reflect on your faults when you are so far from me, and when, besides kind letters and presents, and so forth, you are continually bringing forth your goodness in the most prominent light. Then, too, there are friends always round you who can much better discharge that unpleasant office. I have no doubt their advice is completely at your service;

why then should I intrude mine? Let us have no more nonsense about flattery, Ellen, if you love me. Mr. R. Nussey is going to be married, is he? Well, his wife-elect appeared to me a clever and amiable lady, as far as I could judge from the little I saw of her, and from your account. Now to this flattering sentence must I tack on a list of her faults? You say it is in contemplation for you to leave Rydings; I am sorry for it. Rydings is a pleasant spot, one of the old family halls of England surrounded by lawn and woodland, speaking of past times, and suggesting to me, at least, happy feelings, it would be smooth and easy; but it is the living in other people's houses, the estrangement from one's real character, the adoption of a cold, frigid, apathetic exterior, that is painful.

Martha Taylor thought you grown less, did she? That's like Martha. I am not grown a bit, but as short and dumpy as ever. I wrote to Mary, but have as yet received no answer. You ask me to recommend some books for your perusal. I will do so in as few words as I can. If you like poetry let it be first-rate; Milton, Shakespeare, Thomson, Goldsmith, Pope (if you will, though I don't admire him), Scott, Byron, Campbell, Wordsworth, and Southey. Now, don't be startled at the names of Shakespeare and Byron. Both these were great men, and their works are like themselves. You know how to choose the good and avoid the evil; the finest passages are always the purest, the bad are invariably revolting; you will never wish to read them over twice. Omit the comedies of Shakespeare and the *Don Juan*, perhaps the *Cain* of Byron, though the latter is a magnificent poem, and read the rest fearlessly; that must indeed be a depraved mind which can gather evil from *Henry VIII, Richard III*, from *Macbeth*, and *Hamlet*, and *Julius Cæsar*. Scott's sweet, wild, romantic poetry can do you no harm. Nor can Wordsworth's, nor Campbell's, nor Southey's – the greatest part at least of his; some is certainly objectionable. For history, read Hume, Rollin, and the *Universal History*, if you *can*: I never did. For fiction, read Scott alone; all novels after his are worthless. For biography, read Johnson's *Lives of the Poets*, Boswell's *Life of Johnson*, Southey's *Life of Nelson*, Lockhart's *Life of Burns*, Moore's *Life of Sheridan*, Moore's *Life of Byron*, Wolfe's *Remains*. For natural history, read Bewick, and Audubon, and Goldsmith, and White's *History of Selborne*. For divinity, your brother Henry will advise you there. I can only say adhere to standard authors, and avoid novelty. If you can read this scrawl it will be to the credit of your patience. With love to your sisters, believe me to be, for ever yours,

Charlotte Brontë

11

CHARLOTTE BRONTË TO ELLEN NUSSEY

Haworth,
March 13th, 1835.

Dear Ellen,

I suppose by this time you will be expecting to hear from me. You did not fix any precise period when I should write, so I hope you will not be very angry on the score of delay, etc. Well, here I am, as completely separated from you as if a hundred instead of seventeen miles intervened between us. I can neither hear you, nor see you, nor feel you, you are become a mere thought, an unsubstantial impression on the memory which, however, is happily incapable of erasure. My journey home was rather melancholy, and would have been very much so, but for the presence and conversation of my worthy companion. I found K. a very intelligent man and really not unlike Cato (you will understand the allusion). He told me the adventures of his sailor's life, his shipwreck, and the hurricane he had witnessed in the West Indies, with a much better flow of language than many of far greater pretensions are masters of. I thought he appeared a little dismayed by the wildness of the country round Haworth, and I imagine he has carried back a pretty report of it. He was very inquisitive, and asked several questions respecting the names of places, directions of roads, etc., which I could not answer. I fancy he thought me very stupid.

What do you think of the course Politics are taking? I make this inquiry because I now think you have a wholesome interest in the matter; formerly you did not care greatly about it. Brougham you see is triumphant. Wretch! I am a hearty hater, and if there is any one I thoroughly abhor, it is that man. But the opposition is divided, red hots, and luke warms; and the Duke (par excellence *the* Duke) and Sir Robert Peel show no sign of insecurity, though they have already been twice beat; so 'courage, mon amie'. Heaven defend the right! as the old chevaliers used to say, before they joined battle. Now Ellen, laugh heartily at all this rodomontade, but you have brought it on yourself; don't you remember telling me to write such letters to you as I write to Mary Taylor? Here's a specimen; hereafter should follow a long disquisition on books, but I'll spare you that. Give my sincerest love to your mother and sisters. Every soul in this house unites with me in best wishes to yourself. – I am, dear Ellen, thy friend,

Charlotte

12

CHARLOTTE BRONTË TO ELLEN NUSSEY

Haworth,
July 2nd, 1835.

Dearest Ellen,

I had hoped to have had the extreme pleasure of seeing you at Haworth this summer, but human affairs are mutable, and human resolutions must bend to the course of events. We are all about to divide, break up, separate. Emily is going to school, Branwell is going to London, and I am going to be a governess. This last determination I formed myself, knowing I should have to take the step sometime, and 'better sune as syne', to use the Scotch proverb; and knowing well that papa would have enough to do with his limited income, should Branwell be placed at the Royal Academy, and Emily at Roe Head.[1] Where am I going to reside? you will ask. Within four miles of yourself, dearest, at a place neither of us is unacquainted with, being no other than the identical Roe Head mentioned above. Yes, I am going to teach in the very school where I was myself taught. Miss Wooler made me the offer, and I preferred it to one or two proposals of private governess-ship, which I had before received. I am sad – very sad – at the thought of leaving home; but duty – necessity – these are stern mistresses, who will not be disobeyed. Did I not once say, Ellen – you ought to be thankful for your independence? I felt what I said at the time, and I repeat it now with double earnestness; if anything would cheer me, it is the idea of being so near you. Surely you and Polly will come and see me; it would be wrong in me to doubt it; you were never unkind yet. Emily and I leave home on the 29th of this month; the idea of being together consoles us both somewhat, and, in truth,

[1] Emily returned to Haworth within three months, and was replaced at Roe Head by Anne.

since I must enter a situation, 'My lines have fallen in pleasant places'. I both love and respect Miss Wooler. What did you mean, Ellen, by saying that you knew the reason why I wished to have a letter from your sister Mercy? The sentence hurt me, though I did not quite understand it. My only reason was a desire to correspond with a person I have a regard for. Give my love both to her and to Sarah, and Miss Nussey.

Remember me respectfully to Mrs. Nussey, and believe me, my dearest friend, – Affectionately, warmly yours,

C. Brontë

13

BRANWELL BRONTË
TO THE EDITOR OF 'BLACKWOOD'S MAGAZINE'

Haworth, near Bradford,
Yorks,
December 7th, 1835.

Sir, – Read what I write.

And would to Heaven you would believe in me, for then you would attend to and act upon it!

I have addressed you twice before, and now I do it again. But it is not from affected hypocrisy that I begin my letter with the name of James Hogg; for the writings of that man in your numbers, his speeches in your *Noctes*, when I was a child, laid a hold on my mind which succeeding years have consecrated into a most sacred feeling. I cannot express, though you can understand, the heavenliness of associations connected with such articles as Professor Wilson's, read and re-read while a little child, with all their poetry of language and divine flights into that visionary region of imagination which one very young would believe reality, and which one entering into manhood would look back upon as a glorious dream. I speak so, sir, because as a child 'Blackwood' formed my chief delight, and I feel certain that no child before enjoyed reading as I did, because none ever had such works as *The Noctes*, *Christmas Dreams*, *Christopher in his Sporting Jacket* to read. And even now, 'Millions o' reasonable creatures at this hour – na', no at this hour', etc. 'Long, long ago seems the time when we danced hand in hand with our golden-haired sister, whom all who looked on loved. Long, long ago, the day on which she died. That hour so far more dreadful than any hour than can darken us on earth, when she, her coffin and that velvet pall descended, and descended slowly, slowly into the horrid clay, and we were borne deathlike, and wishing to die, out of the churchyard that from that moment we thought we could never enter more.' Passages like these, sir (and when that last was written my sister died) – passages like these, read then and remembered now, afford feelings which, I repeat, I cannot describe. But one of those who roused these feelings is dead, and neither from himself nor yourself shall I hear him speak again. I quiver for his death, because to me he was a portion of feelings which I suppose nothing can rouse hereafter: because to you he was a contributor of sterling originality, and in the *Noctes* a subject for your unequalled writing. He and others like him gave your Magazine the peculiar character which made it famous; as these men die it will decay unless their places are supplied by others like them. Now, sir, to you I appear writing with conceited assurance: but *I am not*; for I know myself so far as to believe in my own originality, and on that ground to desire admittance into your ranks. And do not wonder that I demand so determinedly: for the remembrances I spoke of have fixed you and your Magazine in such a manner upon my mind that the idea of striving to aid another periodical is *horribly repulsive*. My resolution is to devote my ability to you, and for God's sake, till you see whether or not I can serve you, do not coldly refuse my aid. All, sir, that I desire of you is: *that in answer to this letter you would request a specimen or specimens of my writing, and I even wish that you would name the subject on which you would wish me to write*. In letters previous to this I have perhaps spoken too openly in respect to the extent of my powers. But I did so because I determined to say what I believed. I *know* that I am not one of the wretched writers of the day. I know that I possess strength to assist you beyond some of your own contributors; but I wish to make you the judge in this case and give you the benefit of its decision.

Now, sir, do not act like a commonplace person, but like a man willing to examine for himself. Do not turn from the native truth of my letters, but *prove me*; and if I do not stand the proof, I will not further press myself on you. If I do stand it – why – You have lost an able writer in James Hogg, and God grant you may get one in

Patrick Branwell Brontë[1]

[1] This was Branwell's full name. He was probably called 'Branwell' to avoid confusion with his father, Patrick Brontë.

14

BRANWELL BRONTË
TO THE EDITOR OF 'BLACKWOOD'S MAGAZINE'

Haworth,
April 8th, 1836.

Sir, – Read now at least . . .

The affair which accompanies my letter is certainly sent for insertion in 'Blackwood' as a Specimen which, whether bad or good, I earnestly desire you to look over; it may be disagreeable, but you will thus KNOW whether, in putting it into the fire, you would gain or lose. It would now be impudent in me to speak of my powers, since in five minutes you can tell whether or not they are fudge or nonsense. But this I know that if they are such, I have no intention of stooping under them. New powers I will get if I can, and provided I keep them, you, sir, shall see them.

But don't think, sir, that I write nothing but Miseries. My day is far too much in the morning for such continual shadow. Nor think either (and this I entreat) that I wish to deluge you with poetry. I sent it because it is soon read and comes from the heart. If it goes to yours, print it, and write to me on the subject of contribution. Then I will send prose. But if what I now send is worthless, what I have said has only been conceit and folly, yet CONDEMN NOT UNHEARD

[Patrick Branwell Brontë]

15

CHARLOTTE BRONTË TO ELLEN NUSSEY

Roe Head,
May 10th, 1836.

My Dearest Ellen,

Just now I am not at all comfortable; for if you are thinking of me at all at this moment I know you are thinking of me as an ungrateful and indifferent being. You imagine I do not appreciate the kind, constant heart whose feelings were revealed in your last letter; but I *do*. Why then did I not answer it? you will say. Because I was waiting to receive a letter from Miss Wooler that I might know whether or not I should have time enough to give you an invitation to Haworth, before the School reopened, but Miss Wooler's letter, when it came, summoned me immediately away, and I had no time to write. Do you forgive me? I know you do; you could not persevere in anger against me long; if you would, I defy you. You seemed kindly apprehensive about my health; I am perfectly well now, and never was very ill. I was struck with the note you sent me with the umbrella; it showed a degree of interest about my concerns, which I have no right to expect from any earthly creature. I won't play the hypocrite, I won't answer your kind, gentle, friendly questions in the way you wish me to. Don't deceive yourself by imagining that I have a bit of real goodness about me. My Darling, if I were like you, I should have to face Zionward, though prejudice and error might occasionally fling a mist over the glorious vision before me, for with all your single-hearted sincerity you have your faults, but I am *not like you*. If you knew my thoughts; the dreams that absorb me; and the fiery imagination that at times eats me up and makes me feel society, as it *is*, wretchedly insipid, you would pity me and I dare say despise me. But, Ellen, I know the treasures of the Bible, and love and adore them. I can *see* the Well of Life in all its clearness and brightness; but when I stoop down to drink of the pure waters, they fly from my lips as if I was Tantalus. I have written like a fool. Remember me to your mother and sisters. Good-bye.

Charlotte

Come and see me soon; don't think me mad. This is a silly letter.

16

CHARLOTTE BRONTË TO ELLEN NUSSEY

Roe Head,
1836

My Dear, Dear Ellen,

I am at this moment trembling all over with excitement after reading your note; it is what I never received before – it is the unrestrained pouring out of a warm, gentle, generous heart; it contains sentiments unrestrained by human motives, prompted by the pure God himself; it expresses a noble sympathy which I *do* not, *cannot* deserve. Ellen, Religion has indeed elevated your character. I thank you with energy for his kindness. I will no longer shrink from your questions. I *do* wish to be better than I am. I pray fervently sometimes to be made so. I have stings of conscience –

visitings of remorse – glimpses of Holy, inexpressible things, which formerly I used to be a stranger to. It may all die away, I may be in utter midnight, but I implore a Merciful Redeemer that if this be the real dawn of the Gospel, it may still brighten to perfect day. Do not mistake me, Ellen, do not think I am good, I only wish to be so, I only hate my former flippancy and forwardness. O! I am no better than I ever was. I am in that state of horrid, gloomy uncertainty, that at this moment I would submit to be old, grey-haired, to have passed all my youthful days of enjoyment and be tottering on the verge of the grave, if I could only thereby ensure the prospect of reconcilement to God and Redemption through His Son's merits. I never was exactly careless of these matters, but I have always taken a clouded and repulsive view of them; and now, if possible, the clouds are gathering darker, and a more oppressive despondency weighs continually on my spirits. You have cheered me, my darling; for one moment, for an atom of time, I thought I might call you my own sister, in the spirit, but the excitement is past, and I am now as wretched and hopeless as ever. This very night I will pray as you wish me. May the Almighty hear me compassionately! and I humbly trust He will – for you will strengthen my polluted petition with your own pure requests. All is bustle and confusion round me, the ladies pressing with their sums and their lessons. Miss Wooler is at Rouse Mill. She has said every day this week, I wonder Miss Ellen does not come. If you love me, *do, do, do* come on Friday; I shall watch and wait for you, and if you disappoint me, I shall weep. I wish you could know the thrill of delight which I experienced, when, as I stood at the dining-room window, I saw your brother George as he whirled past toss your little packet over the wall. I dare write no more, I am neglecting my duty. Love to your mother and both your sisters. Thank you again a thousand times for your kindness – farewell, my blessed Ellen.

Charlotte

17

CHARLOTTE BRONTË TO ELLEN NUSSEY

Roe Head,
1836.

Weary with a day's hard work, during which an unusual degree of stupidity has been displayed by my promising pupils, I am sitting down to write a few hurried lines to my dear Ellen. Excuse me if I say nothing but nonsense, for my mind is exhausted and dispirited. It is a stormy evening, and the wind is uttering a continual moaning sound that makes me feel very melancholy. At such times, in such moods as these, Ellen, it is my nature to seek repose in some calm, tranquil idea, and I have now summoned up your image to give me rest. There you sit upright and still in your black dress and white scarf, your pale, marble-like face, looking so serene and kind – just like reality. I wish you would speak to me. If we should be separated – if it should be our lot to live at a great distance, and never to see each other again – in old age how I should conjure up the memory of my youthful days, and what a melancholy pleasure I should feel in dwelling on the recollection of my early friend Ellen Nussey. If I like people it is my nature to tell them so, and I am not afraid of offering incense to your vanity. It is from religion you derive your chief charm, and may its influence always preserve you as pure, as unassuming, and as benevolent in thought and deed as you are now. What am I compared to you? I feel my own utter worthlessness when I make the comparison. I am a very coarse, commonplace wretch, Ellen. I have some qualities which make me very miserable, some feelings that you can have no participation in, that few, very few people in the world can understand. I don't pride myself on these peculiarities, I strive to conceal and suppress them as much as I can, but they burst out sometimes, and those who see the explosion despise me, and I hate myself for days afterwards. We are going to have prayers, so I can write no more of this trash, yet it is too true. I must send this note for want of a better. I don't know what to say. I have just received your epistle and what accompanied it. I can't tell what should induce your sisters to waste their kindness on such a one as me; I'm obliged to them, and I hope you'll tell them so. I'm obliged to you also, more for your note than for your present. The first gave me pleasure, the last something like pain. Give my love to both your sisters, and my thanks. The bonnet is too handsome for me. I dare write no more. When shall we meet again?

C. Brontë

18

CHARLOTTE BRONTË TO ELLEN NUSSEY

Roe Head,
——, 1836.

My notes to you, Ellen, are written in a hurry – I am now snatching an opportunity. Mr. J. Wooler is here, and by his means this will be transmitted to you. I do not blame you for not coming to see me, for I am sure you have been prevented by sufficient reasons, but I do long to see you, and I hope I shall be gratified momentarily at least ere long. Next Friday, if all be well, I shall go to Gomersall; on Sunday, I shall at least catch a glimpse of you. Week after week I have lived on the expectation of your coming. Week after week I have been disappointed. I have not regretted what I said in my last note to you; the confession was wrung from me by sympathy and kindness such as I can never be sufficiently thankful for. I feel in a strange state of mind, still gloomy but not despairing. I keep trying to do right, checking wrong feelings, repressing wrong thoughts – but still, every instant, I feel myself going astray. I have a constant tendency to scorn people who are far better than I am, horror at the idea of becoming one of a certain set – a dread lest, if I made the slightest profession, I should sink at once into Phariseeism, merge wholly into the rank of the self-righteous. In writing at this moment I feel an irksome disgust at the idea of using a single phrase that sounds like religious cant. I abhor myself – I despise myself; if the doctrine of Calvin be true, I am already an outcast. You cannot imagine how hard, rebellious, and intractable all my feelings are. When I begin to study on the subject, I almost grow blasphemous, atheistical in my sentiments. Don't desert me, don't be horrified at me. You know what I am. I wish I could see you, my darling; I have lavished the warmest affections of a very hot, tenacious heart upon you – if you grow cold, it's over. Love to your mother and sisters.

C. *Brontë*

19

CHARLOTTE BRONTË TO ELLEN NUSSEY

Roe Head, 1836.

Last Saturday afternoon, being in one of my sentimental humours, I sat down and wrote to you such a note as I ought to have written to none but Mary, who is nearly as mad as myself; to-day, when I glanced it over, it occurs to me that Ellen's calm eye would look at this with scorn, so I determined to concoct some production more fit for the inspection of common sense. I will not tell you all I think and feel about you, Ellen. I will preserve unbroken that reserve which alone enables me to maintain a decent character for judgment; but for that, I should have long ago been set down by all who know me as a Frenchified fool. You have been very kind to me of late, and gentle, and you have spared me those little sallies of ridicule, which, owing to my miserable and wretched touchiness of character, used formerly to make me wince, as if I had been touched with hot iron. Things that nobody else cares for enter into my mind and rankle there like venom. I know these feelings are absurd, and therefore I try to hide them, but they only sink the deeper for concealment. I'm an idiot! I am informed that your brother George was at Mirfield Church last Sunday. Of course I did not *see* him, though guessed his presence because I heard him cough; my short-sightedness makes my ears very acute. The Miss Woolers told me he was there. They were quite smitten; he was the sole subject of their conversation during the whole of the subsequent evening. Miss Eliza described to me every part of his dress, and likewise that of a gentleman who accompanied him with astonishing minuteness. I laughed most heartily at her graphic details, and so would you if you had been with me.

Ellen, I wish I could live with you always. I begin to cling to you more fondly than ever I did. If we had but a cottage and a competency of our own, I do think we might live and love on till *Death* without being dependent on any third person for happiness. – Farewell, my own dear Ellen.

C. Brontë

20

CHARLOTTE BRONTË TO ELLEN NUSSEY

[December 6th, 1836]

I am sure, Ellen, you will conclude that I have taken a final leave of my senses, to forget to send your bag when I had had it hanging before my eyes in the dressing-room for a whole week. I stood for ten minutes considering before I sent the boy off; I felt sure I had something else to intrust to him besides the books, but I could not recollect what it was. These aberrations of memory warn me pretty intelligibly that I am getting past my prime.

I hope you will not be much inconvenienced by my neglect. I'll wait till to-morrow, to see if George will call for it on his way to Huddersfield, and if he does not, I'll try to get a person to go over with it to Bookroyd on purpose. I am most grieved lest you should think me careless, but I assure you it was merely a temporary fit of absence. I wish exceedingly that I could come to see you before Christmas; but I trust ere another three weeks elapse I shall again have my comforter beside me under the roof of my own dear quiet home. If I could always live with you, if your lips and mine could at the same time drink the same draught at the same pure fountain of mercy, I hope, I trust, I might one day become better, far better than my evil wandering thoughts, my corrupt heart, cold to the spirit and warm to the flesh, will now permit me to be. I often plan the pleasant life which we might lead together, strengthening each other in that power of self-denial, that hallowed and glowing devotion which the past Saints of God often attained to. My eyes fill with tears when I contrast the bliss of such a state, brightened with hopes of the future, with the melancholy state I now live in; uncertain that I have ever felt true contrition, wandering in thought and deed, longing for holiness which I shall never, never attain, smitten at times to the heart with the conviction that – ghastly Calvinistic doctrines are true, darkened, in short, by the very shadows of Spiritual Death! If Christian perfections be necessary to Salvation, I shall never be saved. My heart is a real hot-bed for sinful thoughts, and as to practice, when I decide on an action, I scarcely remember to look to my Redeemer for direction.

I know not how to pray; I cannot bend my life to the grand end of doing good. I go on constantly seeking my own pleasure, pursuing the gratification of my own desires. I forget God, and will not

God forget me? and meantime I know the greatness of Jehovah. I acknowledge the truth, the perfection of His Word. I adore the purity of the Christian faith. My theory is right, my practice horribly wrong. Good-bye, Ellen,

C. Brontë

Write to me again, if you can. Your notes are meat and drink to me. Remember me to the family. I hope Mercy is better [– Clement Shorter].

21

BRANWELL BRONTË
TO THE EDITOR OF 'BLACKWOOD'S MAGAZINE'[1]

January 9th, 1837.

In a former letter I hinted that I was in possession of something, the design of which, whatever might be its execution, would be superior to that of any series of articles which has yet appeared in *Blackwood's Magazine*. But being prose, of course, and of great length, as well as peculiar in character, a description of it by letter would be quite impossible. So surely a journey of three hundred miles shall not deter me from a knowledge of myself and a hope of utterance into the open world.

Now, sir, all I ask you is to permit this interview, and in answer to this letter to say that you will see me, were it only for one half-hour. The fault be mine if you have reason to repent your permission.

Now, is the trouble of writing a single line to outweigh the certainty of doing good to a fellow-creature and the possibility of doing good to yourself? Will you still so wearisomely refuse me a word when you can neither know what you refuse nor whom you are refusing? Do you think your Magazine so perfect that no addition to its power would be either possible or desirable? Is it pride which actuates you – or custom – or prejudice? Be a man, sir!

[1] Mrs Oliphant tells us that not one of these letters of Branwell's was ever answered, but that in spite of the chilling reception Branwell wrote again in September, 1842, 'begging most respectfully to offer the accompanying lines for insertion in *Blackwood's Edinburgh Magazine*'.

and think no more of these things. *Write* to me: tell me that you will receive a visit; and rejoicingly will I take upon myself the labour, which if it succeed, will be an advantage both to you and me, and if it fail, will still be an advantage, because I shall then be assured of the impossibility of succeeding.

[Patrick Branwell Brontë]

22

BRANWELL BRONTË
TO WILLIAM WORDSWORTH

Haworth, near Bradford,
Yorkshire,
January 19th, 1837.

Sir,

I most earnestly entreat you to read and pass your judgment upon what I have sent you, because from the day of my birth to this the nineteenth year of my life I have lived among secluded hills, where I could neither know what I was or what I could do. I read for the same reason that I ate or drank, because it was a real craving of nature. I wrote on the same principle as I spoke – out of the impulse and feelings of the mind; nor could I help it, for what came, came out, and there was the end of it. For as to self-conceit, that could not receive food from flattery, since to this hour not half-a-dozen people in the world know that I have ever penned a line.

But a change has taken place now, sir; and I am arrived at an age wherein I must do something for myself; the powers I possess must be exercised to a definite end, and as I don't know them myself I must ask of others what they are worth. Yet there is not one here to tell me; and still, if they are worthless, time will henceforth be too precious to be wasted on them.

Do pardon me, sir, that I have ventured to come before one whose works I have most loved in our literature, and who most has been with me a divinity of the mind, laying before him one of my writings, and asking of him a judgment of its contents. I must come before some one from whose sentence there is no appeal; and such a one is he who has developed the theory of poetry as well as its practice, and both in such a way as to claim a place in the memory of a thousand years to come.

My aim, sir, is to push out into the open world, and for this I trust not poetry alone; that might launch the vessel, but could not bear her on. Sensible and scientific prose, bold and vigorous efforts in my walk in life, would give a further title to the notice of the world; and then again poetry ought to brighten and crown that name with glory. But nothing of all this can be ever begun without means, and as I don't possess these I must in every shape strive to gain them. Surely, in this day, when there is not a *writing* poet worth a sixpence, the field must be open, if a better man can step forward.

What I send you is the Prefatory Scene of a much longer subject, in which I have striven to develop strong passions and weak principles struggling with a high imagination and acute feelings, till, as youth hardens towards age, evil deeds and short enjoyments end in mental misery and bodily ruin. Now, to send you the whole of this would be a mock upon your patience; what you see does not even pretend to be more than the description of an imaginative child. But read it, sir; and, as you would hold a light to one in utter darkness – as you value your own kind-heartedness – *return* me an *answer*, if but one word, telling me whether I should write on, or write no more. Forgive undue warmth, because my feelings in this matter cannot be cool; and believe me, sir, with deep respect, your really humble servant.

P.B. Brontë

23

ROBERT SOUTHEY
TO CHARLOTTE BRONTË

Keswick,
March, 1837.

Madam,

You will probably, ere this, have given up all expectation of receiving an answer to your letter of December 29. I was on the borders of Cornwall when the letter was written; it found me a fortnight afterwards in Hampshire. During my subsequent movements in different parts of the country, and a tarriance of three busy weeks in London, I had no leisure for replying to it; and now that I am once more at home, and am clearing off the arrears of business which have accumulated during a long absence, it has lain unanswered till the last of a numerous file, not from disrespect or indifference to its contents, but because, in truth, it is not an easy task to answer it, nor a pleasant one to cast a damp over the high spirits and the generous desires of youth. What you are I can only infer from your letter, which appears to be written in sincerity, though I may suspect that you have used a fictitious signature. Be that as it may, the letter and the verses bear the same stamp; and I can well understand the state of mind they indicate. What I am you might have learnt by such of my publications as have come into your hands; and had you happened to be acquainted with me, a little personal knowledge would have tempered your enthusiasm. You might have had your ardour in some degree abated by seeing a poet in the decline of life, and witnessing the effect which age produces upon our hopes and aspirations; yet I am neither a disappointed man nor a discontented one, and you would never have heard from me any chilling sermons upon the text 'All is vanity'.

It is not my advice that you have asked as to the direction of your talents, but my opinion of them; and yet the opinion may be worth little, and the advice much. You evidently possess, and in no inconsiderable degree, what Worthsworth calls the 'faculty of verse'. I am not depreciating it when I say that in these times it is not rare. Many volumes of poems are now published every year without attracting public attention, any one of which, if it had appeared half a century ago, would have obtained a high reputation for its author. Whoever, therefore, is ambitious of distinction in this way ought to be prepared for disappointment.

But it is not with a view to distinction that you should cultivate this talent if you consult your own happiness. I, who have made literature my profession, and devoted my life to it, and have never for a moment repented of the deliberate choice, think myself, nevertheless, bound in duty to caution every young man who applies as an aspirant to me for encouragement and advice against taking so perilous a course. You will say that a woman has no need of such caution; there can be no peril in it for her. In a certain sense this is true; but there is a danger of which I would, with all kindness and all earnestness, warn you. The day dreams in which you habitually indulge are likely to induce a distempered state of mind; and, in proportion as all the ordinary uses of the world seem to you flat and unprofitable, you will be unfitted for them without becoming fitted for anything else. Literature cannot be the business of a woman's life, and it ought not to be. The more she is engaged in her proper duties, the less leisure will she have for it, even as an accomplishment and a recreation. To those duties you have not yet been called, and when you are you will be less eager for celebrity. You will not seek in imagination for excitement, of which the vicissitudes of this life, and the anxieties from which you must not hope to be exempted, be your state what it may, will bring with them but too much.

But do not suppose that I disparage the gift which you possess, nor that I would discourage you from exercising it. I only exhort you so to think of it, and so to use it, as to render it conducive to your own permanent good. Write poetry for its own sake; not in a spirit of emulation, and not with a view to celebrity; the less you aim at that the more likely you will be to deserve and finally to obtain it. So written, it is wholesome both for the heart and soul; it may be made the surest means, next to religion, of soothing the mind, and elevating it. You may embody in it your best thoughts and your wisest feelings, and in so doing discipline and strengthen them.

Farewell, madam. It is not because I have forgotten that I was once young myself, that I write to you in this strain; but because I remember it. You will neither doubt my sincerity, nor my good-will; and, however ill what has here been said may accord with your present views and temper, the longer you live the more reasonable it will appear to you. Though I may be an ungracious adviser, you will allow me, therefore, to subscribe myself, with the best wishes for your happiness here and hereafter, your true friend,

Robert Southey

24

CHARLOTTE BRONTË
TO ROBERT SOUTHEY

Roe Head,
March 16th, 1837.

Sir,

I cannot rest till I have answered your letter, even though by addressing you a second time I should appear a little intrusive; but I must thank you for the kind and wise advice you have condescended to give me. I had not ventured to hope for such a reply; so considerate in its tone, so noble in its spirit. I must suppress what I feel, or you will think me foolishly enthusiastic.

At the first perusal of your letter I felt only shame and regret that I had ever ventured to trouble you with my crude rhapsody; I felt a painful heat rise to my face when I thought of the quires of paper I had covered with what once gave me so much delight, but which now was only a source of confusion; but after I had thought a little, and read it again and again, the prospect seemed to clear. You do not forbid me to write; you do not say that what I write is utterly destitute of merit. You only warn me against the folly of neglecting real duties for the sake of imaginative pleasures; of writing for the love of fame; for the selfish excitement of emulation. You kindly allow me to write poetry for its own sake, provided I leave undone nothing which I ought to do, in order to pursue that single, absorbing, exquisite gratification. I am afraid, sir, you think me very foolish. I know the first letter I wrote to you was all senseless trash from beginning to end; but I am not altogether the idle, dreaming being it would seem to denote.

My father is a clergyman of limited though competent income, and I am the eldest of his children. He expended quite as much in my education as he could afford in justice to the rest. I thought it therefore my duty, when I left school to become a governess. In that capacity I find enough to occupy my thoughts all day long, and my head and hands too, without having a moment's time for one dream of the imagination. In the evenings, I confess, I do think, but I never trouble any one else with my thoughts. I carefully avoid any appearance of preoccupation and eccentricity, which might lead those I live amongst to suspect the nature of my pursuits. Following my father's advice – who from my childhood has counselled me, just in the wise and friendly tone of your letter – I have endeavoured not only attentively to observe all the duties a woman ought to fulfil, but to feel deeply interested in them. I don't always succeed, for sometimes when I'm teaching or sewing I would rather be reading or writing; but I try to deny myself; and my father's approbation amply rewarded me for the privation. Once more allow me to thank you with sincere gratitude. I trust I shall never more feel ambitious to see my name in print; if the wish should rise, I'll look at Southey's letter, and suppress it. It is honour enough for me that I have written to him, and received an answer. That letter is consecrated; no one shall ever see it but papa and my brother and sisters. Again I thank you. This incident, I suppose, will be renewed no more; if I live to be an old woman, I shall remember it thirty years hence as a bright dream. The signature which you suspected of being ficitious is my real name. Again, therefore, I must sign myself.

C. Brontë

P.S. – Pray, sir, excuse me for writing to you a second time; I could not help writing, partly to tell you how thankful I am for your kindness, and partly to let you know that your advice shall not be wasted, however sorrowfully and reluctantly it may at first be followed.

C.B.

25

ROBERT SOUTHEY
TO CHARLOTTE BRONTË

Keswick,
March 22nd, 1837.

Dear Madam,

Your letter has given me great pleasure, and I should not forgive myself if I did not tell you so. You have received admonition as considerately and as kindly as it was given. Let me now request that, if you ever should come to these Lakes while I am living here, you will let me see you. You would then think of me afterwards with the more goodwill, because you would perceive that there is neither severity nor moroseness in the state of mind to which years and observation have brought me.

It is, by God's mercy, in our power to attain a degree of self-government, which is essential to our own happiness, and contributes greatly to that of those around us. Take care of over-excitement, and endeavour to keep a quiet mind (even for your health it is the best advice that can be given you): your moral and spiritual improvement will then keep pace with the culture of your intellectual powers.

And now, madam, God bless you!

Farewell, and believe me to be your sincere friend,

Robert Southey

26

CHARLOTTE BRONTË TO ELLEN NUSSEY

Dewsbury Moor,[1]
October 2nd, 1837.

Dear, dear Ellen,

. . . My sister Emily is gone into a situation as teacher in a large school of near forty pupils, near Halifax. I have had one letter from her since her departure; it gives an appalling account of her duties – hard labour from six in the morning until near eleven at night, with only one half-hour of exercise between. This is slavery. I fear she will never stand it. It gives me sincere pleasure, my dear Ellen, to learn that you have at last found a few associates of congenial minds. I cannot conceive a life more dreary than that passed amidst sights, sounds, and companions all alien to the nature within us. From the tenour of your letter it seems your mind remains fixed as it ever was; in no wise dazzled by novelty or warped by evil example. I am thankful for it. I could not help smiling at the paragraphs which related to ——; there was in them a touch of genuine, unworldly simplicity. Ellen, depend upon it, all people have their dark side – though some possess the power of throwing a fair veil over the defects; close acquaintance slowly removes the screen, and one by one the blots appear, till at length we sometimes see the pattern of perfection all slurred over with blots, that even *partial* affection cannot efface. I hope my next communication with you will be face to face, and not as through a letter darkly. Commending you to the care of One above us all, I remain, still, my *dear* Ellen, – Your friend,

C. Brontë

27

CHARLOTTE BRONTË TO ELLEN NUSSEY

[Haworth]
January 4th, 1838.

Your letter, Ellen, was a welcome surprise, even though it contains something like a reprimand. I had not, however, forgotten

[1] Miss Wooler's school moved to Dewsbury Moor early in 1837.

our agreement; I had prepared a note to be forthcoming against the arrival of your messenger, but things so happened that it was of no avail. You were right in your conjectures respecting the cause of my sudden departure. Anne continued wretchedly ill – neither the pain nor the difficulty of breathing left her – and how could I feel otherwise than very miserable? I looked upon her case in a different light to what I could wish or expect any uninterested person to view it in. Miss Wooler thought me a fool, and by way of proving her opinion treated me with marked coldness. We came to a little éclaircissement one evening. I told her one or two rather plain truths, which set her a-crying, and the next day, unknown to me, she wrote to papa, telling him that I had reproached her bitterly – taken her severely to task, etc., etc. Papa sent for us the day after he had received her letter. Meantime, I had formed a firm resolution – to quit Miss Wooler and her concerns for ever – but just before I went away she took me into her room, and giving way to her feelings, which in general she restrains far too rigidly, gave me to understand that in spite of her cold repulsive manners she had a considerable regard for me and would be very sorry to part with me. If anybody likes me I can't help liking them, and remembering that she had in general been very kind to me, I gave in and said I would come back if she wished me – so we're settled again for the present; but I am not satisfied. I should have respected her far more if she had turned me out of doors instead of crying for two days and two nights together. I was in a regular passion; my '*warm temper*' quite got the better of me – of which I don't boast, for it was a weakness; nor am I ashamed of it, for I had reason to be angry. Anne is now much better, though she still requires a great deal of care. However, I am relieved from my worst fears respecting her.

I approve highly of the plan you mention, except as it regards committing a verse of the psalms to memory; I do not see the direct advantage to be derived from that. We have entered on a new year; will it be stained as darkly as the last, with all our sins, follies, secret vanities, and uncontrolled passions and propensities? I trust not, but I feel in nothing better – neither humbler nor purer. It will want three weeks next Monday to the termination of the holidays. Come to see me, my *dear* Ellen, as soon as you can. However bitterly I sometimes feel towards other people, the recollection of your mild, steady friendship consoles and softens me. I am glad you are not such a weak fool as myself. Give my best love to your mother and sisters, excuse the most hideous scrawl that ever was penned, and believe me always tenderly yours,

C. Brontë

28

CHARLOTTE BRONTË
TO THE REV. HENRY NUSSEY

Haworth,
March 5th, 1839.

My Dear Sir,

Before answering your letter I might have spent a long time in consideration of its subject; but as from the first moment of its reception and perusal I determined on what course to pursue, it seemed to me that delay was wholly unnecessary. You are aware that I have many reasons to feel grateful to your family, that I have peculiar reasons for affection towards one at least of your sisters, and also that I highly esteem yourself – do not therefore accuse me of wrong motives when I say that my answer to your proposal must be a *decided negative*. In forming this decision, I trust I have listened to the dictates of conscience more than to those of inclination. I have no personal repugnance to the idea of a union with you, but I feel convinced that mine is not the sort of disposition calculated to form the happiness of a man like you. It has always been my habit to study the characters of those amongst whom I chance to be thrown, and I think I know yours and can imagine what description of woman would suit you for a wife. The character should not be too marked, ardent, and original, her temper should be mild, her piety undoubted, her spirits even and cheerful, and her *personal attractions* sufficient to please your eyes and gratify your just pride. As for me, you do not know me; I am not the serious, grave, cool-headed individual you suppose; you would think me romantic and eccentric; you would say I was satirical and severe. However, I scorn deceit, and I will never, for the sake of attaining the distinction of matrimony and escaping the stigma of an old maid, take a worthy man whom I am conscious I cannot render happy. Before I conclude, let me thank you warmly for your other proposal regarding the school near Donnington. It is kind in you to take so much interest about me; but the fact is, I could not at present enter upon such a project because I have not the capital necessary to insure success. It is a pleasure to me to hear that you are so comfortably settled and that your health is so much improved. I trust God will continue His kindness towards you. Let me say also that I admire the good sense and absence of flattery and cant which your letter displayed. Farewell. I shall always be glad to hear from you as a *friend*. – Believe me, yours truly,

C. Brontë

29

CHARLOTTE BRONTË TO ELLEN NUSSEY

Haworth,
March 12th, 1839.

My Dearest Ellen,

When your letter was put into my hands, I said, 'She is coming at last, I hope', but when I opened it and found what the contents were, I was vexed to the heart. You need not ask me to go to Brookroyd any more. Once for all, and at the hazard of being called the most stupid little wretch that ever existed, I *won't go* till you have been to Haworth. I don't blame *you*, I believe you would come if you might; perhaps I ought not to blame others, but I am grieved.

Anne goes to Blake Hall on the 8th of April, unless some further unseen cause of delay should occur. I've heard nothing more from Mrs. Thos. Brooke as yet. Papa wishes me to remain at home a little longer, but I begin to be anxious to set to work again; and yet it will be *hard work* after the indulgence of so many weeks, to return to that dreary 'gin-horse' round.

You ask me, my dear Ellen, whether I have received a letter from Henry. I have, about a week since. The contents, I confess, did a little surprise me, but I kept them to myself, and unless you had questioned me on the subject, I would never have adverted to it. Henry says he is comfortably settled at Donnington, that his health is much improved, and that it is his intention to take pupils after Easter. He then intimates that in due time he should want a wife to take care of his pupils, and frankly asks me to be that wife. Altogether the letter is written without cant or flattery, and in a common-sense style, which does credit to his judgment.

Now, my dear Ellen, there were in this proposal some things which might have proved a strong temptation. I thought if I were to marry Henry Nussey, his sister could live with me, and how happy I should be. But again I asked myself two questions: Do I love him as much as a woman ought to love the man she marries? Am I the person best qualified to make him happy? Alas! Ellen, my conscience answered *no* to both these questions. I felt that though I esteemed, though I had a kindly leaning towards him, because he is an amiable and well-disposed man, yet I had not, and could not have, that intense attachment which would make me willing to die for him; and, if ever I marry, it must be in that light of adoration that I will regard my husband. Ten to one I shall never have the chance again; but *n'importe*. Moreover, I was aware that Henry knew so little of me he could hardly be conscious to whom he was writing. Why, it would startle him to see me in my natural home character; he would think I was a wild, romantic enthusiast indeed. I could not sit all day long making a grave face before my husband. I would laugh, and satirize, and say whatever came into my head first. And if he was a clever man, and loved me, the whole world weighed in the balance against his smallest wish should be light as air. Could I, knowing my mind to be such as that, conscientiously say that I would take a grave, quiet, young man like Henry? No, it would have been deceiving him, and deception of that sort is beneath me. So I wrote a long letter back, in which I expressed my refusal as gently as I could, and also candidly avowed my reasons for that refusal. I described to him, too, the sort of character that would suit him for a wife. Write to me soon and say whether you are angry with me or not. – Good-bye, my dear Ellen.

C. Brontë

30

CHARLOTTE BRONTË TO ELLEN NUSSEY

Haworth,
April 15th, 1839.

I could not write to you in the week you requested, as about that time we were very busy in preparing for Anne's departure, Poor child! she left us last Monday; no one went with her; it was her own wish that she might be allowed to go alone, as she thought she could manage better and summon more courage if thrown entirely upon her own resources. We have had one letter from her since she went. She expresses herself very well satisfied, and says that Mrs. Ingham is extremely kind; the two eldest children alone are under her care, the rest are confined to the nursery, with which and its occupants she has nothing to do. Both her pupils are desperate little dunces; neither of them can read, and sometimes they profess a profound ignorance of their alphabet. The worst of it is they are excessively indulged, and she is not empowered to inflict any punishment. She is requested, when they misbehave themselves, to inform their mamma, which she says is utterly out of the question, as in that case she might be making complaints from morning till night. So she alternately scolds, coaxes, and threatens, sticks always to her first word, and gets on as well as she can. I hope she'll do. You would be astonished what a sensible, clever letter she writes; it is only the talking part that I fear. But I do seriously apprehend that Mrs. Ingham will sometimes conclude that she has a natural impediment of speech. For my own part, I am as yet 'wanting a situation,' like a housemaid out of place. By the way, I have lately discovered I have quite a talent for cleaning, sweeping up hearths, dusting rooms, making beds, etc.; so, if everything else fails, I can turn my hand to that, if anybody will give me good wages for little labour. I won't be a cook; I hate cooking. I won't be a nursery-maid, nor a lady's-maid, far less a lady's companion, or a mantua-maker, or a straw-bonnet maker, or a taker-in of plain work. I won't be anything but a housemaid. Setting aside nonsense, I was very glad, my dear Ellen, to learn by your last letter that some improvement had taken place in your health, for occasionally I have felt more uneasy about you than I would willingly confess to yourself. I verily believe that a visit to Haworth would now greatly help to restore you, and there can be no objection on account of cold when the weather is so much milder. However angry you are, I still stick to my resolution that I will go no more to Brookroyd till you have been to Haworth. I think I am right in this determination, and I'll abide by it. It does not arise from resentment, but from reason. I have never for a moment supposed that the reluctance of your friends to allow you to leave home arose from any ill-will to me. It was quite natural, in your precarious state of health, to desire to keep you at home, but that argument does not now hold good. With regard to my visit to Gomersall, I have as yet received no invitation; but if I should be asked, though I should feel it a great act of self-denial to refuse, yet I have almost made up my mind to do so, though the society of the Taylors is one of the most rousing pleasures I have ever known. I wish you good-bye, my darling Ellen, and I tell you once more that I want to see you. Strike out that word *darling*, it is humbug, where's the use of protestations? We've known each other, and *liked* each other a *good while*, that's enough.

C. Brontë

31

CHARLOTTE BRONTË TO EMILY J. BRONTE

Stonegappe,
June 8th, 1839.

Dearest Lavinia,

I am most exceedingly obliged to you for the trouble you have taken in seeking up my things and sending them all right. The box and its contents were most acceptable. I only wished I had asked you to send me some letter-paper. This is my last sheet but two. When you can send the other articles of raiment now manufacturing, I shall be right down glad of them.

I have striven hard to be pleased with my new situation. The country, the house, and the grounds are, as I have said, divine. But, alack-a-day! there is such a thing as seeing all beautiful around you – pleasant woods, winding white paths, green lawns, and blue sunshiny sky – and not having a free moment or a free thought left to enjoy them in. The children are constantly with me, and more riotous, perverse, unmanageable cubs never grew. As for correcting them, I soon quickly found that was entirely out of the question: they are to do as they like. A complaint to Mrs. Sidgwick brings only black looks upon oneself, and unjust, partial excuses to screen the children. I have tried that plan once. It succeeded so notably that I shall try it no more. I said in my last letter that Mrs. Sidgwick did not know me. I now begin to find that she does not intend to know me, that she cares nothing in the world about me except to contrive how the greatest possible quantity of labour may be squeezed out of me, and to that end she overwhelms me with oceans of needlework, yards of cambric to hem, muslin nightcaps to make, and, above all things, dolls to dress. I do not think she likes me at all, because I can't help being shy in such an entirely novel scene, surrounded as I have hitherto been by strange and constantly changing faces. I see now more clearly than I have ever done before that a private governess has no existence, is not considered as a living and rational being except as connected with the wearisome duties she has to fulfil. While she is teaching the children, working for them, amusing them, it is all right. If she steals a moment for herself she is a nuisance. Nevertheless, Mrs. Sidgwick is universally considered an amiable woman. Her manners are fussily affable. She talks a great deal, but as it seems to me not much to the purpose. Perhaps I may like her better after a while. At present I have no call to her. Mr. Sidgwick is in my opinion a hundred times better – less profession, less bustling condescension, but a far kinder heart. It is very seldom that he speaks to me, but when he does I always feel happier and more settled for some minutes after. He never asks me to wipe the children's smutty noses or tie their shoes or fetch their pinafores or set them a chair. One of the pleasantest afternoons I have spent here – indeed, the only one at all pleasant – was when Mr. Sidgwick walked out with his children, and I had orders to follow a little behind. As he strolled on through his fields with his magnificent Newfoundland dog at his side, he looked very like what a frank, wealthy, Conservative gentleman ought to be. He spoke freely and unaffectedly to the people he met, and though he indulged his children and allowed them to tease himself far too much, he would not suffer them grossly to insult others.

I am getting quite to have a regard for the Carter family. At home I should not care for them, but here they are friends. Mr. Carter was at Mirfield yesterday and saw Anne. He says she was looking uncommonly well. Poor girl, *she* must indeed wish to be at home. As to Mrs. Collins' report that Mrs. Sidgwick intended to keep me permanently, I do not think that such was ever her design. Moreover, I would not stay without some alterations. For instance, this burden of sewing would have to be removed. It is too bad for anything. I never in my whole life had my time so fully taken up. Next week we are going to Swarcliffe, Mr. Greenwood's place near Harrogate, to stay three weeks or a month. After that time I hope Miss Hoby will return. Don't show this letter to papa or aunt, only to Branwell. They will think I am never satisfied, wherever I am. I complain to you because it is a relief, and really I have had some unexpected mortifications to put up with. However, things may mend, but Mrs. Sidgwick expects me to do things that I cannot do – to love her children and be entirely devoted to them.'I am really very well. I am so sleepy that I can write no more. I must leave off. Love to all. – Good-bye.

Direct your next despatch – J. Greenwood, Esq., Swarcliffe, near Harrogate.

C. Brontë

32

CHARLOTTE BRONTË TO EMILY J. BRONTË

July –, 1839.

Mine bonnie love, I was as glad of your letter as tongue can express: it is a real, genuine pleasure to hear from home; a thing to be saved till bedtime, when one has a moment's quiet and rest to enjoy it thoroughly. Write whenever you can. I could like to be at home. I could like to work in a mill. I could feel mental liberty. I could like this weight of restraint to be taken off. But the holidays will come. *Corragio.*

33

BRANWELL BRONTË TO JOHN BROWN

[Broughton-in-Furness]
March 13th, 1840.

Old Knave of Trumps,

Don't think I have forgotten you, though I have delayed so long in writing to you. It was my purpose to send you a yarn as soon as I could find materials to spin one with, and it is only just now that I have had time to turn myself round and know where I am. If you saw me now, you would not know me, and you would laugh to hear the character the people give me. Oh, the falsehood and hypocrisy of this world! I am fixed in a little retired town by the sea-shore, among wild, woody hills that rise round me – huge, rocky, and capped with clouds. My employer is a retired County magistrate, a large landowner, and of a right hearty and generous disposition. His wife is a quiet, silent, and amiable woman, and his sons are two fine, spirited lads. My landlord is a respectable surgeon, two days out of seven is as drunk as a lord! His wife is a bustling, chattering, kind-hearted soul; and his daughter! oh! death and damnation! Well, what am I? That is, what do they think I am? A most calm, sedate, sober, abstemious, patient, mild-hearted, virtuous, gentlemanly philosopher – the picture of good works, and the treasure-house of righteous thoughts. Cards are shuffled under the table-cloth, glasses are thrust into the cupboard if I enter the room, I take neither spirits, wine, nor malt liquors. I dress in black, and smile like a saint or martyr. Everybody says, 'what a good young gentleman is Mr. Postlethwaite's tutor!' This is a fact, as I am a living soul, and right comfortably do I laugh at them. I mean to continue in their good opinion. I took a half-year's farewell of old friend whisky at Kendal on the night after I left. There was a party of gentlemen at the Royal Hotel, and I joined them. We ordered in supper and whisky-toddy as 'hot as hell!' They thought I was a physician, and put me in the chair. I gave sundry toasts, that were washed down at the same time, till the room spun round and the candles danced in our eyes. One of the guests was a respectable old gentleman with powdered head, rosy cheeks, fat paunch, and ringed fingers. He gave 'The Ladies', . . . after which he brayed off with a speech; and in two minutes, in the middle of a grand sentence, he stopped, wiped his head, looked wildly round, stammered, coughed, stopped again, and called for his slippers. The waiter helped him to bed. Next a tall Irish squire and a native of the land of Israel began to quarrel about their countries; and, in the warmth of argument, discharged their glasses, each at his neighbour's throat instead of his own. I recommended bleeding, purging, and blistering; but they administered each other a real 'Jem Warder', so I flung my tumbler on the floor, too, and swore I'd join 'Old Ireland!' A regular rumpus ensued, but we were tamed at last. I found myself in bed next morning, with a bottle of porter, a glass, and a corkscrew beside me. Since then I have not tasted anything stronger than milk-and-water, nor, I hope, shall, till I return at Midsummer; when we will see about it. I am getting as fat as Prince William at Springhead, and as godly as his friend, Parson Winterbotham. My hand shakes no longer. I ride to the banker's at Ulverston with Mr. Postlethwaite, and sit drinking tea and talking scandal with old ladies. As to the young ones! I have one sitting by me just now – fair-faced, blue-eyed, dark-haired, sweet eighteen – she little thinks the devil is so near her!

I was delighted to see thy note, old squire, but I do not understand one sentence – you will perhaps know what I mean. . . . How are all about you? I long to hear and see them again. How is the 'Devil's Thumb', whom men call —— ——, and the 'Devil in Mourning', whom they call —— ——. How are —— ——, and

—— ——, and the Doctor; and him who will be used as the tongs of hell – he whose eyes Satan looks out of, as from windows – I mean —— ——, esquire? How are little —— ——, —— 'Long-shanks', —— ——, and the rest of them? Are they married, buried, devilled, and damned? When I come I'll give them a good squeeze of the hand; till then I am too godly for them to think of. That bow-legged devil used to ask me impertinent questions which I answered him in kind. Beelzebub will make of him a walking-stick! Keep to thy teetotalism, old squire, till I return; it will mend thy old body. . . . Does 'Little Nosey' think I have forgotten him? No, by Jupiter! nor his clock either. I'll send him a remembrance some of these days! But I must talk to some one prettier than thee: so good-night, old boy, and believe me thine,

The Philosopher

34

CHARLOTTE BRONTË TO ELLEN NUSSEY

April 7th, 1840.

My Dear Mrs. Menelaus,

I think I am exceedingly good to write to you so soon, indeed I am quite afraid you will begin to consider me intrusive with my frequent letters. I ought by right to let an interval of a quarter of a year elapse between each communication, and I will, in time; never fear me. I shall improve in procrastination as I get older.

My hand is trembling like that of an old man, so I don't expect you will be able to read my writing; never mind, put the letter by and I'll read it to you the next time I see you.

Little Haworth has been all in a bustle about church rates since you were here. We had a most stormy meeting in the schoolroom. Papa took the chair, and Mr. Collins and Mr. Weightman[1] acted as his supporters, one on each side. There was violent opposition, which set Mr. Collins's Irish blood in a ferment, and if papa had not kept him quiet, partly by persuasion and partly by compulsion, he would have given the Dissenters their 'kale through the reek' – a Scotch proverb, which I will explain to you another time. He and

[1] Mr Weightman was a curate at Haworth who is subsequently referred to as 'Miss Weightman' and 'Miss Celia Amelia' – the sisters' nickname for him on account of his dandified manners and appearance.

Mr. Weightman both bottled up their wrath for that time, but it was only to explode with redoubled force at a future period. We had two sermons on dissent, and its consequences, preached last Sunday – one in the afternoon by Mr. Weightman, and one in the evening by Mr. Collins. All the Dissenters were invited to come and hear, and they actually shut up their chapels and came in a body; of course the church was crowded. Miss Celia Amelia delivered a noble, eloquent, High-Church, Apostolical-Succession discourse, in which he banged the Dissenters most fearlessly and unflinchingly. I thought they had got enough for one while, but it was nothing to the dose that was thrust down their throats in the evening. A keener, cleverer, bolder, and more heart-stirring harangue than that which Mr. Collins delivered from Haworth pulpit, last Sunday evening, I never heard. He did not rant; he did not cant; he did not whine; he did not sniggle; he just got up and spoke with the boldness of a man who was impressed with the truth of what he was saying, who has no fear of his enemies and no dread of consequences. His sermon lasted an hour, yet I was sorry when it was done. I do not say that I agree either with him or Mr. Weightman, either in all or half their opinions. I consider them bigoted, intolerant, and wholly unjustifiable on the ground of common sense. My conscience will not let me be either a Puseyite or a Hookist; nay, if I were a Dissenter, I would have taken the first opportunity of kicking or of horsewhipping both the gentlemen for their stern, bitter attack on my religion and its teachers. But in spite of all this, I admired the noble integrity which could dictate so fearless an opposition against so strong an antagonist.

I have been painting a portrait of Agnes Walton, for our friend Miss Celia Amelia. You would laugh to see how his eyes sparkle with delight when he looks at it, like a pretty child pleased with a new plaything. Good-bye to you, let me have no more of your humbug about Cupid, etc. You know as well as I do, it is all groundless trash. Mr. Weightman has given another lecture at the Keighley Mechanics' Institute, and papa has also given a lecture; both are spoken of very highly in the newspaper, and it is mentioned as a matter of wonder that such displays of intellect should emanate from the village of Haworth, situated amongst the bogs and mountains, and, until very lately, supposed to be in a state of semi-barbarism. Such are the words of the newspaper.

C. Brontë

35

BRANWELL BRONTË TO HARTLEY COLERIDGE

Broughton-in-Furness,
Lancashire,
April 20th, 1840.

Sir,

It is with much reluctance that I venture to request, for the perusal of the following lines, a portion of the time of one upon whom I can have no claim, and should not dare to intrude; but I do not, personally, know a man on whom to rely for an answer to the questions I shall put, and I could not resist my longing to ask a man from whose judgment there would be little hope of appeal.

Since my childhood I have been wont to devote the hours I could spare from other and very different employments to efforts at literary composition, always keeping the results to myself, nor have they in more than two or three instances been seen by any other. But I am about to enter active life, and prudence tells me not to waste the time which must make my independence; yet, sir, I like writing too well to fling aside the practice of it without an effort to ascertain whether I could turn it to account, not in *wholly* maintaining myself, but in *aiding* my maintenance, for I do not sigh after fame, and am not ignorant of the folly or the fate of those who, without ability, would depend for their lives upon their pens; but I seek to know, and venture, though with shame, to ask from one whose word I must respect: whether, by periodical or other writing, I could please myself with writing, and make it subservient to living.

I would not, with this view, have troubled you with a composition in verse, but any piece I have in prose would too greatly trespass upon your patience, which, I fear, if you look over the verse, will be more than sufficiently tried.

I feel the egotism of my language, but I have none, sir, in my heart, for I feel beyond all encouragement from myself, and I hope for none from you.

Should you give any opinion upon what I send, it will, however condemnatory, be most gratefully received by, – Sir, your most humble servant,

P.B. Brontë

P.S. – The first piece is only the sequel of one striving to depict the fall from unguided passion into neglect, despair, and death. It ought to show an hour too near those of pleasure for repentance, and too near death for hope. The translations are two out of many made from Horace, and given to assist an answer to the question – would it be possible to obtain remuneration for translations for such as those from that or any other classic author?

36

BRANWELL BRONTË
TO HARTLEY COLERIDGE

Haworth,
June 27th, 1840.

Sir,

You will, perhaps have forgotten me, but it will be long before I forget my first conversation with a man of real intellect, in my first visit to the classic lakes of Westmoreland.

During the delightful day which I had the honour of spending with you at Ambleside, I received permission to transmit to you, as soon as finished, the first book of a translation of Horace, in order that, after a glance over it, you might tell me whether it was worth further notice or better fit for the fire.

I have – I fear most negligently, and amid other very different employments – striven to translate two books, the first of which I have presumed to send to you. And will you, Sir, stretch your past kindness by telling me whether I should amend and pursue the work or let it rest in peace?

Great corrections I feel it wants, but till I feel that the work might benefit me, I have no heart to make them; yet if your judgment prove in any way favourable, I will re-write the whole, without sparing labour to reach perfection.

I dared not have attempted Horace but that I saw the utter worthlessness of all former translations, and thought that a better one, by whomsoever executed, might meet with some little encouragement. I long to clear up my doubts by the judgment of one whose opinion I shall revere, and – but I suppose I am dreaming – one to whom I should be proud indeed to inscribe anything of mine which any publisher would look at, unless, as is likely enough, the work would disgrace the name as much as the name would honour the work.

Amount of remuneration I should not look to – as anything

would be everything – and whatever it might be, let me say that my bones would have no rest unless by written agreement a division should be made of the profits (little or much) between myself and him through whom alone I could hope to obtain a hearing with that formidable personage, a London bookseller.

Excuse my unintelligibility, haste, and appearance of presumption, and – Believe me to be, sir, your most humble and grateful servant,

P.B. Brontë

If anything in this note should displease you, lay it, sir, to the account of inexperience and *not* impudence.

37

CHARLOTTE BRONTË
TO WILLIAM WORDSWORTH

1840

Authors are generally very tenacious of their productions, but I am not so much attached to this but that I can give it up without much distress. No doubt, if I had gone on, I should have made quite a Richardsonian concern of it. . . . I had materials in my head for half-a-dozen volumes. . . . Of course it is with considerable regret I relinquish any scheme so charming as the one I have sketched. It is very edifying and profitable to create a world out of your own brains, and people it with inhabitants, who are so many Melchisedecs, and have no father nor mother but your own imagination. . . . I am sorry I did not exist fifty or sixty years ago, when the *Ladies' Magazine* was flourishing like a green bay tree. In that case, I make no doubt, my aspirations after literary fame would have met with due encouragement, and I should have had the pleasure of introducing Messrs. Percy and West into the very best society, and recording all their sayings and doings in double-columned, close-printed pages. . . . I recollect, when I was a child, getting hold of some antiquated volumes, and reading them by stealth with the most exquisite pleasure. You give a correct description of the patient Grisels of those days. My aunt was one of them; and to this day she thinks the tales of the *Ladies' Magazine* infinitely superior to any trash of modern literature. So do I; for I read them in childhood, and childhood has a very strong faculty of admiration, but a very weak one of criticism. . . . I am pleased that you cannot quite decide whether I am an attorney's clerk or a novel-reading dressmaker. I will not help you at all in the discovery; and as to my handwriting, or the ladylike touches in my style and imagery, you must not draw any conclusion from that – I may employ an amanuensis. Seriously, sir, I am very much obliged to you for your kind and candid letter. I almost wonder you took the trouble to read and notice the novelette of an anonymous scribe, who had not even the manners to tell you whether he was a man or a woman, or whether his 'C.T.' meant Charles Timms or Charlotte Tomkins.

38

CHARLOTTE BRONTË TO ELLEN NUSSEY

July 14th, 1840.

My Dear Ellen,

. . . I am very glad you continue so heart-whole. I rather feared our mutual nonsense might have made a deeper impression on you than was safe. Mr. Weightman left Haworth this morning; we do not expect him back again for some weeks. I am fully convinced, Ellen, that he is a thorough male-flirt; his sighs are deeper than ever, and his treading on toes more assiduous. I find he has scattered his impressions far and wide. Keighley has yielded him a fruitful field of conquest. Sarah Sugden is quite smitten, so is Caroline Dury. She, however, has left, and his Reverence has not yet ceased to idolise her memory. I find he is perfectly conscious of his irresistibleness, and is as vain as a peacock on the subject. I am not at all surprised at all this; it is perfectly natural; a handsome, clever, prepossessing, good-humoured young man will never want troops of victims amongst young ladies – so long as you are not among the number it is all right. He has not mentioned you to me, and I have not mentioned you to him. I believe we fully understand each other on the subject. I have seen little of him lately, and talked precious little to him; and when he was lonely and rather melancholy I had a great pleasure in cheering and amusing him. Now that he has got his spirits up and found plenty of acquaintances, I don't care, and he does not care either.

I have no doubt he will get nobly through his examinations; he is a *clever* lad.

39

CHARLOTTE BRONTË TO ELLEN NUSSEY

July 19th, '41.

My Dear Ellen,

We waited long and anxiously for you on the Thursday that you promised to come. I quite wearied my eyes with watching from the window, eyeglass in hand, and sometimes spectacles on nose. However, you are not to blame; I believe you have done right in going to Earnley; and as to the disappointment, why, all must suffer disappointment at some period or other of their lives. But a hundred things I had to say to you will now be forgotten, and never said. There is a project hatching in this house, which both Emily and I anxiously wished to discuss with you. The project is yet in its infancy, hardly peeping from its shell; and whether it will ever come out a fine full-fledged chicken, or will turn addle, and die before it cheeps, is one of those considerations that are but dimly revealed by the oracles of futurity. Now, don't be nonplussed by all this metaphorical mystery. I talk of a plain and everyday occurrence, though, in Delphic style, I wrap up the information in figures of speech concerning eggs, chickens, etcetera, etceterorum. To come to the point, papa and aunt talk, by fits and starts, of our – *id est*, Emily, Anne, and myself – commencing a school. I have often, you know, said how much I wished such a thing; but I never could conceive where the capital was to come from for making such a speculation. I was well aware, indeed, that aunt had money, but I always considered that she was the last person who would offer a loan for the purpose in question. A loan, however, she *has* offered, or rather intimates that she perhaps *will* offer, in case pupils can be secured, an eligible situation obtained, etc. This sounds very fair, but still there are matters to be considered which throw something of a damp upon the scheme. I do not expect that aunt will risk more than £150 on such a venture; and would it be possible to establish a respectable (not by any means a *showy*) school and to commence housekeeping with a capital of only that amount? Propound the question to your sister Anna, if you think she can answer it; or if not, don't say a word on the subject. As to getting into debt, that is a thing we could none of us reconcile our minds to for a moment. We do not care how modest, how humble a commencement be, so it be made on sure ground, and have a safe foundation. In thinking of all possible and impossible places where we could establish a school, I have thought of Burlington, or rather of the neighbourhood of Burlington. Do you remember whether there was any other school there besides that of Miss J——? This is, of course, a perfectly crude and random idea. There are a hundred reasons why it should be an impracticable one. We have no connections, no acquaintances there; it is far from here, etc. Still, I fancy the ground in the East Riding is less fully occupied than in the West. Much inquiry and consideration will be necessary, of course, before any place is decided on; and I fear much time will elapse before any plan is executed.

Our revered friend, William Weightman, is quite as bonny, pleasant, light-hearted, good-tempered, generous, careless, fickle, and unclerical as ever. He keeps up his correspondence with Agnes Walton. During the last spring he went to Appleby, and stayed upwards of a month.

Write as soon as you can. I shall not leave my present situation till my future prospects assume a more fixed and definite aspect. Good-bye, dear Ellen.

C.B.

40

EMILY BRONTË'S 'BIRTHDAY' NOTE

A PAPER to be opened
when Anne is
25 years old,
or my next birthday after
if
all be well.
Emily Jane Brontë. July the 30th, 1841.

It is Friday evening, near 9 o'clock – wild rainy weather. I am seated in the dining-room, having just concluded tidying our desk boxes, writing this document. Papa is in the parlour – aunt upstairs in her room. She has been reading *Blackwood's Magazine* to papa. Victoria and Adelaide are ensconced in the peat-house. Keeper is in the kitchen – Hero in his cage. We are all stout and hearty, as I hope is the case with Charlotte, Branwell, and Anne, of whom the first is at John White, Esq., Upperwood House, Rawdon; the second is at Luddenden Foot; and the third is, I believe, at Scarborough, inditing perhaps a paper corresponding to this.

A scheme is at present in agitation for setting us up in a school of our own; as yet nothing is determined, but I hope and trust it may go on and prosper and answer our highest expectations. This day four years I wonder whether we shall still be dragging on in our present condition or established to our hearts' content. Time will show.

I guess that at the time appointed for the opening of this paper we, i.e. Charlotte, Anne, and I, shall be all merrily seated in our own sitting-room in some pleasant and flourishing seminary, having just gathered in for the mid-summer ladyday. Our debts will be paid off, and we shall have cash in hand to a considerable amount. Papa, aunt, and Branwell will either have been or be coming to visit us. It will be a fine warm summer evening, very different from this bleak look-out, and Anne and I will perchance slip out into the garden for a few minutes to peruse our papers. I hope either this or something better will be the case.

The *Gondaland* are at present in a threatening state, but there is no open rupture as yet. All the princes and princesses of the Royalty are at the Palace of Instruction. I have a good many books on hand, but I am sorry to say that as usual I make small progress with any. However, I have just made a new regularity paper! and I must *verb sap* to do great things. And now I close, sending from far an exhortation of courage, courage, to exiled and harassed Anne, wishing she was here.

41

ANNE BRONTË'S 'BIRTHDAY' NOTE

[Thorp Green]
July the 30th, A.D. 1841.

This is Emily's birthday. She has now completed her 23rd year, and is, I believe, at home. Charlotte is a governess in the family of Mr. White. Branwell is a clerk in the railroad station at Luddenden Foot, and I am a governess in the family of Mr. Robinson. I dislike the situation and wish to change it for another. I am now at Scarborough. My pupils are gone to bed and I am hastening to finish this before I follow them.

We are thinking of setting up a school of our own, but nothing definite is settled about it yet, and we do not know whether we shall be able to or not. I hope we shall. And I wonder what will be our condition and how or where we shall all be on this day four years hence; at which time, if all be well, I shall be 25 years and 6 months old, Emily will be 27 years old, Branwell 28 years and 1 month, and Charlotte 29 years and a quarter. We are now all separate and not likely to meet again for many a weary week, but we are none of us ill that I know of, and all are doing something for our own livelihood except Emily, who, however, is as busy as any of us, and in reality earns her food and raiment as much as we do.

How little know we what we are
How less what we may be!

Four years ago I was at school. Since then I have been a governess at Blake Hall, left it, come to Thorpe Green, and seen the sea and York Minster. Emily has been a teacher at Miss Patchet's school, and left it. Charlotte has left Miss Wooler's, been a governess at Mrs. Sidgwick's, left her, and gone to Mrs. White's. Branwell has given up painting, been a tutor in Cumberland, left it, and become a clerk on the railroad. Tabby has left us. Martha Brown has come in her place. We have got Keeper, got a sweet little cat and lost it, and also got a hawk. Got a wild goose which has flown away, and three tame ones, one of which has been killed. All these diversities, with many others, are things we did not expect or foresee in the July of 1837. What will the next four years bring forth? Providence only knows. But we ourselves have sustained very little alteration since that time. I have the same faults that I had then, only I have more wisdom and experience, and a little more self-possession than I then enjoyed. How will it be when we open this paper and the one Emily has written? I wonder whether the *Gondaland* will still be flourishing, and what will be their condition. I am now engaged in writing the fourth volume of *Solala Vernon's Life*.

For some time I have looked upon 25 as a sort of era in my existence. It may prove a true presentiment, or it may be only a superstitious fancy; the latter seems most likely, but time will show.

Anne Brontë

42

CHARLOTTE BRONTË
TO ELIZABETH BRANWELL

Upperwood House,
Rawdon,
September 29th, 1841.

Dear Aunt,

I have heard nothing of Miss Wooler yet since I wrote to her intimating that I would accept her offer.[1] I cannot conjecture the reason of this long silence, unless some unforeseen impediment has occurred in concluding the bargain. Meantime, a plan has been suggested and approved by Mr. and Mrs. White, and others, which I wish now to impart to you. My friends recommend me, if I desire to secure permanent success, to delay commencing the school for six months longer, and by all means to contrive, by hook or by crook, to spend the intervening time in some school on the Continent. They say schools in England are so numerous, competition so great, that without some such step towards attaining superiority we shall probably have a very hard struggle, and may fail in the end. They say, moreover, that the loan of £100, which you have been so kind as to offer us, will, perhaps, not be all required now, as Miss Wooler will lend us the furniture; and that, if the speculation is intended to be a good and successful one, half the sum, at least, ought to be laid out in the manner I have mentioned, thereby insuring a more speedy repayment both of interest and principal.

I would not go to France or to Paris. I would go to Brussels, in Belgium. The cost of the journey there, at the dearest rate of travelling, would be £5; living is there little more than half as dear as it is in England, and the facilities for education are equal or superior to any other place in Europe. In half a year, I could acquire a thorough familiarity with French. I could improve greatly in Italian, and even get a dash of German, *i.e.* providing my health continued as good as it is now. Martha Taylor is now staying in Brussels, at a first-rate establishment there. I should not think of going to the Chateau de Kockleberg, where she is resident, as the terms are much too high; but if I wrote to her, she, with the assistance of Mrs. Jenkins, the wife of the British Consul, would be

[1] Miss Wooler had offered her school to Charlotte, who apparently accepted her terms. Nothing, however, came of this project.

able to secure me a cheap and decent residence and respectable protection. I should have the opportunity of seeing her frequently, she would make me acquainted with the city; and, with the assistance of her cousins, I should probably in time be introduced to connections far more improving, polished, and cultivated, than any I have yet known.

These are advantages which would turn to vast account, when we actually commenced a school – and, if Emily could share them with me, only for a single half-year, we could take a footing in the world afterwards which we can never do now. I say Emily instead of Anne; for Anne might take her turn at some future period, if our school answered. I feel certain, while I am writing, that you will see the propriety of what I say; you always like to use your money to the best advantage; you are not fond of making shabby purchases; when you do confer a favour, it is often done in style; and depend upon it £50, or £100, thus laid out, would be well employed. Of course, I know no other friend in the world to whom I could apply on this subject except yourself. I feel an absolute conviction that, if this advantage were allowed us, it would be the making of us for life. Papa will perhaps think it a wild and ambitious scheme; but who ever rose in the world without ambition? When he left Ireland to go to Cambridge University, he was as ambitious as I am now. I want us all to go on. I know we have talents, and I want them to be turned to account. I look to you, aunt, to help us. I think you will not refuse. I know, if you consent, it shall not be my fault if you ever repent your kindness. With love to all, and the hope that you are all well, – Believe me, dear aunt, your affectionate niece.

C. Brontë

43

CHARLOTTE BRONTË TO EMILY J. BRONTË

Upperwood House,
Rawdon,
November 7th, 1841.

Dear E.J.,

You are not to suppose that this note is written with a view of communicating any information on the subject we both have considerably at heart. I have written letters, but I have received no letters in reply yet. Belgium is a long way off, and people are everywhere hard to spur up to the proper speed. Mary Taylor says we can scarcely expect to get off before January. I have wished and intended to write to both Anne and Branwell, but really I have not had time.

Mr. Jenkins I find was mistakenly termed the British Consul at Brussels; he is in fact the English Episcopal clergyman.

I think perhaps we shall find that the best plan will be for papa to write a letter to him by-and-by, but not yet. I will give an intimation when this should be done, and also some idea of what had best be said. Grieve not over Dewsbury Moor. You were cut out there to all intents and purposes, so in fact was Anne; Miss Wooler would hear of neither for the first half-year.

Anne seems omitted in the present plan, but if all goes right I trust she will derive her full share of benefit from it in the end. I exhort all to hope. I believe in my heart this is acting for the best; my only fear is lest others should doubt and be dismayed. Before our half-year in Brussels is completed, you and I will have to seek employment abroad. It is not my intention to retrace my steps home till twelve months, if all continues well and we and those at home retain good health.

I shall probably take my leave of Upperwood about the 15th or 17th of December. When does Anne talk of returning? How is she? What does William Weightman say to these matters? How are papa and aunt, do they flag? How will Anne get on with Martha? Has William Weightman been seen or heard of lately? Love to all. Write quickly. – Good-bye.

C. Brontë

I am well.

44

CHARLOTTE BRONTË TO ELLEN NUSSEY

Brussels,
May, 1842.

Dear Ellen,

It is the fashion nowadays for persons to send shoals of blank paper instead of letters to their friends in a foreign land.

I was twenty-six years old a week or two since, and at this ripe time of life I am a schoolgirl, a complete schoolgirl, and, on the whole, very happy in that capacity. It felt very strange at first to submit to authority instead of exercising it – to obey orders instead of giving them; but I like that state of things. I returned to it with the same avidity that a cow, that has long been kept on dry hay, returns to fresh grass. Don't laugh at my simile. It is natural to me to submit and very unnatural to command.

This is a large school, in which there are about forty *externes* or day-pupils, and twelve *pensonnaires* or boarders. Madame Héger, the head, is a lady of precisely the same cast of mind, degree of cultivation, and quality of intellect as Miss Catherine Wooler. I think the severe points are a little softened, because she has not been disappointed, and consequently soured. In a word, she is a married instead of a maiden lady. There are three teachers in the school – Mademoiselle Blanche, Mademoiselle Sophie, and Mademoiselle Marie. The two first have no particular character. One is an old maid, and the other will be one. Mademoiselle Marie is talented and original, but of repulsive and arbitrary manners, which have made the whole school, except myself and Emily, her bitter enemies. No less than seven masters attend to teach the different branches of education – French, Drawing, Music, Singing, Writing, Arithmetic, and German. All in the house are Catholics except ourselves, one other girl, and the *gouvernante* of Madame's children, an English-woman, in rank something between a lady's-maid and a nursery governess. The difference in country and religion makes a broad line of demarcation between us and all the rest. We are completely isolated in the midst of numbers. Yet I think I am never unhappy; my present life is so delightful, so congenial to my own nature, compared with that of a governess. My time, constantly occupied, passes too rapidly. Hitherto both Emily and I have had good health, and therefore we have been able to work well. There is one individual of whom I have not yet spoken – M. Héger, the husband of Madame. He is a professor of rhetoric, a man of power as to mind, but very choleric and irritable in temperament; a little black being, with a face that varies in expression. Sometimes he borrows the lineaments of an insane tom-cat, sometimes those of a delirious hyena: occasionally, but very seldom, he discards these perilous attractions and assumes an air not above 100 degrees removed from mild and gentleman-like. He is very angry with me just at present, because I have written a translation which he chose to stigmatize as *peu correcte*. He did not tell me so, but wrote the accusation on the margin of my book, and asked in brief, stern phrase, how it happened that my compositions were always better than my translations? adding that the thing seemed to him inexplicable. The fact is, some weeks ago, in a high-flown humour, he forbade me to use either dictionary or grammar in translating the most difficult English compositions into French. This makes the task rather arduous, and compels me now and then to introduce an English word, which nearly plucks the eyes out of his head when he sees it. Emily and he don't draw well together at all. When he is very ferocious with me I cry; that sets all things straight. Emily works like a horse, and she has had great difficulties to contend with, far greater than I have had. Indeed, those who come to a French school for instruction ought previously to have acquired a considerable knowledge of the French language, otherwise they will lose a great deal of time, for the course of instruction is adapted to natives and not to foreigners; and in these large establishments they will not change their ordinary course for one or two strangers. The few private lessons M. Héger has vouchsafed to give us are, I suppose, to be considered a great favour, and I can perceive they have already excited much spite and jealousy in the school.

You will abuse this letter for being short and dreary, and there are a hundred things which I want to tell you, but I have not time. Brussels is a beautiful city. The Belgians hate the English. Their external morality is more rigid than ours. *Do* write to me and cherish Christian charity in your heart! Remember me to Mercy and your Mother, and believe me, my dear Ellen, – Yours, sundered by the sea,

C. Brontë

45

CHARLOTTE BRONTË TO ELLEN NUSSEY

Brussels,
——, 1842.

Dear Ellen,

I began seriously to think you had no particular intention of writing to me again. However, let me make no reproaches, thanking you for your letter. I consider it doubtful whether I shall come home in September or not. Madame Héger has made a proposal for both me and Emily to stay another half-year, offering to dismiss her English master, and to take me as English teacher; also to employ Emily some part of each day in teaching music to a certain number of the pupils. For these services we are to be allowed to continue our studies in French and German, and to have board, etc., without paying for it; no salaries, however, are offered. The proposal is kind, and in a great selfish city like Brussels, and a great selfish school, containing nearly ninety pupils (boarders and day-pupils included), implies a degree of interest which demands gratitude in return. I am inclined to accept it. What think you? I don't deny I sometimes wish to be in England, or that I have brief attacks of home-sickness; but, on the whole, I have borne a very valiant heart so far; and I have been happy in Brussels, because I have always been fully occupied with the employments that I like. Emily is making rapid progress in French, German, music and drawing. Monsieur and Madame Héger begin to recognize the valuable parts of her character, under her singularities.

If the national character of the Belgians is to be measured by the character of most of the girls in this school, it is a character singularly cold, selfish, animal, and inferior. They are very mutinous and difficult for the teachers to manage; and their principles are rotten to the core. We avoid them, which is not difficult to do, as we have the brand of Protestantism and Anglicanism upon us. People talk of the danger which Protestants expose themselves to in going to reside in Catholic countries, and thereby running the chance of changing their faith. My advice to all Protestants who are tempted to do anything so besotted as to turn Catholics is, to walk over the sea on to the Continent; to attend Mass sedulously for a time; to note well the mummeries thereof; also the idiotic, mercenary aspect of all the priests; and *then*, if they are still disposed to consider Papistry in any other light than a most feeble, childish piece of humbug, let them turn Papists at once – that's all. I consider Methodism, Quakerism, and the extremes of High and Low Churchism foolish, but Roman Catholicism beats them all. At the same time, allow me to tell you that there are some Catholics who are as good as any Christians can be to whom the Bible is a sealed book, and much better than many Protestants. – Believe me present occasionally in spirit when absent in the flesh.

C.B.

46

BRANWELL BRONTË
TO FRANCIS H. GRUNDY

October 29th, 1842.

My Dear Sir,

As I don't want to lose a real friend, I write in deprecation of the tone of your letter. Death only has made me neglectful of your kindness, and I have lately had so much experience with him, that your sister would not now blame me for indulging in gloomy visions either of this world or another. I am incoherent, I fear, but I have been waking two nights witnessing such agonising suffering as I would not wish my worst enemy to endure; and I have now lost the guide and director of all the happy days connected with my childhood. I have suffered such sorrow since I last saw you at Haworth, that I do not now care if I were fighting in India or —, since, when the mind is depressed, danger is the most effectual cure. But you don't like croaking, I know well, only I request you to understand from my two notes that I have not forgotten you, but myself. – Yours, etc.,

P.B. Brontë

47

CHARLOTTE BRONTË TO ELLEN NUSSEY

Haworth,
November 10th, 1842.

My Dear Ellen,

I was not yet returned to England when your letter arrived. We received the first news of aunt's illness, Wednesday, Nov. 2nd. We decided to come home directly. Next morning a second letter informed us of her death. We sailed from Antwerp on Sunday; we travelled day and night and got home on Tuesday morning – and of course the funeral and all was over. We shall see her no more. Papa is pretty well. We found Anne at home; she is pretty well also. You say you have had no letter from me for a long time. I wrote to you three weeks ago. When you answer this note, I will write to you more in detail. Martha Taylor's[1] illness was unknown to me

[1] Martha was the sister of Charlotte's school-friend, Mary Taylor.

till the day before she died. I hastened to Kockleberg the next morning – unconscious that she was in great danger – and was told that it was finished. She had died in the night. Mary was taken away to Bruxelles. I have seen Mary frequently since. She is in no ways crushed by the event; but while Martha was ill she was to her more than a mother – more than a sister: watching, nursing, cherishing her so tenderly, so unweariedly. She appears calm and serious now: no bursts of violent emotion, no exaggeration of distress. I have seen Martha's grave – the place where her ashes lie in a foreign country. Aunt, Martha Taylor, and Mr. Weightman are now all gone; how dreary and void everything seems. Mr. Weightman's illness was exactly what Martha's was – he was ill the same length of time and died in the same manner. Aunt's disease was internal obstruction; she also was ill a fortnight.

Good-bye, my dear Ellen.

C. Brontë

48

CHARLOTTE BRONTË TO ELLEN NUSSEY

Brussels,
January 30th, 1843.

Dear Ellen,

I left Leeds for London last Friday at nine o'clock[1]; owing to delay we did not reach London till ten at night – two hours after time. I took a cab the moment I arrived at Euston Square, and went forthwith to London Bridge Wharf. The packet lay off that wharf, and I went on board the same night. Next morning we sailed. We had a prosperous and speedy voyage, and landed at Ostend at seven o'clock next morning. I took the train at twelve and reached Rue d'Isabelle at seven in the evening. Madame Héger received me with great kindness. I am still tired with the continued excitement of three days' travelling. I had no accident, but of course some anxiety. Miss Dixon called this afternoon. Mary Taylor had told her I should be in Brussels the last week in January. You can tell Joe Taylor she looks very elegant and ladylike. I am going there on Sunday, D.V. Address – Miss Brontë, Chez Mme. Héger, 32 Rue d'Isabelle, Bruxelles. – Good-bye, dear.

C.B.

[1] Emily did not accompany Charlotte on her second sojourn in Brussels.

49

CHARLOTTE BRONTË TO BRANWELL BRONTË

Brussels,
May 1st, 1843.

Dear Branwell,

I hear you have written a letter to me. This letter, however, as usual, I have never received, which I am exceedingly sorry for, as I have wished very much to hear from you. Are you sure that you put the right address and that you paid the English postage, 1s. 6d.? Without that, letters are never forwarded. I heard from papa a day or two since. All appears to be going on reasonably well at home. I grieve only that Emily is so solitary; but, however, you and Anne will soon be returning for the holidays, which will cheer the house for a time. Are you in better health and spirits, and does Anne continue to be pretty well? I understand papa has been to see you. Did he seem cheerful and well? Mind when you write to me you answer these questions, as I wish to know. Also give me a detailed account as to how you get on with your pupil and the rest of the family. I have received a general assurance that you do well and are in good odour, but I want to know particulars.

As for me, I am very well and wag on as usual. I perceive, however, that I grow exceedingly misanthropic and sour. You will say that this is no news, and that you never knew me possessed of the contrary qualities – philanthropy and sugariness. *Das ist wahr* (which being translated means, that is true); but the fact is, the people here are no go whatsoever. Amongst 120 persons which compose the daily population of this house, I can discern only one or two who deserve anything like regard. This is not owing to foolish fastidiousness on my part, but to the absence of decent qualities on theirs. They have not intellect or politeness or good-nature or good-feeling. They are nothing. I don't hate them – hatred would be too warm a feeling. They have no sensations themselves and they excite none. But one wearies from day to day of caring nothing, fearing nothing, liking nothing, hating nothing, being nothing, doing nothing – yes, I teach and sometimes get red in the face with impatience at their stupidity. But don't think I ever scold or fly into a passion. If I spoke warmly, as warmly as I sometimes used to do at Roe Head, they would think me mad. Nobody ever gets into a passion here. Such a thing is not known. The phlegm that thickens their blood is too gluey to boil. They are very false in their relations with each other, but they rarely quarrel, and friendship is a folly they are unacquainted with. The black swan, M. Héger, is the only sole veritable exception to this rule (for Madame, always cool and always reasoning, is not quite an exception). But I rarely speak to Monsieur now, for not being a pupil I have little or nothing to do with him. From time to time he shows his kind-heartedness by loading me with books, so that I am still indebted to him for all the pleasure or amusement I have. Except for the total want of companionship I have nothing to complain of. I have not too much to do, sufficient liberty, and I am rarely interfered with. I lead an easeful, stagnant, silent life, for which, when I think of Mrs. Sidgwick, I ought to be very thankful. Be sure you write to me soon, and beg of Anne to inclose a small billet in the same letter; it will be a real charity to do me this kindness. Tell me everything you can think of. It is a curious metaphysical fact that always in the evening when I am in the great dormitory alone, having no other company than a number of beds with white curtains, I always recur as fanatically as ever to the old ideas, the old faces, and the old scenes in the world below.

Give my love to Anne. – And believe me, yourn!

Dear Anne, – Write to me. – Your affectionate Schwester,

C.B.

50

EMILY BRONTË TO ELLEN NUSSEY

May 22nd, '43.

Dear Miss Ellen,

I should be wanting in common civility if I did not thank you for your kindness in letting me know of an opportunity to send 'postage free'.

I have written as you directed, though if 'next Tuesday' means to-morrow, I fear it will be too late to go with Mr.____. Charlotte has never mentioned a word about coming home. If you would go over for half a year, perhaps you might be able to bring her back with you, otherwise she might vegetate there till the age of Methusaleh for mere lack of courage to face the voyage.

All here are in good health; so was Anne according to her last account. The holidays will be here in a week or two, and then, if she be willing, I will get her to write you a proper letter, a feat that I have never performed. – With love and good wishes.

Emily J. Brontë

51

CHARLOTTE BRONTË
TO EMILY J. BRONTË

Brussels,
May 29th, 1843.

Dear E.J.,

The reason of the unconscionable demand for money is explained in my letter to papa. Would you believe it, Mdlle. Mühl demands as much for one pupil as for two, namely, 10 francs per month. This, with the 5 francs per month to the Blanchisseuse, makes havoc in £16 per annum. You will perceive I have begun again to take German lessons. Things wag on much as usual here. Only Mdlle. Blanche and Mdlle. Haussé are at present on a system of war without quarter. They hate each other like two cats. Mdlle. Blanche frightens Mdlle. Haussé by her white passions (for they quarrel venomously). Mdlle. Haussé complains that when Mdlle. Blanche is in fury, '*elle n'a pas de lèvres*'. I find also that Mdlle. Sophie dislikes Mdlle. Blanche extremely. She says she is heartless, insincere, and vindictive, which epithets, I assure you, are richly deserved. Also I find she is the regular spy of Mme Héger, to whom she reports everything. Also she invents – which I should not have thought. I have now the entire charge of the English lessons. I have given two lessons to the first class. Hortense Jannoy was a picture on these occasions; her face was black as a 'blue-piled thunder-loft', and her two ears were red as raw beef. To all questions asked her reply was, '*je ne sais pas*'. It is a pity but her friends could meet with a person qualified to cast out a devil. I am richly off for companionship in these parts. Of late days, M. and Mde. Héger rarely speak to me, and I really don't pretend to care a fig for any body else in the establishment. You are not to suppose by that expression that I am under the influence of *warm* affection for Mme. Héger. I am convinced she does not like me – why, I can't tell, nor do I think she herself has any definite reason for the aversion; but for one thing, she cannot comprehend why I do not make intimate friends of Mesdames Blanche, Sophie, and Haussé.

M. Héger is wonderously influenced by Madame, and I should not wonder if he disapproves very much of my unamiable want of sociability. He has already given me a brief lecture on universal *bienveillance*, and, perceiving that I don't improve in consequence, I fancy he has taken to considering me as a person to be let alone – left to the error of her ways; and consequently he has in a great measure withdrawn the light of his countenance, and I get on from day to day in a Robinson-Crusoe-like condition – very lonely. That does not signify. In other respects I have nothing substantial to complain of, nor is even this a cause for complaint. Except the loss of M. Héger's goodwill (if I have lost it) I care for none of 'em. I hope you are well and hearty. Walk out often on the moors. Sorry am I to hear that Hannah is gone, and that she has left you burdened with the charge of the little girl, her sister. I hope Tabby will continue to stay with you – give my love to her. Regards to the fighting gentry, and to old asthma. – Your

C.B.

I have written to Branwell, though I never got a letter from him.

52

CHARLOTTE BRONTË
TO EMILY J. BRONTË

Bruxelles,
September 2nd, 1843.

Dear E.J.,

Another opportunity of writing to you coming to pass, I shall improve it by scribbling a few lines. More than half the holidays are now past, and rather better than I expected. The weather has been exceedingly fine during the last fortnight, and yet not so Asiatically hot as it was last year at this time. Consequently I have tramped about a great deal and tried to get a clearer acquaintance with the streets of Bruxelles. This week, as no teacher is here except Mdlle. Blanche, who is returned from Paris, I am always alone except at mealtimes, for Mdlle. Blanche's character is so false and so contemptible I can't force myself to associate with her. She perceives my utter dislike and never now speaks to me – a great relief.

However, I should inevitably fall into the gulf of low spirits if I stayed always by myself here without a human being to speak to, so I go out and traverse the Boulevards and streets of Bruxelles sometimes for hours together. Yesterday I went on a pilgrimage to the cemetery, and far beyond it on to a hill where there was nothing but fields as far as the horizon. When I came back it was evening; but I had such a repugnance to return to the house, which contained nothing that I cared for, I still kept threading the streets in the neighbourhood of the Rue d'Isabelle and avoiding it. I found myself opposite to Ste. Gudule, and the bell, whose voice you know, began to toll for evening *salut*. I went in, quite alone (which procedure you will say is not much like me), wandered about the aisles where a few old women were saying their prayers, till vespers began. I stayed till they were over. Still I could not leave the church or force myself to go home – to school I mean. An odd whim came into my head. In a solitary part of the Cathedral six or seven people still remained kneeling by the confessionals. In two confessionals I saw a priest. I felt as if I did not care what I did, provided it was not absolutely wrong, and that it served to vary my life and yield a moment's interest. I took a fancy to change myself into a Catholic and go and make a real confession to see what it was like. Knowing me as you do, you will think this odd, but when people are by themselves they have singular fancies. A penitent was occupied in confessing. They do not go into the sort of pew or cloister which the priest occupies, but kneel down on the steps and confess through a grating. Both the confessor and the penitent whisper very low, you can hardly hear their voices. After I had watched two or three penitents go and return, I approached at last and knelt down in a niche which was just vacated. I had to kneel there ten minutes waiting, for on the other side was another penitent invisible to me. At last they went away and a little wooden door inside the grating opened, and I saw the priest leaning his ear towards me. I was obliged to begin, and yet I did not know a word of the formula with which they always commence their confessions. It was a funny position. I felt precisely as I did when alone on the Thames at midnight. I commenced with saying I was a foreigner and had been brought up a Protestant. The priest asked if I was a Protestant then. I somehow could not tell a lie, and said 'yes'. He replied that in that case I could not '*jouir du bonheur de la confesse*'; but I was determined to confess, and at last he said he would allow me because it might be the first step towards returning to the true church. I actually did confess, a real confession. When I had done he told me his address, and said that every morning I was to go to the rue du Parc – to his house – and he would reason with me and try to convince me of the error and enormity of being a Protestant!!! I promised faithfully to go. Of course, however, the adventure stops there, and I hope I shall never see the priest again. I think you had better not tell papa of this. He will not understand that it was only a freak, and will perhaps think I am going to turn Catholic. Trusting that you and papa are well, and also Tabby and the Holyes,[1] and hoping you will write to me immediately, – I am, yours,

C.B.

53

CHARLOTTE BRONTË TO ELLEN NUSSEY

October 13th, 1843.

Dear Ellen,

. . . Mary Taylor is getting on well, as she deserves to do. I often hear from her. Her letters and yours are one of my few pleasures. She urges me very much to leave Brussels and go to her; but at present, however tempted to take such a step, I should not feel justified in doing so. To leave a certainty for a complete uncertainty, would be to the last degree imprudent. Notwithstanding that, Brussels is indeed desolate to me now. Since Mary Dixon left, I have had no friend. I had, indeed, some very kind acquaintances in the family of Dr. Wheelwright, but they too are gone now. They left in the latter part of August, and I am completely alone. I cannot count the Belgians as anything. Madame Héger is a politic, plausible, and interested person. I no longer trust to her. It is a curious position to be so utterly solitary in the midst of numbers. Sometimes the solitude oppresses me to an excess. One day, lately, I felt as if I could bear it no longer, and I went to Madame Héger and gave her notice. If it had depended on her I should certainly have soon been at liberty; but M. Héger, having heard of what was in agitation, sent for me the day after, and pronounced with vehemence his decision that I should not leave. I could not, at that time, have persevered in my intention without exciting him to passion; so I promised to stay a little while longer. How long that will be I do not know. I should not like to return to England to do

[1] A reference to the curates.

nothing. I am too old for that now; but if I could hear of a favourable opportunity for commencing a school, I think I should embrace it. I have much to say – many little odd things, queer and puzzling enough – which I do not like to trust to a letter, but which one day perhaps, or rather one evening – if ever we should find ourselves by the fireside at Haworth or at Brookroyd, with our feet on the fender, curling our hair – I may communicate to you. We have as yet no fires here, and I suffer much from cold; otherwise I am well in health. Mr. George Dixon will take this letter to England. He is a pretty-looking and pretty-behaved young man, apparently constructed without a backbone; by which I don't allude to his corporal spine, which is all right enough, but to his character.

Farewell, dear Ellen. Give my love to your mother and sisters, and good wishes to Mr. George; anything you like to yourself, dear Nell.

C.B.

54

CHARLOTTE BRONTË TO ELLEN NUSSEY

Brussels,
Nov. 15th, 1843.

Dear Ellen,

. . . To-day the weather is gloomy, and I am stupefied with a bad cold and headache. I have nothing to tell you, my dear Ellen. One day is like another in this place. I know you, living in the country, can hardly believe it possible life can be monotonous in the centre of a brilliant capital like Brussels; but so it is. I feel it most on holidays, when all the girls and teachers go out to visit, and it sometimes happens that I am left, during several hours, quite alone, with four great desolate school rooms at my disposition. I try to read, I try to write; but in vain. I then wander about from room to room, but the silence and loneliness of all the house weighs down one's spirits like lead. You will hardly believe that Madame Héger (good and kind as I have described her) never comes near me on these occasions. I own, I was astonished the first time I was left alone thus; when everybody else was enjoying the pleasures of a fête-day with their friends, and she knew I was quite by myself, and never took the least notice of me. Yet, I understand, she praises me very much to everybody, and says what excellent lessons I give. She is not colder to me than she is to the other teachers; but they are less dependent on her than I am. They have relations and acquaintances in Brussels. You remember the letter she wrote me, when I was in England? How kind and affectionate that was? Is it not odd? I fancy I begin to perceive the reason of this mighty distance and reserve; it sometimes makes me laugh, and at other times nearly cry. When I am sure of it, I will tell it you. In the meantime, the complaints I make at present are for your ear only – a sort of relief which I permit myself. In all other respects I am well satisfied with my position, and you may say so to people who inquire after me (if any one does). Write to me, dear Nell, whenever you can. You do a good deed when you send me a letter, for you comfort a very desolate heart. Good-bye. – Love to your mother and sisters.

C.B.

55

CHARLOTTE BRONTË TO EMILY J. BRONTE

Brussels,
December 19th, 1843.

Dear E.J.,

I have taken my determination. I hope to be at home the day after New Year's Day. I have told Mme. Héger. But in order to come home I shall be obliged to draw on my cash for another £5. I have only £3 at present, and as there are several little things I should like to buy before I leave Brussels – which you know cannot be got as well in England – £3 would not suffice. Low spirits have afflicted me much lately, but I hope all will be well when I get home – above all, if I find papa and you and B. and A. well. I am not ill in body. It is only the mind which is a trifle shaken – for want of comfort.

I shall try to cheer up now. – Good-bye.

C.B.

56

CHARLOTTE BRONTË TO ELLEN NUSSEY

Haworth,
January 23rd, 1844.

My Dear Ellen,

It was a great disappointment to me to hear that you were in the south of England. I had counted upon seeing *you soon*, as one of the great pleasures of my return; now, I fear, our meeting will be postponed for an indefinite time.

Every one asks me what I am going to do, now that I am returned home; and every one seems to expect that I should immediately commence a school. In truth, it is what I should wish to do. I desire it above all things. I have sufficient money for the undertaking, and I hope now sufficient qualifications to give me a fair chance of success; yet I cannot yet permit myself to enter upon life – to touch the object which seems now within my reach, and which I have been so long straining to attain. You will ask me why. It is on Papa's account; he is now, as you know, getting old, and it grieves me to tell you that he is losing his sight. I have felt for some months that I ought not to be away from him; and I feel now that it would be too selfish to leave him (at least as long as Branwell and Anne are absent) in order to pursue selfish interests of my own. With the help of God I will try to deny myself in this matter, and to wait.

I suffered much before I left Brussels. I think, however long I live, I shall not forget what the parting with M. Héger cost me; it grieved me so much to grieve him, who has been so true, kind, and disinterested a friend. At parting he gave me a kind of diploma certifying my abilities as a teacher, sealed with the seal of the Athénée Royal, of which he is professor. I was surprised also at the degree of regret expressed by my Belgian pupils, when they knew I was going to leave. I did not think it had been in their phlegmatic nature. When do you think I shall see you? I have, of course, much to tell you, and I dare say you have much also to tell me, of things which we should neither of us wish to commit to paper. I am much disquieted at not having heard from Mary Taylor for so long a time. Joe called at Rue d'Isabelle with a letter from you, but I was already gone. I do not know whether you feel as I do, but there are times now when it appears to me as if all my ideas and feelings, except a few friendships and affections, are changed from what they used to be; something in me which used to be enthusiasm, is tamed down and broken. I have fewer illusions; what I wish for now is active exertion – a stake in life. Haworth seems such a lonely, quiet spot, buried away from the world. I no longer regard myself as young – indeed, I shall soon be twenty-eight; and it seems as if I ought to be working and braving the rough realities of the world, as other people do. It is, however, my duty to restrain this feeling at present, and I will endeavour to do so. Write to me soon, my dear Ellen, and believe as far as regards yourself, your *unchanged* friend,

C. Brontë

Remember me with kindness to your brother Henry. Anne and Branwell have just left us to return to York. They are both wondrously valued in their situations.[1]

57

CHARLOTTE BRONTË TO M. HÉGER
(*Translated from the French*)

July 24th, 1844.

Monsieur,

I am well aware that it is not my turn to write to you, but as Mrs. Wheelwright is going to Brussels and is kind enough to take charge of a letter – it seems to me that I ought not to neglect so favourable an opportunity of writing to you.

I am very pleased that the school-year is nearly over and that the holidays are approaching. I am pleased on your account, Monsieur – for I am told that you are working too hard and that your health has suffered somewhat in consequence. For that reason I refrain from uttering a single complaint for your long silence – I would rather remain six months without receiving news from you than add one grain to the weight, already too heavy, which overwhelms you. I know well that it is now the period of compositions, that it will soon be that of examinations, and later on of prizes – and during all that time you are condemned to breathe the stifling atmosphere of the class-rooms – to wear yourself out – to explain,

[1] Branwell was tutor and Anne governess in the same household, at Thorp Green.

to question, to talk all day, and then in the evening you have all those wretched compositions to read, to correct, almost to re-write – Ah, Monsieur! I once wrote you a letter that was less than reasonable, because sorrow was at my heart; but I shall do so no more. I shall try to be selfish no longer; and even while I look upon your letters as one of the greatest felicities known to me, I shall await the receipt of them in patience until it pleases you and suits you to send me any. Meanwhile, I may well send you a little letter from time to time – you have authorised me to do so.

I greatly fear that I shall forget French, for I am firmly convinced that I shall see you again some day. I know not how or when, but it must be, for I wish it so much, and then I should not wish to remain dumb before you – it would be too sad to see you and not be able to speak to you. To avoid such a misfortune I learn every day by heart half a page of French from a book written in familiar style, and I take pleasure in learning this lesson, Monsieur; as I pronounce the French words it seems to me as if I were chatting with you.

I have just been offered a situation as first governess in a large school in Manchester, with a salary of £100 (*i.e.*, 2,500 francs) per annum. I cannot accept it, for in accepting it I should have to leave my father, and that I cannot do. Nevertheless I have a plan (when one lives retired the brain goes on working; there is the desire of occupation, the wish to embark on an active career). Our parsonage is rather a large house – with a few alterations there will be room for five or six boarders. If I could find this number of children of good family I should devote myself to their education. Emily does not care much for teaching, but she would look after the housekeeping, and, although something of a recluse, she is too good-hearted not to do all she could for the well-being of the children. Moreover, she is very generous, and as for order, economy, strictness – and diligent work – all of them things very essential in a school – I willingly take that upon myself.

That, Monsieur, is my plan, which I have already explained to my father, and which he approves. It only remains to find the pupils – rather a difficult thing, for we live rather far from towns, and people do not greatly care about crossing the hills which form as it were a barrier around us. But the task that is without difficulty is almost without merit; there is great interest in triumphing over obstacles. I do not say I shall succeed, but I shall try to succeed – the effort alone will do me good. There is nothing I fear so much as idleness, the want of occupation, inactivity, the lethargy of the faculties; when the body is idle, the spirit suffers painfully.

I should not know this lethargy if I could write. Formerly I passed whole days and weeks and months in writing, not wholly without result, for Southey and Coleridge – two of our best authors, to whom I sent certain manuscripts – were good enough to express their approval; but now my sight is too weak to write. Were I to write much I should become blind. This weakness of sight is a terrible hindrance to me. Otherwise, do you know what I should do, Monsieur? I should write a book, and I should dedicate it to my literature-master – to the only master I ever had – to you, Monsieur. I have often told you in French how much I respect you – how much I am indebted to your goodness, to your advice. I should like to say it once in English. But that cannot be – it is not to be thought of. The career of letters is closed to me – only that of teaching is open. It does not offer the same attractions; never mind, I shall enter it, and if I do not go far it will not be from want of industry. You, too, Monsieur – you wished to be a barrister – destiny or Providence made you a professor; you are happy in spite of it.

Please convey to Madame the assurance of my esteem. I fear that Maria, Louise, Claire have already forgotten me. Prospère and Victorine never knew me well; I remember well all five of them, especially Louise. She had so much character, so much naïveté in her little face. Good-bye, Monsieur – Your grateful pupil.

C. Brontë

I have not begged you to write to me soon as I fear to importune you – but you are too kind to forget that I wish it all the same – yes, I wish it greatly. Enough; after all, do as you wish, Monsieur. If, then, I received a letter, and if I thought that you had written it *out of pity*, I should feel deeply wounded.

It seems that Mrs. Wheelwright is going to Paris before going to Brussels, but she will post my letter at Boulogne. Once more good-bye, Monsieur; it hurts to say good-bye even in a letter. Oh, it is certain that I shall see you again one day – it must be so – for as soon as I shall have earned enough money to go to Brussels I shall go there, and I shall see you again if only for a moment.

58

CHARLOTTE BRONTË TO M. HÉGER
(*Translated from the French*)

October 24th, 1844.

Monsieur,

I am in high glee this morning, and that has rarely happened to me these last two years. It is because a gentleman of my acquaintance is going to Brussels, and has offered to take charge of a letter for you – which letter he will deliver to you himself, or else his sister, so that I shall be certain that you have received it.

I am not going to write a long letter; in the first place, I have not the time – it must leave at once; and then, I am afraid to worry you. I would only ask of you if you heard from me at the beginning of May and again in the month of August? For six months I have been awaiting a letter from Monsieur – six months' waiting is very long, you know. However, I do not complain, and I shall be richly rewarded for a little sorrow if you will now write a letter and give it to this gentleman, or to his sister, who will hand it to me without fail.

I shall be satisfied with the letter however brief it be, only do not forget to tell me of your health, Monsieur, and how Madame and the children are, and the governesses and pupils.

My father and my sister send you their respects. My father's infirmity increases little by little. Nevertheless, he is not yet entirely blind. My sisters are well, but my poor brother is always ill.

Farewell, Monsieur; I am depending on soon having your news. The idea delights me, for the remembrance of your kindness will never fade from my memory, and, as long as that remembrance endures, the respect with which it has inspired me will endure likewise, – Your very devoted pupil,

C. Brontë

I have just had bound all the books you gave me when I was at Brussels. I take delight in contemplating them; they make quite a little library. To begin with, there are the complete works of Bernardian de St. Pierre – the Pensées de Pascal – a book of poetry, two German books – and (worth all the rest) two discourses of Monsieur le Professeur Héger, delivered at the distribution of prizes of the Athenée Royal.

59

CHARLOTTE BRONTË TO M. HÉGER
(*Translated from the French*)

January 8th, 1845.

Mr. Taylor has returned. I asked him if he had a letter for me. 'No; nothing.' 'Patience,' said I, 'his sister will be here soon.' Miss Taylor has returned. 'I have nothing for you from Monsieur Héger,' says she; 'neither letter nor message.'

Having realized the meaning of these words, I said to myself what I should say to another similarly placed: 'You must be resigned, and above all do not grieve at a misfortune which you have not deserved.' I strove to restrain my tears, to utter no complaint.

But when one does not complain, when one seeks to dominate oneself with a tyrant's grip, the faculties start into rebellion, and one pays for external calm with an internal struggle that is almost unbearable.

Day and night I find neither rest nor peace. If I sleep I am disturbed by tormenting dreams in which I see you, always severe, always grave, always incensed against me.

Forgive me then, Monsieur, if I adopt the course of writing to you again. How can I endure life if I make no effort to ease its sufferings?

I know that you will be irritated when you read this letter. You will say once more that I am neurotic – that I have black thoughts, etc. So be it, Monsieur; I do not seek to justify myself; I submit to every sort of reproach. All I know is that I cannot, that I will not, resign myself to lose wholly the friendship of my master. I would rather suffer the greatest physical pain than always have my heart lacerated by smarting regrets.

If my master withdraws his friendship from me entirely I shall be altogether without hope; if he gives me a little – just a little – I shall be satisfied – happy; I shall have reasons for living on, for working.

Monsieur, the poor have not need of much to sustain them – they ask only for the crumbs that fall from the rich man's table. But if they are refused the crumbs they die of hunger. Nor do I, either, need much affection from those I love. I should not know what to do with a friendship entire and complete – I am not used to it. But you showed me of yore a *little* interest, when I was your pupil in

Brussels, and I hold on to the maintenance of that *little* interest – I hold on to it as I would hold on to life.

You will tell me perhaps, 'I take not the slightest interest in you, Mademoiselle Charlotte. You are no longer an inmate of my House; I have forgotten you'.

Well, Monsieur, tell me so frankly. It will be a shock to me. It matters not. It would be less dreadful than uncertainty.

I shall not re-read this letter. I send it as I have written it. Nevertheless, I have a hidden consciousness that some people, cold and common sense, in reading it would say, 'She is talking nonsense'. I would avenge myself on such persons in no other way than by wishing them one single day of the torments which I have suffered for eight months. We should then see if they would not talk nonsense too.

One suffers in silence so long as one has the strength so to do, and when that strength gives out one speaks without too carefully measuring one's words.

I wish Monsieur happiness and prosperity.

C.B.

60

CHARLOTTE BRONTË TO ELLEN NUSSEY

July 31st, '45.

Dear Ellen,

. . . I got home very well. There was a gentleman in the railroad carriage whom I recognized by his features immediately as a foreigner and Frenchman. So sure was I of it, that I ventured to say to him in French – 'Monsieur est français, n'est-ce pas?' He gave a start of surprise, and answered immediately in his own tongue; he appeared still more astonished, and even puzzled, when after a few minutes' further conversation, I inquired if he had not passed the greater part of his life in Germany. He said the surmise was correct. I had guessed it from his speaking French with the German accent.

It was ten o'clock at night when I got home. I found Branwell ill, he is so very often owing to his own fault. I was not therefore shocked at first, but when Anne informed me of the immediate cause of his present illness, I was greatly shocked. He had last Thursday received a note from Mr. Robinson sternly dismissing him, intimating that he had discovered his proceedings, which he characterized as bad beyond expression, and charging him on pain of exposure to break off instantly and for ever all communication with every member of his family. We have had sad work with Branwell since. He thought of nothing but stunning or drowning his distress of mind. No one in the house could have rest. At last we have been obliged to send him from home for a week, with some one to look after him; he has written to me this morning, and expresses some sense of contrition for his frantic folly; he promises amendment on his return, but so long as he remains at home I scarce dare hope for peace in the house. We must all, I fear, prepare for a season of distress and disquietude. When I left you I was strongly impressed with the feeling that I was going back to sorrow. . . . Good-bye, dear Nell,

C. Brontë

61

EMILY BRONTË'S 'BIRTHDAY' NOTE

Haworth,
Thursday, July 30th, 1845.

My birthday – showery, breezy, cool. I am twenty-seven years old to-day. This morning Anne and I opened the papers we wrote four years since, on my twenty-third birthday. This paper we intend, if all be well, to open on my thirtieth – three years hence, in 1848. Since the 1841 paper the following events have taken place. Our school scheme has been abandoned, and instead Charlotte and I went to Brussels on the 8th of February, 1842.

Branwell left his place at Luddenden Foot. C. and I returned from Brussels, November 8th, 1842, in consequence of aunt's death.

Branwell went to Thorp Green as a tutor, where Anne still continued, January, 1843.

Charlotte returned to Brussels the same month, and after staying a year, came back again on New Year's Day 1844.

Anne left her situation at Thorp Green of her own accord, June 1845.

Anne and I went our first long journey by ourselves together, leaving home on the 30th of June, Monday, sleeping at York, returning to Keighley Tuesday evening, sleeping there and walking home on Wednesday morning. Though the weather was broken we enjoyed ourselves very much, except during a few hours at Bradford. And during our excursion we were, Ronald Macalgin, Henry Angora, Juliet Angusteena, Rosabella Esmaldan, Ella and Julian Egremont, Catharine Navarre, and Cordelia Fitzapnnold, escaping from the palaces of instruction to join the Royalists who are hard driven at present by the victorious Republicans. The Gondals still flourish bright as ever. I am at present writing a work on the First War. Anne has been writing some articles on this, and a book by Henry Sophona. We intend sticking firm by the rascals as long as they delight us, which I am glad to say they do at present. I should have mentioned that last summer the school scheme was revived in full vigour. We had prospectuses printed, despatched letters to all acquaintances imparting our plans, and did our little all; but it was found no go. Now I don't desire a school at all, and none of us have any great longing for it. We have cash enough for our present wants, with a prospect of accumulation. We are all in decent health, only that papa has a complaint in his eyes, and with the exception of B., who, I hope, will be better and do better hereafter. I am quite contented for myself: not as idle as formerly, altogether as hearty, and having learnt to make the most of the present and long for the future with the fidgetiness that I cannot do all I wish; seldom or ever troubled with nothing to do, and merely desiring that everybody could be as comfortable as myself and as undesponding, and then we should have a very tolerable world of it.

By mistake I find we have opened the paper on the 31st instead of the 30th. Yesterday was much such a day as this, but the morning was divine.

Tabby, who was gone in our last paper, is come back, and has lived with us two years and a half, and is in good health. Martha, who also departed, is here too. We have got Flossy; got and lost Tiger; lost the hawk Hero, which, with the geese, was given away, and is doubtless dead, for when I came back from Brussels I inquired on all hands and could hear nothing of him. Tiger died early last year. Keeper and Flossy are well, also the canary acquired four years since. We are now all at home, and likely to be there some time. Branwell went to Liverpool on Tuesday to stay a week. Tabby has just been teasing me to turn as formerly to 'Pilloputate'. Anne and I should have picked the black currants if it had been fine and sunshiny. I must hurry off now to my turning and ironing. I have plenty of work on hands, and writing, and am altogether full of business. With best wishes for the whole house till 1848, July 30th, and as much longer as may be, – I conclude.

Emily Brontë

62

ANNE BRONTË'S 'BIRTHDAY' NOTE

Thursday, July the 31st, 1845. Yesterday was Emily's birthday, and the time when we should have opened our 1841 paper, but by mistake we opened it to-day instead. How many things have happened since it was written – some pleasant, some far otherwise. Yet I was then at Thorp Green, and now I am only just escaped from it. I was wishing to leave it then, and if I had known that I had four years longer to stay how wretched I should have been; but during my stay I have had some very unpleasant and undreamt-of experience of human nature. Others have seen more changes. Charlotte has left Mr. White's and been twice to Brussels, where she stayed each time nearly a year. Emily has been there too, and stayed nearly a year. Branwell has left Luddenden Foot, and been a tutor at Thorp Green, and had much tribulation and ill-health. He was very ill on Thursday, but he went with John Brown to Liverpool, where he now is, I suppose; and we hope he will be better and do better in future. This is a dismal, cloudy wet evening. We have had so far a very cold, wet summer. Charlotte has lately been to Hathersage, in Derbyshire, on a visit of three weeks to Ellen Nussey. She is now sitting sewing in the dining-room. Emily is ironing upstairs. I am sitting in the dining-room in the rocking-chair before the fire with my feet on the fender. Papa is in the parlour. Tabby and Martha are, I think, in the kitchen. Keeper and Flossy are, I do not know where. Little Dick is hopping in his cage. When the last paper was written we were thinking of setting up a school. The scheme has been dropt, and long after taken up again, and dropt again, because we could not get pupils. Charlotte is thinking about getting another situation. She wishes to go to Paris. Will she go? She has let Flossy in, by-the-by, and he is now lying on the sofa. Emily is engaged in writing the Emperor Julius's Life. She has read some of it, and I want very much to hear the rest. She is writing some poetry, too. I wonder what it is about? I have begun the third volume of *Passages in the Life of an Individual*. I wish I had finished it. This afternoon I began to set about making my grey figured silk frock that was dyed at Keighley. What sort of a hand shall I make of it? E. and I have a great deal of work to do. When shall we sensibly diminish it? I want to get a habit of early rising. Shall I succeed? We have not yet finished our *Gondal Chronicles* that we began three years and a half ago. When will they be done? The Gondals are at present in a sad state. The Republicans are uppermost, but the Royalists are not quite overcome. The young sovereigns, with their brothers and sisters, are still at the Palace of Instruction. The Unique Society, about half a year ago, were wrecked on a desert island as they were returning from Gaul. They are still there, but we have not played at them much yet. The Gondals in general are not in first-rate playing condition. Will they improve? I wonder how we shall all be, and where and how situated, on the thirtieth of July, 1848, when, if we are all alive, Emily will be just 30. I shall be in my 29th year, Charlotte in her 33rd and Branwell in his 32nd; and what changes shall we have seen and known; and shall we be much changed ourselves? I hope not, for the worse at least. I, for my part, cannot well be flatter or older in mind than I am now. Hoping for the best, I conclude.

Anne Brontë

63

CHARLOTTE BRONTË TO ELLEN NUSSEY

Sep. 8th, '45.

Dear Ellen,

You will wonder why I have not sent the French newspaper. I did not finish reading it till yesterday. I am glad you have got home, and yet I scarcely know why I should be. I neither intend to go and see you soon, nor to ask you to come and see us. Branwell makes no effort to seek a situation, and while he is at home I will invite no one to come and share our discomfort. I was much struck with —. I could not live with one so cold and narrow, though she were correct as a mathematical straight line, and upright as perpendicularity itself. Emily and Anne regret, as I do, that we cannot ask you to come to Haworth; we think during this fine weather how we should enjoy your company. – Write to me soon, dear Nell.

C. Brontë

64

BRANWELL BRONTË TO FRANCIS H. GRUNDY

October, 1845.

I fear you will burn my present letter on recognizing the handwriting; but if you will read it through, you will perhaps rather pity than spurn the distress of mind which could prompt my communication, after a silence of nearly three (to me) eventful years. While very ill and confined to my room, I wrote to you two months ago, hearing that you were resident engineer of the Skipton Railway, to the inn at Skipton. I never received any reply, and as to my letter asked only for one day of your society to ease a very weary mind in the company of a friend who always had what I always wanted, but most want now, cheerfulness. I am sure you never received my letter, or your heart would have prompted an answer.

Since I last shook hands with you in Halifax, two summers ago, my life till lately has been one of apparent happiness and indulgence. You will ask, 'Why does he complain then?' I can only reply by showing the under-current of distress which bore my bark to a whirlpool, despite the surface waves of life that seemed floating me to peace. In a letter begun in the spring of 1844 and never finished, owing to incessant attacks of illness, I tried to tell you that I was tutor to the son of —, a wealthy gentleman whose wife is sister to the wife of —, M.P., for the county of —, and the cousin of Lord —. This lady (though her husband detested me) showed me a degree of kindness which, when I was deeply grieved one day at her husband's conduct, ripened into declarations of more than ordinary feeling. My admiration of her mental and personal attractions, my knowledge of her unselfish sincerity, her sweet temper, and unwearied care for others, with but unrequited return where most should have been given . . . although she is seventeen years my senior, all combined to an attachment on my part, and led to reciprocations which I had little looked for. During nearly three years I had daily 'troubled pleasure soon chastised by fear'. Three months since I received a furious letter from my employer, threatening to shoot me if I returned from my vacation, which I was passing at home; and letters from her lady's maid and physician informed me of the outbreak, only checked by her firm courage and resolution that whatever harm came to her, none should come to me . . . I have lain during nine long weeks utterly shattered in body and broken down in mind. The probability of her becoming free to give me herself and estate never rose to drive away the prospect of her decline under her present grief. I dreaded, too, the wreck of my mind and body, which, God knows, during a short life have been severely tried. Eleven continuous nights of sleepless horror reduced me to almost blindness, and being taken into Wales to recover, the sweet scenery, the sea, the sound of music caused me fits of unspeakable distress. You will say, 'What a fool!' but if you knew the many causes I have for sorrow which I cannot even hint at here, you would perhaps pity as well as blame. At the kind request of Mr. Macaulay and Mr. Baines, I have striven to arouse my mind by writing something worthy of being read, but I really cannot do so. Of course, you will despise the writer of all this. I can only answer that the writer does the same, and would not wish to live if he did not hope that work and change may yet restore him.

Apologizing sincerely for what seems like whining egotism, and hardly daring to hint about days when in your company I could sometimes sink the thoughts which 'remind me of departed days', I fear departed never to return, I remain, etc.

P.B. Brontë

65

CHARLOTTE BRONTË TO M. HÉGER
(*Translated from the French*)

November 18th, 1845.

Monsieur,

The six months of silence have run their course. It is now the 18th of Novr.; my last letter was dated (I think) the 18th of May. I may therefore write to you without failing in my promise.

The summer and autumn seemed very long to me; truth to tell, it has needed painful efforts on my part to bear hitherto the self-denial which I have imposed on myself. You, Monsieur, you cannot conceive what it means; but suppose for a moment that one of your children was separated from you, 160 leagues away, and that you had to remain six months without writing to him, without receiving news of him, without hearing him spoken of, without knowing aught of his health, then you would understand easily all the harshness of such an obligation. I tell you frankly that I have tried meanwhile to forget you, for the remembrance of a person whom one thinks never to see again, and whom, nevertheless, one greatly esteems, frets too much the mind; and when one has suffered that kind of anxiety for a year or two, one is ready to do anything to find peace once more. I have done everything; I have sought occupations; I have denied myself absolutely the pleasure of speaking about you – even to Emily; but I have been able to conquer neither my regrets or my impatience. That, indeed, is humiliating – to be unable to control one's own thoughts, to be the slave of a regret, of a memory, the slave of a fixed and dominant idea which lords it over the mind. Why cannot I have just as much friendship for you, as you for me – neither more nor less? Then should I be so tranquil, so free – I could keep silence then for ten years without an effort.

My father is well but his sight is almost gone. He can neither read nor write. Yet the doctors advise waiting a few months more before attempting an operation. The winter will be a long night for him. He rarely complains; I admire his patience. If Providence wills the same calamity for me, may He at last vouchsafe me as much patience with which to bear it! It seems to me, Monsieur, that there is nothing more galling in great physical misfortunes than to be compelled to make all those about us share in our sufferings. The ills of the soul one can hide, but those which attack the body and destroy the faculties cannot be concealed. My father allows me now to read to him and write for him; he shows me, too, more confidence than he has ever shown before, and that is a great consolation.

Monsieur, I have a favour to ask of you: when you reply to this letter, speak to me a little of yourself, not of me; for I know that if you speak of me it will be to scold me, and this time I would see your kindly side. Speak to me therefore of your children. Never was your brow severe when Louise and Claire and Prosper were by your side. Tell me also something of the School, of the pupils, of the Governesses. Are Mesdemoiselles Blanche, Sophie, and Justine still at Brussels? Tell me where you travelled during the holidays – did you go to the Rhine? Did you not visit Cologne or Coblentz? Tell me, in short, my master, what you will, but tell me something. To write to an ex-assistant governess (No! I refuse to remember my employment as assistant governess – I repudiate it) – anyhow, to write to an old pupil cannot be a very interesting occupation for you, I know; but for me it is life. Your last letter was stay and prop to me – nourishment for half a year. Now I need another and you will give it me; not because you bear me friendship – you cannot have much – but because you are compassionate of soul and you would condemn no one to prolonged suffering to save yourself a few moments' trouble. To forbid me to write to you, to refuse to answer me, would be to tear from me my only joy on earth, to deprive me of my last privilege – a privilege I never shall consent willingly to surrender. Believe me, my master, in writing to me it is a good deed that you will do. So long as I believe you are pleased with me, so long as I have hope of receiving news from you, I can be at rest and not too sad. But when a prolonged and gloomy silence seems to threaten me with the estrangement of my master – when day by day I await a letter, and when day by day disappointment comes to fling me back into overwhelming sorrow, and the sweet delight of seeing your handwriting and reading your counsel escapes me as a vision that is vain, then fever claims me – I lose appetite and sleep – I pine away.

May I write to you again next May: I would rather wait a year, but it is impossible – it is too long.

C. Brontë

(*Postcript in English.*)

I must say one word to you in English. I wish I could write to you more cheerful letters, for when I read this over I find it to be somewhat gloomy – but forgive me, my dear master – do not be irritated at my sadness – according to the words of the Bible: 'Out of the fulness of the heart, the mouth speaketh,' and truly I find it difficult to be cheerful so long as I think I shall never see you more. You will perceive by the defects in this letter than I am forgetting the French language – yet I read all the French books I can get, and learn daily a portion by heart – but I have never heard French spoken but once since I left Brussels – and then it sounded like music in my ears – every word was most precious to me because it reminded me of you – I love French for your sake with all my heart and soul.

Farewell, my dear Master – may God protect you with special care and crown you with peculiar blessings.

C.B.

66

CHARLOTTE BRONTË TO AYLOTT & JONES

January 28th, 1846.

Gentlemen,

May I request to be informed whether you would undertake the publication of a collection of short poems in one volume, 8vo.[1]

If you object to publishing the work at your own risk, would you undertake it on the author's account? – I am, gentlemen, your obedient humble servant,

C. Brontë

Address – Rev. P. Brontë, Haworth, Bradford, Yorkshire.

67

CHARLOTTE BRONTË TO AYLOTT & JONES

Feb. 6th, 1846.

Gentlemen,

I send you the M.S. as you desired.

You will perceive that the poems are the work of three persons, relatives; their separate pieces are distinguished by their respective signatures.

C. Brontë

68

CHARLOTTE BRONTË TO ELLEN NUSSEY

March 3rd, 1846.

Dear Ellen,

I reached home a little after two o'clock, all safe and right, yesterday; I found papa very well; his sight much the same. Emily and Anne were gone to Keighley to meet me; unfortunately, I had returned by the old road, while they were gone by the new, and we missed each other. They did not get home till half-past four, and were caught in a heavy shower of rain which fell in the afternoon. I am sorry to say

[1] The poems were published under the pseudonyms 'Currer, Ellis, and Acton Bell'.

Anne has taken a little cold in consequence, but I hope she will soon be well. Papa was much cheered by my report of Mr. Carr's opinion, and of old Mrs. Carr's experience; but I could perceive he caught gladly at the idea of deferring the operations a few months longer. I went into the room where Branwell was, to speak to him, about an hour after I got home; it was very forced work to address him. I might have spared myself the trouble, as he took no notice, and made no reply; he was stupified. My fears were not in vain. I hear that he had got a sovereign from papa while I have been away, under pretence of paying a pressing debt; he went immediately and changed it at a public-house, and has employed it as was to be expected. Emily concluded her account by saying he was a hopeless being; it is too true. In his present state, it is scarcely possible to stay in the room where he is. What the future has in store I do not know. I hope Mary and Miss B — got home without any wet; give my love to your mother and sisters. Let me hear from you if possible on Thursday. – Believe me, dear Nell, yours faithfully,

C.B.

69

CHARLOTTE BRONTË TO AYLOTT & JONES

April 6th, 1846.

Gentlemen,,

C., E., and A. Bell are now preparing for the press a work of fiction,[1] consisting of three distinct and unconnected tales, which may be published either together, as a work of three volumes, of the ordinary novel size, or separately as single volumes, as shall be deemed most advisable.

It is not their intention to publish these tales on their own account. They direct me to ask you whether you would be disposed to undertake the work, after having, of course, by due inspection of the MS., ascertained that its contents are such as to warrant an expectation of success.

An early answer will oblige, as, in case of your negativing the proposal, inquiry must be made of other publishers. – I am, gentlemen, yours truly,

C. Brontë

[1] *The Professor* by Charlotte, *Wuthering Heights* by Emily, and *Agnes Grey* by Anne.

70

CHARLOTTE BRONTË TO ELLEN NUSSEY

June 17th, '46.

Dear Ellen,

I was glad to perceive by the tone of your last letter, that you are beginning to be a little more settled and comfortable. I should think Dr. Belcombe is quite right in opposing George's removal home. We, I am sorry to say, have been somewhat more harassed than usual lately. The death of Mr. Robinson, which took place about three weeks or a month ago, served Branwell for a pretext to throw all about him into hubbub and confusion with his emotions, etc., etc. Shortly after, came news from all hands that Mr. Robinson had altered his will before he died and effectually prevented all chance of a marriage between his widow and Branwell, by stipulating that she should not have a shilling if she ever ventured to reopen any communication with him. Of course, he then became intolerable. To papa he allows rest neither day nor night, and he is continually screwing money out of him, sometimes threatening that he will kill himself if it is withheld from him. He says Mrs. Robinson is now insane; that her mind is a complete wreck owing to remorse for her conduct towards Mr. Robinson (whose end it appears was hastened by distress of mind) and grief for having lost him. I do not know how much to believe of what he says, but I fear she is very ill. Branwell declares that he neither can nor will do anything for himself; good situations have been offered him more than once, for which, by a fortnight's work, he might have qualified himself, but he will do nothing, except drink and make us all wretched. I had a note from Ellen Taylor a week ago, in which she remarks that letters were received from New Zealand a month since, and that all was well. I should like to hear from you again soon. I hope one day to see Brookroyd again, though I think it will not be yet – these are not times of amusement. Love to all.

C.B.

71

CHARLOTTE BRONTË TO AYLOTT & JONES

July 10th, 1846.

Gentlemen,

I am directed by the Messrs. Bell to acknowledge the receipt of the *Critic* and the *Athenæum* containing notices of the poems.

They now think that a further sum of £10 may be devoted to advertisements, leaving it to you to select such channels as you deem most advisable.

They would wish the following extract from the *Critic* to be appended to each advertisement: –

'They in whose hearts are chords strung by Nature to sympathize with the beautiful and the true, will recognize in these compositions the presence of more genius than it was supposed this utilitarian age had devoted to the loftier exercises of the intellect.'

They likewise request you to send copies of the poems to *Fraser's Magazine*, *Chambers's Edinburgh Journal*, the *Globe*, and *Examiner*. – I am, gentlemen, yours truly,

C. Brontë

72

CHARLOTTE BRONTË TO ELLEN NUSSEY

December 13th, '46.

Dear Ellen,

I hope you are not frozen up in Northamptonshire; the cold here is dreadful. I do not remember such a series of North-Pole days. England might really have taken a slide up into the Arctic Zone: the sky looks like ice; the earth is frozen; the wind is as keen as a two-edged blade. I cannot keep myself warm. We have all had severe colds and coughs in consequence of the severe weather. Poor Anne has suffered greatly from asthma, but is now, I am glad to say, rather better. She had two nights last week when her cough and difficulty of breathing were painful indeed to hear and witness, and must have been most distressing to suffer; she bore it, as she does all affliction, without one complaint, only sighing now and then when nearly worn out. She has an extraordinary heroism of endurance. I admire, but I certainly could not imitate her. . . . You say I am to tell you plenty. What would you have me say? Nothing happens at Haworth, nothing, at least, of a pleasant kind. One little incident occurred about a week ago to sting us to life; but if it gives no more pleasure for you to hear than it did for us to witness, you will scarcely thank me for adverting to it. It was merely the arrival of a sheriff's officer on a visit to Branwell, inviting him either to pay his debts or take a trip to York. Of course his debts had to be paid. It is not agreeable to lose money, time after time, in this way; but it is ten times worse to witness the shabbiness of his behaviour on such occasions; but where is the use of dwelling on such subjects? It will make him no better. . . . I send you the last French newspaper; several have missed coming. Do you intend paying a visit to Sussex before you return home? Write again soon; your last epistle was very interesting. – I am, dear Nell, yours in spirit and flesh.

C.B.

73

CHARLOTTE BRONTË TO THOMAS DE QUINCEY[1]

June 16th, 1847.

Sir,

My relatives, Ellis and Acton Bell, and myself, heedless of the repeated warnings of various respectable publishers, have committed the rash act of printing a volume of poems.

The consequences predicted have, of course, overtaken us: our book is found to be a drug; no man needs it or heeds it. In the space of a year our publisher has disposed but of two copies, and by what painful efforts he succeeded in getting rid of these two, himself only knows.

Before transferring the edition to the trunkmakers, we have decided on distributing as presents a few copies of what we cannot sell; and we beg to offer you one in acknowledgment of the pleasure and profit we have often and long derived from your works. – I am, sir, yours very respectfully,

Currer Bell

[1] A similar letter was written to Wordsworth, Tennyson, and Lockhart.

74

CHARLOTTE BRONTË
TO MESSRS. SMITH, ELDER AND CO.

August 24th, 1847.

I now send you per rail a MS. entitled *Jane Eyre*, a novel in three volumes, by Currer Bell. I find I cannot prepay the carriage of the parcel, as money for that purpose is not received at the small station-house where it is left. If, when you acknowledge the receipt of the MS., you would have the goodness to mention the amount charged on delivery, I will immediately transmit it in postage-stamps. It is better in future to address Mr. Currer Bell, under cover to Miss Brontë, Haworth, Bradford, Yorkshire, as there is a risk of letters otherwise directed not reaching me at present. To save trouble, I enclose an envelope.

Currer Bell

75

ANNE BRONTË TO ELLEN NUSSEY

Haworth,
October 4th, '47.

My Dear Miss Nussey,

Many thanks to you for your unexpected and welcome epistle. Charlotte is well, and meditates writing to you. Happily for all parties the east wind no longer prevails. During its continuance she complained of its influence as usual. I too suffered from it in some degree, as I always do, more or less; but this time, it brought me no reinforcement of colds and coughs which is what I dread the most. Emily considers it a very uninteresting wind, but it does not affect her nervous system. Charlotte agrees with me in thinking the — a very provoking affair. You are quite mistaken about her parasol, she affirms she brought it back and I can bear witness to the fact, having seen it yesterday in her possession. As for my book, I have no wish to see it again till I see you along with it, and then it will be welcome enough for the sake of the bearer. We are all here much as you left us. I have no news to tell you, except that Mr. Nicholls begged a holiday and went to Ireland three or four weeks ago, and is not expected back till Saturday, but that, I dare say, is no news at all. We were all and severally pleased and gratified for your kind and judiciously selected presents, from papa down to Tabby, or down to myself, perhaps I ought rather to say. The crab-cheese is excellent and likely to be very useful, but I don't intend to need it. It is not choice, but necessity has induced me to choose such a tiny sheet of paper for my letter, having none more suitable at hand; but perhaps it will contain as much as you need wish to read, and I to write, for I find I have nothing more to say, except that your little Tabby must be a charming little creature. And —, and that is all, for as Charlotte is writing, or about to write to you herself, I need not send any messages from her. Therefore, accept my best love. I must not omit the Major's[1] compliments. – And believe me to be your affectionate friend,

Anne Brontë

76

CHARLOTTE BRONTË TO W.S. WILLIAMS

Haworth,
October 28th, 1847.

Dear Sir,

Your last letter was very pleasant to me to read, and is very cheering to reflect on. I feel honoured in being approved by Mr. Thackeray, because I approve Mr. Thackeray. This may sound presumptuous perhaps, but I mean that I have long recognized in his writings genuine talent, such as I admired, such as I wondered at and delighted in. No author seems to distinguish so exquisitely as he does dross from ore, the real from the counterfeit. I believed too he had deep and true feelings under his seeming sternness. Now I am sure he has. One good word from such a man is worth pages of praise from ordinary judges.

You are right in having faith in the reality of Helen Burns's character; she was real enough. I have exaggerated nothing there. I abstained from recording much that I remember respecting her, lest the narrative should sound incredible. Knowing this, I could not but smile at the quiet self-complacent dogmatism with which one of the journals lays it down that 'such creations as Helen Burns are

[1] Emily was nicknamed 'the Major' because on one occasion she guarded Ellen Nussey from the attentions of Mr Weightman during a walk.

very beautiful but very untrue'.

The plot of *Jane Eyre* may be a hackneyed one. Mr. Thackeray remarks that it is familiar to him. But having read comparatively few novels I never chanced to meet with it, and I thought it original. The work referred to by the critic of the *Athenæum* I had not the good fortune to hear of.

The *Weekly Chronicle* seems inclined to identify me with Mrs. Marsh. I never had the pleasure of perusing a line of Mrs. Marsh's in my life, but I wish very much to read her works, and shall profit by the first opportunity of doing so. I hope I shall not find I have been an unconscious imitator.

I would still endeavour to keep my expectations low respecting the ultimate success of *Jane Eyre*. But my desire that it should succeed augments, for you have taken much trouble about the work, and it would grieve me seriously if your active efforts should be baffled and your sanguine hopes disappointed. Excuse me if I again remark that I fear they are rather *too* sanguine: it would be better to moderate them. What will the critics of the monthly reviews and magazines be likely to see in *Jane Eyre* (if indeed they deign to read it), which will win from them even a stinted modicum of approbation? It has no learning, no research, it discusses no subject of public interest. A mere domestic novel will, I fear, seem trivial to men of large views and solid attainments.

Still, efforts so energetic and indefatigable as yours ought to realize a result in some degree favourable, and I trust they will. – I remain, dear sir, yours respectfully,

C. Bell

I have just received the *Tablet* and the *Morning Advertiser*. Neither paper seems inimical to the book, but I see it produces a very different effect on different natures. I was amused at the analysis in the *Tablet*, it is oddly expressed in some parts. I think the critic did not always seize my meaning; he speaks, for instance, of 'Jane's inconceivable alarm at Mr. Rochester's repelling manner.' I do not remember that.

77

CHARLOTTE BRONTË TO G.H. LEWES

November 6th, 1847.

Dear Sir,

Your letter reached me yesterday. I beg to assure you that I appreciate fully the intention with which it was written, and I thank you sincerely both for its cheering commendation and valuable advice.

You warn me to beware of melodrama, and you exhort me to adhere to the real. When I first began to write, so impressed was I with the truth of the principles you advocate, that I determined to take Nature and Truth as my sole guides, and to follow to their very footprints; I restrained imagination, eschewed romance, repressed excitement; over-bright colouring, too, I avoided, and sought to produce something which should be soft, grave, and true.

My work (a tale in one volume) being completed, I offered it to a publisher. He said it was original, faithful to nature, but he did not feel warranted in accepting it; such a work would not sell. I tried six publishers in succession; they all told me it was deficient in 'startling incident' and 'thrilling excitement', that it would never suit the circulating libraries, and as it was on those libraries the success of works of fiction mainly depended, they could not undertake to publish what would be overlooked there.

Jane Eyre was rather objected to at first, on the same grounds, but finally found acceptance.

I mention this to you, not with a view of pleading exemption from censure, but in order to direct your attention to the root of certain literary evils. If, in your forthcoming article in *Fraser*, you would bestow a few words of enlightenment on the public who support the circulating libraries, you might, with your powers, do some good.

You advise me, too, not to stray far from the ground of experience, as I become weak when I enter the region of fiction; and you say 'real experience is perennially interesting, and to all men'.

I feel that this also is true; but, dear sir, is not the real experience of each individual very limited? And, if a writer dwells upon that solely or principally, is he not in danger of repeating himself, and also becoming an egotist? Then, too, imagination is a strong, restless faculty, which claims to be heard and exercised: are we to be quite deaf to her cry, and insensate to her struggles? When she shows us bright pictures, are we never to look at them, and try to reproduce them? And when she is eloquent, and speaks rapidly and urgently in our ear, are we not to write to her dictation?

I shall anxiously search the next number of *Fraser* for your opinions on these points. – Believe me, dear sir, yours gratefully,

C. Bell

78

CHARLOTTE BRONTË TO W.S. WILLIAMS

November 10th, 1847.

Dear Sir,

I have received the *Britannia* and the *Sun*, but not the *Spectator*, which I rather regret, as censure, though not pleasant, is often wholesome.

Thank you for your information regarding Mr. Lewes. I am glad to hear that he is a clever and sincere man: such being the case, I can await his critical sentence with fortitude; even if it goes against me I shall not murmur; ability and honesty have a right to condemn where they think condemnation is deserved. From what you say, however, I trust rather to obtain at least a modified approval.

Your account of the various surmises respecting the identity of the brothers Bell amused me much: were the enigma solved it would probably be found not worth the trouble of solution; but I will let it alone: it suits ourselves to remain quiet, and certainly injures no one else.

The reviewer who noticed the little book of poems, in the *Dublin Magazine*, conjectured that the *soi-disant* three personages were in reality but one, who, endowed with an unduly prominent organ of self-esteem, and consequently impressed with a somewhat weighty notion of his own merits, thought them too vast to be concentrated in a single individual, and accordingly divided himself into three, out of consideration, I suppose, for the nerves of the much-to-be-astounded public! This was an ingenious thought in the reviewer – very original and striking, but not accurate. We are three.

A prose work, by Ellis and Acton, will soon appear: it should have been out, indeed, long since; for the first proof-sheets were already in the press at the commencement of last August, before Currer Bell had placed the MS. of *Jane Eyre* in your hands. Mr. Newby, however, does not do business like Messrs. Smith & Elder;

a different spirit seems to preside at Mortimer Street to that which guides the helm at 65 Cornhill. . . . My relations have suffered from exhausting delay and procrastination, while I have to acknowledge the benefits of a management at once businesslike and gentlemanlike, energetic and considerate.

I should like to know if Mr. Newby often acts as he has done to my relations, or whether this is an exceptional instance of his method. Do you know, and can you tell me anything about him? You must excuse me for going to the point at once, when I want to learn anything; if my questions are impertinent you are, of course, at liberty to decline answering them. – I am yours respectfully,

C. Bell

79

CHARLOTTE BRONTË TO W.S. WILLIAMS

December 21st, 1847.

Dear Sir,

I am, for my own part, dissatisfied with the preface I sent – I fear it savours of flippancy. If you see no objection I should prefer substituting the enclosed. It is rather more lengthy, but it expresses something I have long wished to express.

Mr. Smith is kind indeed to think of sending me *The Jar of Honey*. When I receive the book I will write to him. I cannot thank you sufficiently for your letters, and I can give you but a faint idea of the pleasure they afford me; they seem to introduce such light and life to the torpid retirement where we live like dormice. But, understand this distinctly, you must never write to me except when you have both leisure and inclination. I know your time is too fully occupied and too valuable to be often at the service of any one individual.

You are not far wrong in your judgment respecting *Wuthering Heights* and *Agnes Grey*. Ellis has a strong, original mind, full of strange though sombre power. When he writes poetry that power speaks in language at once condensed, elaborated, and refined, but in prose it breaks forth in scenes which shock more than they attract. Ellis will improve, however, because he knows his defects. *Agnes Grey* is the mirror of the mind of the writer. The orthography and punctuation of the books are mortifying to a degree: almost all the errors that were corrected in the proof-sheets appear intact in what should have been the fair copies. If Mr. Newby always does business in this way, few authors would like to have him for their publisher a second time. – Believe me, dear sir, yours respectfully,

C. Bell

80

CHARLOTTE BRONTË TO G.H. LEWES

Haworth,
January 12th, 1848.

Dear Sir,

I thank you, then, sincerely for your generous review; and it is with the sense of double content I express my gratitude, because I am now sure the tribute is not superfluous or obtrusive. You were not severe on *Jane Eyre*; you were very lenient. I am glad you told me my faults plainly in private, for in your public notice you touch on them so lightly, I should perhaps have passed them over, thus indicated, with too little reflection.

I mean to observe your warning about being careful how I undertake new works; my stock of materials is not abundant, but very slender; and besides, neither my experience, my acquirements, nor my powers are sufficiently varied to justify my ever becoming a frequent writer. I tell you this because your article in *Fraser* left in me an uneasy impression that you were disposed to think better of the author of *Jane Eyre* than that individual deserved; and I would rather you had a correct than a flattering opinion of me, even though I should never see you.

If I ever *do* write another book, I think I will have nothing of what you call 'melodrama'; I *think* so, but I am not sure. I *think*, too, I will endeavour to follow the counsel which shines out of Miss Austen's 'mild eyes', 'to finish more and be more subdued'; but neither am I sure of that. When authors write best, or, at least, when they write most fluently, an influence seems to waken in them, which becomes their master – which will have its own way – putting out of view all behests but its own, dictating certain words, and insisting on their being used, whether vehement or measured in their nature; new-moulding characters, giving unthought-of turns to incidents, rejecting carefully elaborated old ideas, and suddenly creating and adopting new ones.

Is it not so? And should we try to counteract this influence? Can we indeed counteract it?

I am glad that another work of yours will soon appear; most curious shall I be to see whether you will write up to your own principles, and work out your own theories. You did not do it altogether in *Ranthorpe* – at least, not in the latter part; but the first portion was, I think, nearly without fault; then it had a pith, truth, significance in it which gave the book sterling value; but to write so one must have seen and known a great deal, and I have seen and known very little.

Why do you like Miss Austen so very much? I am puzzled on that point. What induced you to say that you would have rather written *Pride and Prejudice* or *Tom Jones*, than any of the Waverley Novels?

I had not seen *Pride and Prejudice* till I read that sentence of yours, and then I got the book. And what did I find? An accurate daguerreotyped portrait of a commonplace face; a carefully fenced, highly cultivated garden, with neat borders and delicate flowers; but no glance of a bright, vivid physiognomy, no open country, no fresh air, no blue hill, no bonny beck. I should hardly like to live with her ladies and gentlemen, in their elegant but confined houses. These observations will probably irritate you, but I shall run the risk.

Now I can understand admiration of George Sand; for though I never saw any of her works which I admired throughout (even *Consuelo*, which is the best, or the best that I have read, appears to me to couple strange extravagance with wondrous excellence), yet she has a grasp of mind which, if I cannot fully comprehend, I can very deeply respect: she is sagacious and profound; Miss Austen is only shrewd and observant.

Am I wrong; or were you hasty in what you said? If you have time I should be glad to hear further on this subject; if not, or if you think the question frivolous, do not trouble yourself to reply. – I am yours respectfully,

C. Bell

81

CHARLOTTE BRONTË TO ELLEN NUSSEY

May 3rd, 1848.

Dear Ellen,

All I can say to you about a certain matter is this: the report – if report there be – and if the lady who seems to have been rather mystified, had not dreamt what she fancied had been told to her – must have had its origin in some absurd misunderstanding. I have given *no one* a right either to affirm, or hint, in the most distant manner, that I am 'publishing' – (humbug!) Whoever has said it – if any one has, which I doubt – is no friend of mine. Though twenty books were ascribed to me, I should own none. I scout the idea utterly. Whoever, after I have distinctly rejected the charge, urges it upon me, will do an unkind and an ill-bred thing. The most profound obscurity is infinitely preferable to vulgar notoriety; and that notoriety I neither seek nor will have. If then any Birstallian or Gomersallian should presume to bore you on the subject – to ask you what 'novel' Miss Brontë has been 'publishing' – you can just say, with the distinct firmness of which you are perfect mistress, when you choose, that you are authorized by Miss Brontë to say, that she repels and disowns every accusation of the kind. You may add, if you please, that if any one has her confidence, you believe you have, and she has made no drivelling confessions to you on the subject. I am not absolutely at a loss to conjecture from what source this rumour has come; and I fear it has far from a friendly origin. I am not certain, however, and I should be very glad if I could gain certainty. Should you hear anything more, let me know it. I was astonished to hear of Miss Dixon being likely to go to the West Indies; probably this too is only rumour. Your offer of Simeon's *Life* is a very kind one, and I thank you for it. I dare say papa would like to see the work very much, as he knew Mr. Simeon. Laugh or scold Ann out of the publishing notion; and believe me through all chances and changes, whether calumniated or let alone, – Yours faithfully,

C. Brontë

82

BRANWELL BRONTË TO J.B. LEYLAND

June 17th, 1848.

My Dear Sir,

Mr. Nicholson has sent to my Father a demand for the settlement of my bill owed to him, immediately, under penalty of a Court Summons.

I have written to inform him that I shall soon be able to pay him the balance left in full – for that I will write to Dr. Crosby, and request an advance through his hands which I am sure to obtain, when I will remit my amount owed, at once, to the Old Cock.[1]

I have also given John Brown this morning Ten shillings which John will certainly place in Mr. N's hands on Wednesday next.

If he refuses my offer and presses me with law, I am RUINED. I have had five months of such utter sleeplessness, violent cough and frightful agony of mind that jail would destroy me for ever.

I earnestly beg you to see Nicholson and tell him that my receipt of money on asking, through Dr. Crosby, is morally certain.

If you conveniently can, see Mrs. Sugden of the Talbot, and tell her that on receipt of the money I expect so shortly I will transmit her the whole or part of the account I owe her.

Excuse this scrawl. Long have I resolved to write to you a letter of five or six pages, but intolerable mental wretchedness and corporeal weakness have utterly prevented me.

I shall [not] bother you again if this painful business only gets settled.

At present, believe me, Dear Sir, Yours Sincerely, but nearly worn out,

P.B. Brontë

83

BRANWELL BRONTË
TO JOHN BROWN, SEXTON, HAWORTH.

[1848] Sunday, Noon.

Dear John,

I shall feel very much obliged to you if [you] can contrive to get me Five pence worth of Gin in a proper measure.

[1] An inn at Halifax.

Should it be speedily got I could perhaps take it from you or Billy at the lane top, or, what would be quite as well, sent out for, to you.

I anxiously ask the favour because I know the good it will do me.

Punctually at Half-past Nine in the morning you will be paid the 5d. out of a shilling given me then. – Yours,

P.B.B.

84

CHARLOTTE BRONTË TO MARY TAYLOR

Haworth,
September 4th, 1848.

Dear Polly,

I write you a great many more letters than you write me, though whether they all reach you, or not, Heaven knows! I dare say you will not be without a certain desire to know how our affairs get on; I will give you therefore a notion as briefly as may be. Acton Bell has published another book; it is in three volumes, but I do not like it quite so well as *Agnes Grey* – the subject not being such as the author had pleasure in handling; it has been praised by some reviews and blamed by others. As yet, only £25 have been realized for the copyright, and as Acton Bell's publisher is a shuffling scamp, I expected no more.

About two months since I had a letter from my publishers – Smith and Elder – saying that *Jane Eyre* had had a great run in America, and that a publisher there had consequently bid high for the first sheets of a new work by Currer Bell, which they had promised to let him have.

Presently after came another missive from Smith and Elder; their American correspondent had written to them complaining that the first sheets of a new work by Currer Bell had been already received, and not by their house, but by a rival publisher, and asking the meaning of such false play; it enclosed and extract from a letter from Mr. Newby (A. and C. Bell's publisher) affirming that to the best of his belief *Jane Eyre*, *Wuthering Heights*, and *Agnes Grey*, and *The Tenant of Wildfell Hall* (the new work) were all the production of one author.

This was a lie, as Newby had been told repeatedly that they were the production of three different authors, but the fact was he wanted to make a dishonest move in the game to make the public and the trade believe that he had got hold of Currer Bell, and thus cheat Smith and Elder by securing the American publisher's bid.

The upshot of it was that on the very day I received Smith and Elder's letter, Anne and I packed up a small box, sent it down to Keighley, set out ourselves after tea, walked through a snowstorm to the station, got to Leeds, and whirled up by the night train to London with the view of proving our separate identity to Smith and Elder, and confronting Newby with his *lie*.

We arrived at the Chapter Coffee-House (our old place, Polly, we did not well know where else to go) about eight o'clock in the morning. We washed ourselves, had some breakfast, sat a few minutes, and then set off in queer inward excitement to 65 Cornhill. Neither Mr. Smith nor Mr. Williams knew we were coming – they had never seen us – they did not know whether we were men or women, but had always written to us as men.

We found 65 to be a large bookseller's shop, in a street almost as bustling as the Strand. We went in, walked up to the counter. There were a great many young men and lads here and there; I said to the first I could accost. 'May I see Mr. Smith?' He hesitated, looked a little surprised. We sat down and waited a while, looking at some books on the counter, publications of theirs well known to us, of many of which they sent us copies as presents. At last we were shown up to Mr. Smith. 'Is it Mr. Smith?' I said, looking up through my spectacles at a tall young man. 'It is.' I then put his own letter into his hand directed to Currer Bell. He looked at it and then at me again. 'Where did you get this?' he said. I laughed at his perplexity – a recognition took place. I gave my real name: Miss Brontë. We were in a small room – ceiled with a great skylight – and there explanations were rapidly gone into; Mr. Newby being anathematized, I fear, with undue vehemence. Mr. Smith hurried out and returned quickly with one whom he introduced as Mr. Williams, a pale, mild, stooping man of fifty, very much like a faded Tom Dixon. Another recognition and a long, nervous shaking of hands. Then followed talk – talk – talk; Mr. Williams being silent, Mr. Smith loquacious.

Mr. Smith said we must come and stay at his house, but we were not prepared for a long stay and declined this also; as we took our leave he told us he should bring his sisters to call on us that evening. We returned to our inn, and I paid for the excitement of the interview by a thundering headache and harassing sickness.

Towards evening, as I got no better and expected the Smiths to call, I took a strong dose of sal-volatile. It roused me a little; still, I was in grievous bodily case when they were announced. They came in, two elegant young ladies, in full dress, prepared for the Opera – Mr. Smith himself in evening costume, white gloves, etc. We had by no means understood that it was settled we were to go to the Opera, and were not ready. . . . Moreover, we had no fine, elegant dresses with us, or in the world. However, on brief rumination I thought it would be wise to make no objections – I put my headache in my pocket, we attired ourselves in the plain, high-made country garments we possessed, and went with them to their carriage, where we found Mr. Williams. They must have thought us queer, quizzical-looking beings, especially me with my spectacles. I smiled inwardly at the contrast, which must have been apparent, between me and Mr. Smith as I walked with him up the crimson-carpeted staircase of the Opera House and stood amongst a brilliant throng at the box door, which was not yet open. Fine ladies and gentlemen glanced at us with a slight, graceful superciliousness quite warranted by the circumstances. Still, I felt pleasantly excited in spite of headache and sickness and conscious clownishness, and I saw Anne was calm and gentle, which she always is.

The performance was Rossini's opera of the *Barber of Seville*, very brilliant, though I fancy there are things I should like better. We got home after one o'clock; we had never been in bed the night before, and had been in constant excitement for twenty-four hours. You may imagine we were tired.

The next day, Sunday, Mr. Williams came early and took us to church. He was so quiet, but so sincere in his attentions, one could not but have a most friendly leaning towards him. He has a nervous hesitation in speech, and a difficulty in finding appropriate language in which to express himself, which throws him into the background in conversation; but I had been his correspondent and therefore knew with what intelligence he could write, so that I was not in danger of undervaluing him. In the afternoon Mr. Smith came in his carriage with his mother, to take us to his house to dine. Mr. Smith's residence is at Bayswater, six miles from Cornhill; the rooms, the drawing-room especially, looked splendid to us. There was no company – only his mother, his two grown-up sisters, and his brother, a lad of twelve or thirteen, and a little sister, the youngest of the family, very like himself. They are all dark-eyed, dark-haired, and have clear, pale faces. The mother is a portly, handsome woman of her age, and all the children more or less well-looking – one of the daughters decidedly pretty. We had a fine dinner, which neither Anne nor I had appetite to eat, and were glad when it was over. I always feel under an awkward constraint at table. Dining out would be hideous to me.

Mr. Smith made himself very pleasant. He is a *practical* man. I wish Mr. Williams were more so, but he is altogether of the contemplative, theorizing order. Mr. Williams has too many abstractions.

On Monday we went to the Exhibition of the Royal Academy and the National Gallery, dined again at Mr. Smith's, then went home with Mr. Williams to tea and saw his comparatively humble but neat residence and his fine family of eight children. A daughter of Leigh Hunt's was there. She sang some little Italian airs which she had picked up among the peasantry in Tuscany, in a manner that charmed me.

On Tuesday morning we left London laden with books which Mr. Smith had given us, and got safely home. A more jaded wretch than I looked when I returned it would be difficult to conceive. I was thin when I went, but was meagre indeed when I returned; my face looked grey and very old, with strange, deep lines ploughed in it; my eyes stared unnaturally. I was weak and yet restless. In a while, however, the bad effects of excitement went off and I regained my normal condition. We saw Mr. Newby, but of him more another time. Good-bye. God bless you. Write.

C.B.

85

CHARLOTTE BRONTË TO W.S. WILLIAMS

Haworth,
July 31st, 1848.

My Dear Sir,

I have lately been reading *Modern Painters*, and I have derived from the work much genuine pleasure and, I hope, some edification; at any rate, it made me feel how ignorant I had previously been on the subject which it treats. Hitherto I have only had instinct to guide me in judging of art; I feel more as if I had been walking blindfold – this book seems to give me eyes. I *do* wish I had pictures within reach by which to test the new sense. Who can read these glowing descriptions of Turner's works without longing to see them? However eloquent and convincing the language in which another's opinion is placed before you, you still wish to judge for yourself. I like this author's style much: there is both energy and beauty in it; I like himself too; because he is such a hearty admirer. He does not give Turner half-measure of praise or veneration, he eulogizes, he reverences him (or rather his genius) with his whole soul. One can sympathize with that sort of devout, serious admiration (for he is no rhapsodist) – one can respect it; and yet possibly many people would laugh at it. I am truly obliged to Mr. Smith for giving me this book, not having often met with one that has pleased me more.

You will have seen some of the notices of *Wildfell Hall*. I wish my sister felt the unfavourable ones less keenly. She does not *say* much, for she is of a remarkably taciturn, still, thoughtful nature, reserved even with her nearest of kin, but I cannot avoid seeing that her spirits are depressed sometimes. The fact is, neither she nor any of us expected that view to be taken of the book which has been taken by some critics. That it had faults of execution, faults of art, was obvious, but faults of intention or feeling could be suspected by none who knew the writer. For my own part, I consider the subject unfortunately chosen – it was one the author was not qualified to handle at once vigorously and truthfully. The simple and natural – quiet description and simple pathos are, I think, Acton Bell's forte. I liked *Agnes Grey* better than the present work.

Permit me to caution you not to speak of my sisters when you write to me. I mean, do not use the word in the plural. Ellis Bell will not endure to be alluded to under any other appellation than the *nom de plume*. I committed a grand error in betraying his identity to you and Mr. Smith. It was inadvertent – the words 'we are three sisters' escaped me before I was aware. I regretted the avowal the moment I had made it; I regret it bitterly now, for I find it is against every feeling and intention of Ellis Bell. . . .

C. Brontë

86

CHARLOTTE BRONTË TO W.S. WILLIAMS

October 2nd, 1848.

My Dear Sir,

'We have buried our dead out of sight.' A lull begins to succeed the gloomy tumult of last week. It is not permitted us to grieve for him who is gone as others grieve for those they lose. The removal of our only brother must necessarily be regarded by us rather in the light of a mercy than a chastisement. Branwell was his father's and his sisters' pride and hope in boyhood, but since manhood the case has been otherwise. It has been our lot to see him take a wrong bent; to hope, expect, wait his return to the right path; to know the sickness of hope deferred, the dismay of prayer baffled; to experience despair at last – and now to behold the sudden early obscure close of what might have been a noble career.

I do not weep from a sense of bereavement – there is no prop withdrawn, no consolation torn away, no dear companion lost – but for the wreck of talent, the ruin of promise, the untimely dreary extinction of what might have been a burning and a shining light. My brother was a year my junior. I had aspirations and ambitions for him once, long ago – they have perished mournfully. Nothing remains of him but a memory of errors and sufferings. There is such a bitterness of pity for his life and death, such a yearning for the emptiness of his whole existence as I cannot describe. I trust time will allay these feelings.

My poor father naturally thought more of his *only* son than of his daughters, and, much and long as he had suffered on his account, he cried out of his loss like David for that of Absalom – my son! my son! – and refused at first to be comforted. And then when I ought to have been able to collect my strength and be at hand to support him, I fell ill with an illness whose approaches I had felt for some time previously, and of which the crisis was hastened by the awe and trouble of the death-scene – the first I had ever witnessed. The past has seemed to me a strange week. Thank God, for my father's sake, I am better now, though still feeble. I wish indeed I had more general physical strength – the want of it is sadly in my way. I cannot do what I would do for want of sustained animal spirits and efficient bodily vigour.

My unhappy brother never knew what his sisters had done in literature – he was not aware that they had ever published a line.

We could not tell him of our efforts for fear of causing him too deep a pang of remorse for his own time misspent, and talents misapplied. Now he will *never* know. I cannot dwell longer on the subject at present – it is too painful.

I thank you for your kind sympathy, and pray earnestly that your sons may all do well, and that you may be spared the sufferings my father has gone through. – Yours sincerely,

C. Brontë

87

CHARLOTTE BRONTË TO W.S. WILLIAMS

November 22nd, 1848.

My Dear Sir,

I put your most friendly letter into Emily's hands as soon as I had myself perused it, taking care, however, not to say a word in favour of homœopathy – that would not have answered. It is best usually to leave her to form her own judgment, and *especially* not to advocate the side you wish her to favour; if you do, she is sure to lean in the opposite direction, and ten to one will argue herself into non-compliance. Hitherto she has refused medicine, rejected medical advice; no reasoning, no entreaty, has availed to induce her to see a physician. After reading your letter she said, 'Mr. Williams's intention was kind and good, but he was under a delusion: Homœopathy was only another form of quackery.' Yet she may reconsider this opinion and come to a different conclusion; her second thoughts are often the best.

The *North American Review* is worth reading; there is no mincing the matter there. What a bad set the Bells must be! What appalling books they write! To-day, as Emily appeared a little easier, I thought the *Review* would amuse her, so I read it aloud to her and Anne. As I sat between them at our quiet but now somewhat melancholy fireside, I studied the two ferocious authors. Ellis, the 'man of uncommon talents, but dogged, brutal, and morose', sat leaning back in his easy-chair drawing his impeded breath as he best could, and looking, alas! piteously pale and wasted; it is not his wont to laugh, but he smiled half-amused and half in scorn as he listened. Acton was sewing, no emotion ever stirs him to loquacity, so he only smiled too, dropping at the same time a single word of calm amazement to hear his character so darkly portrayed. I wonder what the reviewer would have thought of his own sagacity could he have beheld the pair as I did. Vainly, too, might he have looked round for the masculine partner in the firm of 'Bell & Co.' How I laugh in my sleeve when I read the solemn assertions that *Jane Eyre* was written in partnership, and that it 'bears the marks of more than one mind and one sex'.

The wise critics would certainly sink a degree in their own estimation if they knew that yours or Mr. Smith's was the first masculine hand that touched the MS. of *Jane Eyre*, and that till you or he read it no masculine eye had scanned a line of its contents, no masculine ear heard a phrase from its pages. However, the view they take of the matter rather pleases me than otherwise. If they like, I am not unwilling they should think a dozen ladies and gentlemen aided at the compilation of the book. Strange patchwork it must seem to them – this chapter being penned by Mr., and that by Miss or Mrs. Bell; that character or scene being delineated by the husband, that other by the wife! The gentleman, of course, doing the rough work, the lady getting up the finer parts. I admire the idea vastly. . . .

I must abruptly bid you good-bye for the present. – Yours sincerely,

Currer Bell

88

CHARLOTTE BRONTË TO ELLEN NUSSEY

[1848].

My Dear Ellen,

I mentioned your coming here to Emily as a mere suggestion, with the faint hope that the prospect might cheer her, as she really esteems you perhaps more than any other person out of this house. I found, however, it would not do; any, the slightest excitement or putting out of the way is not to be thought of, and indeed I do not think the journey in this unsettled weather, with the walk from Keighley and walk back, at all advisable for yourself. Yet I should have liked to see you, and so would Anne. Emily continues much the same; yesterday I thought her a little better, but to-day she is not so well. I hope still – for I *must* hope – she is dear to me as life – if I let the faintness of despair reach my heart I shall become worthless. The attack was, I believe, in the first place, inflammation of the lungs; it ought to have been met promptly in time. She is too intractable. I *do* wish I knew her state and feelings more clearly. The fever is not so high as it was, but the pain in the side, the cough, the emaciation are there still.

Take *care* of yourself, dear Ellen, for the sake of all who have any affection for you. I believe these influenza colds are most insidious things. I think I scarcely need make a reference to the absurd rumour about the fortune, etc. In what it had its rise I do not know. I am not aware that we have a relation in the world in a position to leave a handsome fortune to anybody. I think you must have been mistaken in saying that the Miss Woolers spread so groundless a report, they are not such gossips.

Remember me kindly to all at Brookroyd, and believe me, yours faithfully,

C. Brontë

89

CHARLOTTE BRONTË TO ELLEN NUSSEY

Tuesday,
December 19th, 1848.

Dear Ellen,

I should have written to you before, if I had had one word of hope to say; but I had not. She grows daily weaker. The physician's opinion was expressed too obscurely to be of use. He sent some medicine which she would not take. Moments so dark as these I have never known. I pray for God's support to us all. Hitherto He has granted it. – Yours faithfully,

C. Brontë

90

CHARLOTTE BRONTË TO ELLEN NUSSEY

December 23rd, 1848.

My Dear Ellen,

Emily suffers no more from pain or weakness now. She will never suffer more in this world. She is gone, after a hard, short conflict. She died on *Tuesday*, the very day I wrote to you. I thought it very possible she might be with us still for weeks; and a few hours afterwards she was in eternity. Yes; there is no Emily in time or on earth now. Yesterday we put her poor, wasted, mortal frame quietly under the church pavement. We are very calm at present. Why should we be otherwise? The anguish of seeing her suffer is over; the spectacle of the pains of death is gone by; the funeral day is past. We feel she is at peace. No need now to tremble for the hard frost and the keen wind. Emily does not feel them. She died in a time of promise. We saw her taken from life in its prime. But it is God's will, and the place where she is gone is better than she has left.

God has sustained me, in a way that I marvel at, through such agony as I had not conceived. I now look to Anne, and wish she were well and strong; but she is neither; nor is papa. Could you now come to us for a few days? I would not ask you to stay long. Write and tell me if you could come next week, and by what train. I would try to send a gig for you to Keighley. You will, I trust, find us tranquil. Try to come. I never so much needed the consolation of a friend's presence. Pleasure, of course, there would be none for you in the visit, except what your kind heart would teach you to find in doing good to others.

91

CHARLOTTE BRONTË TO ELLEN NUSSEY

January 15th, 1849.

Dear Ellen,

I can scarcely say that Anne is worse, nor can I say she is better. She varies often in the course of a day, yet each day is passed pretty much the same. The morning is usually the best time; the afternoon and evening the most feverish. Her cough is the most troublesome at night, but it is rarely violent. The pain in her arm still disturbs her. She takes the cod-liver oil and carbonate of iron regularly; she finds them both nauseous, but especially the oil. Her appetite is small indeed. Do not fear that I shall relax in my care of her. She is too precious to me not to be cherished with all the fostering strength I have. Papa, I am thankful to say, has been a good deal better this last day or two.

As to your queries about myself, I can only say, that if I continue as I am I shall do very well. I have not yet got rid of the pains in my chest and back. They oddly return with every change of weather;

and are still sometimes accompanied with a little soreness and hoarseness, but I combat them steadily with pitch plasters and bran tea. I should think it silly and wrong indeed not to be regardful of my own health at present; it would not do to be ill *now*.

I avoid looking forward or backward, and try to keep looking upward. This is not the time to regret, dread, or weep. What I have and ought to do is very distinctly laid out for me; what I want, and pray for, is strength to perform it. The days pass in a slow, dark march; the nights are the test; the sudden wakings from restless sleep; the revived knowledge that one lies in her grave, and another not at my side, but in a separate and sick bed. However, God is over all. – Yours sincerely,

C. Brontë

92

CHARLOTTE BRONTË TO ELLEN NUSSEY

March 29th, '49.

Dear Ellen,

I read your kind note to Anne, and she wishes me to thank you sincerely for your friendly proposal. She feels, of course, that it would not do to take advantage of it, by quartering an invalid upon the inmates of Brookroyd; but she intimates there is another way in which you might serve her, perhaps with some benefit to yourself as well as to her. Should it, a month or two hence, be deemed advisable that she should go either to the seaside or to some inland watering-place, and should papa be disinclined to move, and I consequently obliged to remain at home, she asks, could you be her companion? Of course I need not add that in case of such an arrangement being made, you would be put to no expense. This, dear Ellen, is Anne's proposal; I make it to comply with her wish; but for my own part, I must add that I see serious objections to your accepting it, objections I cannot name to her. She continues to vary; is sometimes worse, and sometimes better, as the weather changes, but on the whole I fear she loses strength. Papa says her state is most precarious; she may be spared for some time, or a sudden alteration might remove her ere we are aware. Were such an alteration to take place while she was far from home, and alone with you, it would be too terrible. The idea of it distresses me inexpressibly, and I tremble whenever she alludes to the project of a journey. In short, I wish we could gain time, and see how she gets on. If she leaves home, it certainly should not be in the capricious month of May, which is proverbially trying to the weak. June would be a safer month. If we could reach June, I should have good hopes of her getting through the summer. Write such an answer to this note as I can show Anne. You can write any additional remarks to me on a separate piece of paper. Do not regard yourself as confined to discussing only our sad affairs. I am interested in all that interests you. Love to your mother, sisters, and Miss Ringrose. – Yours faithfully,

C.B.

93

ANNE BRONTË TO ELLEN NUSSEY

April 5th, 1849.

My Dear Miss Nussey,

I thank you greatly for your kind letter, and your ready compliance with my proposal as far as the *will* can go at least. I see, however, that your friends are unwilling that you should undertake the responsibility of accompanying me under present circumstances. But I do not think there would be any great responsibility in the matter. I know, and everybody knows, that you would be as kind and helpful as any one could possibly be, and I hope I should not be very troublesome. It would be as a companion, not as a nurse, that I should wish for your company; otherwise I should not venture to ask it. As for your kind and often repeated invitation to Brookroyd, pray give my sincere thanks to your mother and sisters, but tell them I could not think of inflicting my presence upon them as I now am. It is very kind of them to make so light of the trouble, but still there must be more or less, and certainly no pleasure, from the society of a silent invalid stranger. I hope, however, that Charlotte will by some means make it possible to accompany me after all. She is certainly very delicate, and greatly needs a change of air and scene to renovate her constitution. And then your going with me before the end of May is apparently out of the question, unless you are disappointed in your visitors; but I should be reluctant to wait till then if the weather would at all permit an earlier departure. You say May is a trying month, and so say others. The early part is often cold enough, I acknowledge, but according to my experience, we are almost certain of some fine warm days in the latter half, when the laburnums and lilacs are in bloom; whereas June is often cold, and July generally wet. But I have a more serious reason than this for my impatience of delay. The doctors say that change of air or removal to a better climate would hardly ever fail of success in consumptive cases, if the remedy be taken *in time*; but the reason why there are so many disappointments is that it is generally deferred till it is too late. Now I would not commit this error; and, to say the truth, though I suffer much less from pain and fever than I did when you were with us, I am decidedly weaker, and very much thinner. My cough still troubles me a good deal, especially in the night, and, what seems worse than all, I am subject to great shortness of breath on going up stairs or any slight exertion. Under these circumstances, I think there is no time to be lost. I have no horror of death: if I thought it inevitable, I think I could quietly resign myself to the prospect, in the hope that you, dear Miss Nussey, would give as much of your company as you possibly could to Charlotte, and be a sister to her in my stead. But I wish it would please God to spare me not only for papa's and Charlotte's sakes, but because I long to do some good in the world before I leave it. I have many schemes in my head for future practice, humble and limited indeed, but still I should not like them all to come to nothing, and myself to have lived to so little purpose. But God's will be done. Remember me respectfully to your mother and sisters, and believe me, dear Miss Nussey, yours most affectionately,

Anne Brontë

94

CHARLOTTE BRONTË TO ELLEN NUSSEY

April 12th, '49.

Dear Ellen,

I read Anne's letter to you; it was touching enough, as you say. If there was no hope beyond this world, no eternity, no life to come, Emily's fate, and that which threatens Anne, would be heart-breaking. I cannot forget Emily's death-day; it becomes a more fixed, a darker, a more frequently recurring idea in my mind than ever. It was very terrible. She was torn, conscious, panting, reluctant, though resolute, out of a happy life. But it *will not do* to dwell on these things.

I am glad your friends object to your going with Anne; it would never do. To speak the truth, even if your mother and sisters had consented, I never could. It is not that there is any laborious attention to pay her; she requires, and will accept, but little nursing; but there would be hazard, and anxiety of mind, beyond what you ought to be subject to. If, a month or six weeks hence, she continues to wish for a change as much as she does now, I shall (D.V.) go with her myself. It will certainly be paramount duty; other care must be made subservient to that. I have consulted Mr. Teale, he does not object, and recommends Scarborough, which was Anne's own choice. I trust affairs may be so ordered, that you may be able to be with us at least part of the time. . . . Whether in lodgings or not I should wish to be boarded. Providing oneself is, I think, an insupportable nuisance. I don't like keeping provisions in a cupboard, locking up, being pillaged, and all that. It is a petty, wearing annoyance. Best regards to all at Brookroyd. I am, dear Ellen, yours faithfully,

C.B.

95

CHARLOTTE BRONTË TO W.S. WILLIAMS

No. 2 Cliff, Scarboro',
May 27th, 1849.

My Dear Sir,

The date above will inform you why I have not answered your last letter more promptly. I have been busy with preparations for departure and with the journey. I am thankful to say we reached our destination safely, having rested one night at York. We found assistance wherever we needed it; there was always an arm ready to do for my sister what I was not quite strong enough to do: lift her in and out of the carriages, carry her across the line, etc.

It made her happy to see both York and its Minster, and Scarboro' and its bay once more. There is yet no revival of bodily strength – I fear indeed the slow ebb continues. People who see her tell me I must not expect her to last long – but it is something to cheer her mind.

Our lodgings are pleasant. As Anne sits at the window she can look down on the sea, which this morning is calm as glass. She says if she could breathe more freely she would be comfortable at this moment – but she cannot breathe freely.

My friend Ellen is with us. I find her presence a solace. She is a calm, steady girl – not brilliant, but good and true. She suits and has always suited me well. I like her, with her phlegm, repose, sense, and sincerity, better than I should like the most talented without these qualifications.

If ever I see you again I should have pleasure in talking over with you the topics you allude to in your last – or rather, in hearing *you* talk them over. We see these things through a glass darkly – or at least I see them thus. So far from objecting to speculation on, or discussion of, the subject, I should wish to hear what others have to say. By *others*, I mean only the serious and reflective – levity in such matters shocks as much as hypocrisy.

Write to me. In this strange place your letters will come like the visits of a friend. Fearing to lose the post, I will add no more at present. – Believe me, yours sincerely,

C. Brontë

96

CHARLOTTE BRONTË TO W.S. WILLIAMS

2 Cliff, Scarboro',
June 4th, 1849.

My Dear Sir,

I hardly know what I said when I wrote last. I was then feverish and exhausted. I am now better and, I believe, quite clear.

You have been informed of my dear sister Anne's death. Let me now add that she died without severe struggle, resigned, trusting in God – thankful for release from a suffering life – deeply assured that a better existence lay before her. She believed, she hoped – and declared her belief and hope with her last breath. Her quiet, Christian death did not rend my heart as Emily's stern, simple undemonstrative end did. I let Anne go to God, and felt He had a right to her. I could hardly let Emily go. I wanted to hold her back then, and I want her back now. Anne, from her childhood, seemed preparing for an early death. Emily's spirit seemed strong enough to bear her to fulness of years. They are both gone, and so is poor Branwell, and Papa has now me only – the weakest, puniest, least promising of his six children. Consumption had taken the whole five.

For the present Anne's ashes rest apart from the others. I have buried her here at Scarboro', to save Papa the anguish of the return and a third funeral.

I am ordered to remain at the seaside awhile. I cannot rest here, but neither can I go home. Possibly I may not write again soon – attribute my silence neither to idleness nor negligence. No letters will find me at Scarboro' after the 7th. I do not know what my next address will be. I shall wander a week or two on the East Coast, and only stop at quiet, lonely places. No one need be anxious about me as far as I know. Friends and acquaintance seem to think *this* the worst time of suffering. They are surely mistaken. Anne reposes now – what have the long desolate hours of her patient pain and fast decay been?

Why life is so blank, brief, and bitter I do not know. Why younger and far better than I are snatched from it with projects unfulfilled I cannot comprehend, but I believe God is wise – perfect – merciful.

I have heard from Papa. He and the servants knew when they parted from Anne they would see her no more. All tried to be resigned. I knew it likewise, and I wanted her to die where she would be happiest. She loved Scarboro'. A peaceful sun gilded her evening – Yours sincerely,

C. Brontë

97

CHARLOTTE BRONTË TO ELLEN NUSSEY

Haworth,
July 14th, 1849.

I do not much like giving you an account of myself. I like better to go out of myself, and talk of something more cheerful. My cold, wherever I got it, whether at Easton or elsewhere, is not vanished yet. It began in my head; then I had a sore throat, and then a sore chest, with a cough, but only a trifling cough, which I still have at times. The pains between my shoulders likewise annoyed me much. Say nothing about it, for I confess I am too much disposed to be nervous. This nervousness is a horrid phantom. I dare communicate no ailment to papa; his anxiety harrasses me inexpressibly.

My life is what I expected it to be. Sometimes when I wake in the morning, and know that Solitude, Remembrance, and Longing are to be almost my sole companions all day through, that at night I shall go to bed with them, that they will keep me sleepless, that next morning I shall wake to them again; sometimes, Ellen, I have a heavy heart of it. But crushed I am not yet; nor robbed of elasticity, nor of hope, nor quite of endeavour. Still I have some strength to fight the battle of life. I am aware, and can acknowledge, I have many comforts, many mercies. Still I can *get on*. But I do hope and pray, that never may you, or any one I love, be placed as I am. To sit in a lonely room, the clock ticking loud through a still house, and to have open before the mind's eye the record of the last year, with its shocks, sufferings, losses, is a trial.

I write to you freely, because I believe you will hear me with moderation, that you will not take alarm or think me in any way worse off than I am. My love to your mother and sisters, and believe me yours sincerely,

C.B.

98

CHARLOTTE BRONTË TO W.S. WILLIAMS

August 24th, 1849.

My Dear Sir,

I think the best title for the book would be *Shirley*, without any explanation or addition – the simpler and briefer, the better.

If Mr. Taylor calls here on his return to town he might take charge of the MS.; I would rather intrust it to him than send it by the ordinary conveyance. Did I see Mr. Taylor when I was in London? I cannot remember him.

I would with pleasure offer him the homely hospitalities of the Parsonage for a few days, if I could at the same time offer him the company of a brother, or if my father were young enough and strong enough to walk with him on the moors and show him the neighbourhood, or if the peculiar retirement of papa's habits were not such as to render it irksome to him to give much of his society to a stranger, even in the house. Without being in the least misanthropical or sour-natured, papa habitually prefers solitude to society, and custom is a tyrant whose fetters it would now be impossible for him to break. Were it not for difficulties of this sort, I believe I should ere this have asked you to come down to Yorkshire. Papa, I know, would receive any friend of Mr. Smith's with perfect kindness and goodwill, but I likewise know that, unless greatly put out of his way, he could not give a guest much of his company, and that, consequently, his entertainment would be but dull.

You will see the force of these considerations, and understand why I only ask Mr. Taylor to come for a day instead of requesting the pleasure of his company for a longer period; you will believe me also, and so will he, when I say I shall be most happy to see him. He will find Haworth a strange, uncivilized little place, such as, I dare say, he never saw before. It is twenty miles distant from Leeds; he will have to come by rail to Keighley (there are trains every two hours I believe). He must remember that at a station called Shipley the carriages are changed, otherwise they will take him on to Skipton or Colne, or I know not where. When he reaches Keighley, he will yet have four miles to travel; a conveyance may be hired at the Devonshire Arms – there is no coach or other regular communication.

I should like to hear from him before he comes, and to know on what day to expect him, that I may have the MS. ready; if it is not quite finished I might send the concluding chapter or two by post.

I advise you to send this letter to Mr. Taylor – it will save you the trouble of much explanation, and will serve to apprise him of what lies before him; he can then weigh well with himself whether it would suit him to take so much trouble for so slight an end. – Believe me, my dear sir, yours sincerely,

C. Brontë

99

CHARLOTTE BRONTË TO W.S. WILLIAMS

September 21st, 1849.

My Dear Sir,

I am obliged to you for preserving my secret, being at least as anxious as ever (*more* anxious I cannot well be) to keep quiet. You asked me in one of your letters lately whether I thought I should escape identification in Yorkshire. I am so little known that I think I shall. Besides, the book is far less founded on the Real than perhaps appears. It would be difficult to explain to you how little actual experience I have had of life, how few persons I have known, and how very few have known me.

As an instance how the characters have been managed take that of Mr. Helstone. If this character had an original it was in the person of a clergyman who died some years since at the advanced age of eighty. I never saw him except once – at the consecration of a church – when I was a child of ten years old. I was then struck with his appearance and stern, martial air. At a subsequent period I heard him talked about in the neighbourhood where he had resided: some mentioned him with enthusiasm, others with detestation. I listened to various anecdotes, balanced evidence against evidence, and drew an inference. The original of Mr. Hall I have seen; he knows me slightly; but he would as soon think I had closely observed him or taken him for a character – he would as soon, indeed, suspect me of writing a book – a novel – as he would his dog Prince. Margaret Hall called *Jane Eyre* a 'wicked book', on the authority of the *Quarterly*; an expression which, coming from her, I will here confess, struck somewhat deep. It opened my eyes to the harm the *Quarterly* had done. Margaret would not have called it 'wicked' if she had not been told so.

No matter – whether known or unknown – misjudged or the contrary – I am resolved not to write otherwise. I shall bend as my powers tend. The two human beings who understood me, and whom I understood, are gone. I have some that love me yet, and whom I love without expecting, or having a right to expect, that they shall perfectly understand me. I am satisfied; but I must have my own way in the matter of writing. The loss of what we possess nearest and dearest to us in this world produces an effect upon the character: we search out what we have yet left that can support, and, when found, we cling to it with a hold of new-strung tenacity. The faculty of imagination lifted me when I was sinking, three months ago; its active exercise has kept my head above water since; its results cheer me now, for I feel they have enabled me to give pleasure to others. I am thankful to God, who gave me the faculty; and it is for me a part of my religion to defend this gift and to profit by its possession. – Yours sincerely,

Charlotte Brontë

100

CHARLOTTE BRONTË TO GEORGE SMITH

October 4th, 1849.

My Dear Sir,

I must not thank you for, but acknowledge the receipt of, your letter. The business is certainly very bad; worse than I thought, and much worse than my father has any idea of. In fact, the little railway property I possessed, according to original prices, formed already a small competency for me, with my views and habits. Now scarcely any portion of it can, with security, be calculated upon. I must open this view of the case to my father by degrees; and, meanwhile, wait patiently till I see how affairs are likely to turn. . . . However the matter may terminate, I ought perhaps to be rather thankful than dissatisfied. When I look at my own case, and compare it with that of thousands besides, I scarcely see room for a murmur. Many, very many, are by the late strange railway system deprived almost of their daily bread. Such, then, as have only lost provision laid up for the future should take care how they complain. The thought that *Shirley* has given pleasure at Cornhill yields me much quiet comfort. No doubt, however, you are, as I am, prepared for critical severity; but I have good hopes that the vessel is sufficiently sound of construction to weather a gale or two, and to make a prosperous voyage for you in the end.

C. Brontë

101

CHARLOTTE BRONTË TO W.S. WILLIAMS

November 1st, 1849.

My Dear Sir,

I reached home yesterday, and found your letter and one from Mr. Lewes, and one from the Peace Congress Committee, awaiting my arrival. The last document it is now too late to answer, for it was an invitation to Currer Bell to appear on the platform at their meeting at Exeter Hall last Tuesday! A wonderful figure Mr. Currer Bell would have cut under such circumstances! Should the 'Peace Congress' chance to read *Shirley* they will wash their hands of its author.

I am glad to hear that Mr. Thackeray is better, but I did not know he had been seriously ill, I thought it was only a literary indisposition. You must tell me what he thinks of *Shirley* if he gives you any opinion on the subject.

I am also glad to hear that Mr. Smith is pleased with the commercial prospects of the work. I try not to be anxious about its literary fate; and if I cannot be quite stoical, I think I am still tolerably resigned.

Mr. Lewes does not like the opening chapter, wherein he resembles you.

I have permitted myself the treat of spending the last week with my friend Ellen. Her residence is in a far more populous and stirring neighbourhood than this. Whenever I go there I am unavoidably forced into society – clerical society chiefly.

During my late visit I have too often had reason, sometimes in a pleasant, sometimes in a painful form, to fear that I no longer walk invisible. *Jane Eyre*, it appears, has been read all over the district – a fact of which I never dreamt – a circumstance of which the possibility never occurred to me. I met sometimes with new deference, with augmented kindness; old schoolfellows and old teachers, too, greeted me with generous warmth. And again, ecclesiastical brows lowered thunder at me. When I confronted one or two large-made priests, I longed for the battle to come on. I wish they would speak out plainly. You must not understand that my schoolfellows and teachers were of the Clergy Daughters' School – in fact, I was never there but for one little year as a very little girl. I am certain I have long been forgotten; though for myself, I remember all and everything clearly: early impressions are ineffaceable.

I have just received the *Daily News*. Let me speak the truth – when I read it my heart sickened over it. It is not a good review, it is unutterably false. If *Shirley* strikes all readers as it has struck that one, but – I shall not say what follows.

On the whole I am glad a decidedly bad notice has come first – a notice whose inexpressible ignorance first stuns and then stirs me. Are there no such men as the Helstones and Yorkes?

Yes, there are.

Is the first chapter disgusting or vulgar?

It is not, it is real.

As for the praise of such a critic, I find it silly and nauseous, and I scorn it.

Were my sisters now alive they and I would laugh over this

notice; but they sleep, they will wake no more for me, and I am a fool to be so moved by what is not worth a sigh. – Believe me, yours sincerely,

C.B.

You must spare me if I seem hasty, I fear I really am not so firm as I used to be, nor so patient. Whenever any shock comes, I feel that almost all supports have been withdrawn.

102

CHARLOTTE BRONTË TO G.H. LEWES

November 1st, 1849.

My Dear Sir,

It is about a year and a half since you wrote to me; but it seems a longer period, because since then it has been my lot to pass some black milestones in the journey of life. Since then there have been intervals when I have ceased to care about literature and critics and fame; when I have lost sight of whatever was prominent in my thoughts at the first publication of *Jane Eyre*; but now I want these things to come back vividly, if possible: consequently it was a pleasure to receive your note. I wish you did not think me a woman. I wish all reviewers believed 'Currer Bell' to be a man; they would be more just to him. You will, I know, keep measuring me by some standard of what you deem becoming to my sex; where I am not what you consider graceful you will condemn me. All mouths will be open against that first chapter, and that first chapter is as true as the Bible, nor is it exceptionable. Come what will, I cannot, when I write, think always of myself and of what is elegant and charming in femininity; it is not on those terms, or with such ideas, I ever took pen in hand: and if it is only on such terms my writing will be tolerated, I shall pass away from the public and trouble it no more. Out of obscurity I came, to obscurity I can easily return. Standing afar off, I now watch to see what will become of *Shirley*. My expectations are very low, and my anticipations somewhat sad and bitter; still, I earnestly conjure you to say honestly what you think; flattery would be worse than vain; there is no consolation in flattery. As for condemnation, I cannot, on reflection, see why I should much fear it; there is no one but myself to suffer therefrom, and both happiness and suffering in this life soon pass away. Wishing you all success in your Scottish expedition, – I am, dear sir, yours sincerely,

C. Bell

103

CHARLOTTE BRONTË TO W.S. WILLIAMS

November 20th, 1849.

My Dear Sir,

You said that if I wished for any copies of *Shirley* to be sent to individuals I was to name the parties. I have thought of one person to whom I should much like a copy to be offered – Harriet Martineau. For her character – as revealed in her works – I have a lively admiration, a deep esteem. Will you enclose with the volume the accompanying note?

The letter you forwarded this morning was from Mrs. Gaskell, authoress of *Mary Barton*; she said I was not to answer it, but I cannot help doing so. The note brought the tears to my eyes. She is a good, she is a great woman. Proud am I that I can touch a chord of sympathy in souls so noble. In Mrs. Gaskell's nature it mournfully pleases me to fancy a remote affinity to my sister Emily. In Miss Martineau's mind I have always felt the same, though there are wide differences. Both these ladies are above me – certainly far my superiors in attainments and experience. I think I could look up to them if I knew them. – I am, dear sir, yours sincerely.

C. Brontë

104

CHARLOTTE BRONTË TO ELLEN NUSSEY

Westbourne Place,
Bishop's Road, London.
December 1849.

Dear Ellen,

I have just remembered that as you do not know my address, you cannot write to me till you get it; it is as above. I came to this big Babylon last Thursday, and have been in what seems to me a sort of whirl ever since, for changes, scenes, and stimulus which would be a trifle to others, are much to me. I found when I mentioned to

Mr. Smith my plan of going to Dr. Wheelwright's it would not do at all, he would have been seriously hurt; he made his mother write to me, and thus I was persuaded to make my principal stay at his house. I have found no reason to regret this decision. Mrs. Smith received me at first like one who had received the strictest orders to be scrupulously attentive. I had fires in my bedroom evening and morning, wax candles, etc., etc. Mrs. Smith and her daughters seemed to look upon me with a mixture of respect and alarm. But all this is changed, that is to say, the attention and politeness continue as great as ever, but the alarm and estrangement are quite gone. She treats me as if she liked me, and I begin to like her much; kindness is a potent heartwinner. I had not judged too favourably of her son on a first impression; he pleases me much. I like him better even as a son and brother than as a man of business. Mr. Williams, too, is really most gentlemanly and well-informed. His weak points he certainly has, but these are not seen in society. Mr. Taylor – the little man – has again shown his parts; in fact, I suspect he is of the Helstone[1] order of men – rigid, despotic, and self-willed. He tries to be very kind and even to express sympathy sometimes, but he does not manage it. He has a determined, dreadful nose in the middle of his face which when poked into my countenance cuts into my soul like iron. Still he is horribly intelligent, quick, searching, sagacious, and with a memory of relentless tenacity. To turn to Williams after him, or to Smith himself, is to turn from granite to easy down or warm fur. I have seen Thackeray.

No more at present from yours, etc.,

C. Brontë

105

CHARLOTTE BRONTË TO G.H. LEWES

January 19th, 1850.

My Dear Sir,

I will tell you why I was so hurt by that review in the *Edinburgh* – not because its criticism was keen or its blame sometimes severe; not because its praise was stinted (for, indeed, I think you give me quite as much praise as I deserve), but because after I had said earnestly that I wished critics would judge me as an *author*, not as

[1] A character in *Shirley*.

a woman, you so roughly – I even thought so cruelly – handled the question of sex. I dare say you meant no harm, and perhaps you will not now be able to understand why I was so grieved at what you will probably deem such a trifle; but grieved I was, and indignant too.

There was a passage or two which you did quite wrong to write.

However, I will not bear malice against you for it; I know what your nature is: it is not a bad or unkind one, though you would often jar terribly on some feelings with whose recoil and quiver you could not possibly sympathize. I imagine you are both enthusiastic and implacable, as you are at once sagacious and careless; you know much and discover much, but you are in such a hurry to tell it all you never give yourself time to think how your reckless eloquence may affect others; and, what is more, if you knew how it did affect them, you would not much care.

However, I shake hands with you: you have excellent points; you can be generous. I still feel angry, and think I do well to be angry; but it is the anger one experiences for rough play rather than for foul play. – I am yours, with a certain respect, and more chagrin,

Currer Bell

106

CHARLOTTE BRONTË TO REV. P. BRONTË

76 Gloucester Terrace,
Hyde Park Gardens,
June 4th, 1850.

Dear Papa,

I was very glad to get your letter this morning, and still more glad to learn that your health continues in some degree to improve. I fear you will feel the present weather somewhat debilitating, at least if it is as warm in Yorkshire as in London. I cannot help grudging these fine days on account of the roofing of the house. It is a great pity the workmen were not prepared to begin a week ago.

Since I wrote I have been to the Opera; to the Exhibition of the Royal Academy, where there were some fine paintings, especially a large one by Landseer of the Duke of Wellington on the field of Waterloo, and a grand, wonderful picture of Martin's from Campbell's poem of the 'Last Man', showing the red sun fading out of the sky, and all the soil of the foreground made up of bones and skulls. The secretary of the Zoological Society also sent me an honorary ticket of admission to their gardens, which I wish you could see. There are animals from all parts of the world enclosed in great cages in the open air amongst trees and shrubs – lions, tigers, leopards, elephants, numberless monkeys, camels, five or six camelopards, a young hippopotamus with an Egyptian for its keeper; birds of all kinds – eagles, ostriches, a pair of great condors from the Andes, strange ducks and water-fowl which seem very happy and comfortable, and build their nests among the reeds and edges of the lakes where they are kept. Some of the American birds make inexpressible noises.

There are also all sorts of living snakes and lizards in cages, some great Ceylon toads not much smaller than Flossy, some large foreign rats nearly as large and fierce as little bull-dogs. The most ferocious and deadly-looking things in the place were these rats, a laughing hyena (which every now and then uttered a hideous peal of laughter such as a score of maniacs might produce) and a cobra di capello snake. I think this snake was the worst of all: it had the eyes and face of a fiend, and darted out its barbed tongue sharply and incessantly.

I am glad to hear that Tabby and Martha are pretty well. Remember me to them, and – Believe me, dear papa, your affectionate daughter,

C. *Brontë*

I hope you don't care for the notice in *Sharpe's Magazine*; it does not disturb me in the least. Mr. Smith says it is of no consequence whatever in a literary sense. Sharpe, the proprietor, was an apprentice of Mr. Smith's father.

107

CHARLOTTE BRONTË TO MRS. GASKELL

August 27th, 1850.

Papa and I have just had tea; he is sitting quietly in his room, and I in mine; 'storms of rain' are sweeping over the garden and churchyard: as to the moors, they are hidden in thick fog. Though alone I am not unhappy; I have a thousand things to be thankful for, and, amongst the rest, that this morning I received a letter from you, and that this evening I have the privilege of answering it.

I do not know the *Life of Sydney Taylor*, whenever I have the opportunity I will get it. The little French book you mention shall also take its place on the list of books to be procured as soon as possible. It treats a subject interesting to all women – perhaps more especially to single women, though, indeed, mothers like you study it for the sake of their daughters. The *Westminster Review* is not a periodical I see regularly, but some time since I got hold of a number – for last January, I think – in which there was an article entitled 'Woman's Mission' (the phrase is hackneyed), containing a great deal that seemed to me just and sensible. Men begin to regard the position of woman in another light than they used to do; and a few men, whose sympathies are fine and whose sense of justice is strong, think and speak of it with a candour that commands my admiration. They say, however – and, to an extent, truly – that the amelioration of our condition depends on ourselves. Certainly there are evils which our own efforts will best reach; but as certainly there are other evils – deep-rooted in the foundations of the social system – which no efforts of ours can touch; of which we cannot complain; of which it is advisable not too often to think.

I have read Tennyson's *In Memoriam*,[1] or rather part of it; I closed the book when I had got about half-way. It is beautiful; it is mournful; it is monotonous. Many of the feelings expressed bear, in their utterance, the stamp of truth; yet, if Arthur Hallam had been somewhat nearer Alfred Tennyson – his brother instead of his friend – I should have distrusted this rhymed, and measured, and printed monument of grief. What change the lapse of years may work I do not know; but it seems to me that bitter sorrow, while recent, does not flow out in verse.

I promised to send you Wordsworth's *Prelude*,[2] and, accordingly, despatch it by this post; the other little volume shall follow in a day or two. I shall be glad to hear from you whenever you have time to write to me, *but you are never on any account to do this except when inclination prompts and leisure permits*. I should never thank you for a letter which you had felt it a task to write.

[1] Tennyson's *In Memoriam* was published in 1850.
[2] Wordsworth's *Prelude* was also printed, posthumously, in 1850.

108

CHARLOTTE BRONTË TO G.H. LEWES

October 17th, 1850.

I am sure you will have thought me very dilatory in returning the books you so kindly lent me; the fact is, having some other books to send, I retained yours to enclose them in the same parcel.

Accept my thanks for some hours of pleasant reading. Balzac was for me quite a new author; and in making his acquaintance, through the medium of *Modeste Mignon* and *Illusions Perdues*, you cannot doubt I have felt some interest. At first I thought he was going to be painfully minute, and fearfully tedious; one grew impatient of his long parade of detail, his slow revelation of unimportant circumstances, as he assembled his personages on the stage; but by-and-by I seemed to enter into the mystery of his craft, and to discover, with delight, where his force lay: is it not in the analysis of motive, and in a subtle perception of the most obscure and secret workings of the mind? Still, admire Balzac as we may, I think we do not like him; we rather feel towards him as towards an ungenial acquaintance who is for ever holding up in strong light our defects, and who rarely draws forth our better qualities.

Truly I like George Sand better.

Fantastical, fanatical, unpractical enthusiastic as she often is – far from truthful as are many of her views of life – misled, as she is apt to be, by her feelings – George Sand has a better nature than M. de Balzac; her brain is larger, her heart warmer than his. The *Lettres d'un Voyageur* are full of the writer's self, and I never felt so strongly, as in the perusal of this work, that most of her very faults spring from the excess of her good qualities: it is this excess which has often hurried her into difficulty, which has prepared for her enduring regret.

But I believe her mind is of that order which disastrous experience teaches, without weakening, or too much disheartening, and, in that case, the longer she lives the better she will grow. A hopeful point in all her writings is the scarcity of false French sentiment; I wish I could say its absence; but the weed flourishes here and there even in the *Lettres*.

C.B.

109

CHARLOTTE BRONTË TO ELLEN NUSSEY

October, 1850.

Dear Ellen,

There is nothing wrong, and I am writing you a line as you desire, merely to say that I *am* busy just now. Mr. Smith wishes to reprint some of Emily's and Anne's works, with a few little additions from the papers they have left; and I have been closely engaged in revising, transcribing, preparing a preface, notice, etc. As the time for doing this is limited, I am obliged to be industrious. I found the task at first exquisitely painful and depressing; but regarding it in the light of a *sacred duty*, I went on, and now can bear it better. It is work, however, that I cannot do in the evening, for if I did I should have no sleep at night. Papa, I am thankful to say, is in improved health, and so, I think, am I; I trust you are the same.

I have just received a kind letter from Miss Martineau. She has got back to Ambleside, and had heard of my visit to the Lakes. She expressed her regret, etc., at not being at home.

I trust you are well. I am very decent indeed in bodily health, and am both angry and surprised at myself for not being in better spirits; for not growing accustomed, or at least resigned, to the solitude and isolation of my lot. But my late occupation left a result for some days, and indeed still, very painful. The reading over of papers, the renewal of remembrances brought back the pang of bereavement, and occasioned a depression of spirits well-nigh intolerable. For one or two nights, I scarcely knew how to get on till morning; and when morning came, I was still haunted with a sense of sickening distress. I tell you these things, because it is absolutely necessary to me to have some *relief*. You will forgive me, and not trouble yourself, or imagine that I am one whit *worse*, than I say. It is quite a mental ailment, and I believe and hope it is better now. I think so, because I can *speak* about it, which I never can when grief is at its worst.

I thought to find occupation and interest in writing, when alone at home, but hitherto my efforts have been vain; the deficiency of every stimulus is so complete. You will recommend me, I dare say, to go from home; but that does no good, even if I could again leave papa with an easy mind (thank God! he is better). I cannot describe what a time of it I had after my return from London, Scotland, etc.

There was a reaction that sunk me to the earth; the deadly silence, solitude, desolation, were awful; the craving for companionship, the hopelessness of relief, were what I should dread to feel again.

Dear Nell, when I think of you, it is with a compassion and tenderness that scarcely cheer me. Mentally, I fear, you also are too lonely and too little occupied. It seems our doom, for the present at least. May God in His mercy help us to bear it. – Yours faithfully,

C. Brontë

110

CHARLOTTE BRONTË TO JAMES TAYLOR

November 6th, 1850.

My Dear Sir,

I have just finished reading the Life of Dr. Arnold, but now when I wish, in accordance with your request, to express what I think of it, I do not find the task very easy; proper terms seem wanting. This is not a character to be dismissed with a few laudatory words; it is not a one-sided character; pure panegyric would be inappropriate. Dr. Arnold (it seems to me) was not quite saintly; his greatness was cast in a mortal mould; he was a little severe – almost a little hard; he was vehement and somewhat oppugnant. Himself the most indefatigable of workers, I know not whether he could have understood or made allowance for a temperament that required more rest, yet not to one man in twenty thousand is given his giant faculty of labour; by virtue of it he seems to me the greatest of Working Men. Exacting he might have been then on this point, and granting that he were so, and a little hasty, stern and positive, those were his sole faults (if indeed that can be called a fault which in no shape degrades the individual's own character but is only apt to oppress and overstrain the weaker nature of his neighbours). Afterwards come his good qualities. About these there is nothing dubious. Where can we find justice, firmness, independence, earnestness, sincerity, fuller and purer than in him?

But this is not all, and I am glad of it. Besides high intellect and stainless rectitude, his letters and his life attest his possession of the most true-hearted affection. Without this, however we might admire, we could not love him, but with it I think we love him much. A hundred such men, fifty, nay, ten or five such righteous men might save any country, might victoriously champion any cause.

I was struck, too, by the almost unbroken happiness of his life; a happiness resulting chiefly, no doubt, from the right use to which he put that health and strength which God had given him, but also owing partly to a singular exemption from those deep and bitter griefs which most human beings are called on to endure. His wife was what he wished; his children were healthy and promising; his own health was excellent; his undertakings were crowned with success; even Death was kind, for however sharp the pains of his last hours, they were but brief. God's blessing seems to have accompanied him from the cradle to the grave. One feels thankful to know that it has been permitted to any man to live such a life.

When I was in Westmoreland last August, I spent an evening at Fox How, where Mrs. Arnold and her daughters still reside. It was twilight as I drove to the place, and almost dark ere I reached it; still I could perceive that the situation was exquisitely lovely. The house looked like a nest half buried in flowers and creepers, and, dusk as it was, I could feel that the valley and the hills round were beautiful as imagination could dream. Mrs. Arnold seemed an amiable, and must once have been a very pretty, woman; her daughters I liked much. There was present also a son of Chevalier Bunsen, with his wife or rather bride. I had not then read Dr. Arnold's Life; otherwise, the visit would have interested me even more than it actually did.

Mr. Williams told me (if I mistake not) that you had recently visited the 'Lake Country'. I trust you enjoyed your excursion, and that our English Lakes did not suffer too much by comparison in your memory with the Scottish Lochs. – I am, my dear sir, yours sincerely,

C. Brontë

111

CHARLOTTE BRONTË TO ELLEN NUSSEY

The Knoll, Ambleside,
December 18th, 1850.

Dear Ellen,

I can write to you now, for I am away from home, and relieved temporarily, at least, by change of air and scene, from the heavy burden of depression which, I confess, has for nearly three months been sinking me to the earth. I shall never forget last autumn! Some days and nights have been cruel; but now, having once told you this, I need say no more on the subject. My loathing of solitude grew extreme; my recollection of my sisters intolerably poignant. I am better now. I am at Miss Martineau's[1] for a week. Her house is very pleasant, both within and without; arranged at all points with admirable neatness and comfort. Her visitors enjoy the most perfect liberty; what she claims for herself she allows them. I rise at my own hour, breakfast alone (she is up at five, and takes a cold bath, and a walk by starlight, and has finished breakfast and got to her work by seven o'clock). I pass the morning in the drawing-room, she in her study. At two o'clock we meet; work, talk, and walk together till five, her dinner-hour; spend the evening together, when she converses fluently and abundantly, and with the most complete frankness. I go to my own room soon after ten; she sits up writing letters till twelve. She appears exhaustless in strength and spirits, and indefatigable in the faculty of labour. She is a great and a good woman; of course not without peculiarities, but I have seen none as yet that annoy me. She is both hard and warm-hearted, abrupt and affectionate, liberal and despotic. I believe she is not at all conscious of her own absolutism. When I tell her of it, she denies the charge warmly; then I laugh at her. I believe she almost rules Ambleside. Some of the gentry dislike her, but the lower orders have a great regard for her. I will not stay more than a week because about Christmas relatives and guests will come. Sir J. and Lady Shuttleworth are coming here to dine on Thursday. Write to me and say how you are. Kind regards to all. – Yours faithfully,

C. Brontë

112

CHARLOTTE BRONTË TO ELLEN NUSSEY

April 23rd, 1851.

My Dear Ellen,

. . . I have heard from Mr. Taylor to-day, a quiet little note; he returned to London a week since on Saturday, he has since kindly chosen and sent me a parcel of books. He leaves England May 20th; his note concludes with asking whether he has any chance of

[1] Harriet Martineau, economist and novelist.

seeing me in London before that time. I must tell him that I have already fixed June for my visit, and therefore, in all human probability we shall see each other no more.

There is still a want of plain mutual understanding in this business, and there is sadness and pain in more ways than one. My conscience, I can truly say, does not *now* accuse me of having treated Mr. Taylor with injustice or unkindness. What I once did wrong in this way, I have endeavoured to remedy both to himself and in speaking of him to others, Mr. Smith to wit, though I more than doubt whether that last opinion will ever reach him; I am sure he has estimable and sterling qualities, but with every disposition and with every wish, with every intention even, to look on him in the most favourable point of view at his last visit, it was impossible to me in my inward heart, to think of him as one that might one day be acceptable as a husband. It would sound harsh were I to tell even *you* of the estimate I felt compelled to form respecting him; dear Nell, I looked for something of the gentleman – something I mean of the *natural* gentleman; you know I can dispense with acquired polish, and for looks, I know myself too well to think that I have any right to be exacting on that point. I could not find one gleam, I could not see one passing glimpse, of true good-breeding; it is hard to say, but it is true. In mind too; though clever, he is second-rate; thoroughly second-rate. One does not like to say these things, but one had better be honest. Were I to marry him, my heart would bleed in pain and humiliation; I could not, *could* not look up to him. No – if Mr. Taylor be the only husband fate offers to me, single I must always remain. But yet, at times I grieve for him, and perhaps it is superfluous, for I cannot think he will suffer much; a hard nature, occupation and change of scene will befriend him.

I am glad to hear that you have lost that horrid tic, and hope your cold is by this time well. Papa continues much better. – With kind regards to all, I am, dear Nell, your middle-aged friend,

C. Brontë

Write soon.

113

CHARLOTTE BRONTË TO THE REV. P. BRONTË

76 Gloucester Terrace,
Hyde Park, London,
May 30th, 1851.

Dear Papa,

I have now heard one of Mr. Thackeray's lectures and seen the great Exhibition. On Thursday afternoon I went to hear the lecture. It was delivered in a large and splendid kind of saloon – that in which the great balls of Almack's are given. The walls were all painted and gilded, the benches were sofas stuffed and cushioned and covered with blue damask. The audience was composed of the *élite* of London society. Duchesses were there by the score, and amongst them the great and beautiful Duchess of Sutherland, the Queen's Mistress of the Robes. Amidst all this Thackeray just got up and spoke with as much simplicity and ease as if he had been speaking to a few friends by his own fireside. The lecture was truly good: he has taken pains with composition. It was finished without being in the least studied; a quiet humour and graphic force enlivened it throughout. He saw me as I entered the room, and came straight up and spoke very kindly. He then took me to his mother, a fine, handsome old lady, and introduced me to her. After the lecture somebody came behind me, leaned over the bench, and said, 'Will you permit me, as a Yorkshireman, to introduce myself to you?' I turned round, was puzzled at first by the strange face I met, but in a minute I recognized the features, 'You are the Earl of Carlisle,' I said. He smiled and assented. He went on to talk for some time in a courteous, kind fashion. He asked after you, recalled the platform electioneering scene at Haworth, and begged to be remembered to you. Dr. Forbes came up afterwards, and Mr. Monckton Milnes, a Yorkshire Member of Parliament, who introduced himself on the same plea as Lord Carlisle.

Yesterday we went to the Crystal Palace.[1] The exterior has a strange and elegant but somewhat unsubstantial effect. The interior is like a mighty Vanity Fair. The brightest colours blaze on all sides; and ware of all kinds, from diamonds to spinning jennies and printing presses, are there to be seen. It was very fine, gorgeous, animated, bewildering, but I liked Thackeray's lecture better.

[1] The Great Exhibition in Hyde Park. – [*Clement Shorter.*]

I hope, dear papa, that you are keeping well. With kind regards to Tabby and Martha, and hopes that they are well too, – I am, your affectionate daughter,

C. Brontë

114

CHARLOTTE BRONTË TO ELLEN NUSSEY

Haworth,
August 25th, '52.

Dear Ellen,

I am thankful to say that papa's convalescence seems now to be quite confirmed. There is scarcely any remainder of the inflammation in his eyes. He begins even to look forward to resuming his duty ere long, but caution must be observed on that head.

Martha has been very willing and helpful during papa's illness. Poor Tabby is ill herself at present, with English cholera, which with influenza has been almost universally prevalent in this district; I have myself had a touch of the last, but it went off very gently on the whole, affecting my chest and liver less than any cold has done for the last three years.

I write to you about yourself rather under constraint and in the dark, for your letters, dear Ellen, are most remarkably oracular, dropping nothing but hints; which tie my tongue a good deal. Your last postcript is quite Sybilline. I can hardly guess what checks you in writing to me. There is certainly no one in this house or elsewhere to whom I should show your notes, and I do not imagine they are in any peril in passing through the post.

Perhaps you think that as *I* generally write with some reserve, you ought to do the same. *My* reserve, however, has its foundation not in design, but in necessity. I am silent because I have literally *nothing to say*. I might indeed repeat over and over again that my life is a pale blank and often a very weary burden, and that the Future sometimes appals me; but what end could be answered by such repetition except to weary you and enervate myself?

The evils that now and then wring a groan from my heart, lie in position; not that I am a *single* woman and likely to remain a *single* woman, but because I am a *lonely* woman and likely to be *lonely*. But it cannot be helped and therefore *imperatively must be borne*, and borne too with as few words about it as may be.

I write all this just to prove to you that whatever you would freely *say* to me, you may just as freely write.

Understand, I remain just as resolved as ever not to allow myself the holiday of a visit from you, *till* I have done my work. After labour, pleasure; but while work is lying at the wall undone, I never yet could enjoy recreation. – Yours very faithfully,

C. Brontë

115

CHARLOTTE BRONTË TO GEORGE SMITH[1]

October 30th, 1852.

My Dear Sir,

You must notify honestly what you think of *Villette* when you have read it. I can hardly tell you how I hunger to hear some opinion beside my own, and how I have sometimes desponded, and almost despaired, because there was no one to whom to read a line, or of whom to ask a counsel. *Jane Eyre* was not written under such circumstances, nor were two-thirds of *Shirley*. I got so miserable about it, I could bear no allusion to the book. It is not finished yet; but now I hope. As to the anonymous publication, I have this to say: If the withholding of the author's name should tend materially to injure the publisher's interest, to interfere with booksellers' orders, etc., I would not press the point; but if no such detriment is contingent I should be much thankful for the sheltering shadow of an incognito. I seem to dread the advertisements – the large-lettered 'Currer Bell's New Novel', or 'New Work by the author of *Jane Eyre*'. These, however, I feel well enough, are the transcendentalisms of a retired wretch; so you must speak frankly. . . . I shall be glad to see *Colonel Esmond*. My objection to the second volume lay here: I thought it contained decidedly too much History – too little Story.

You will see that *Villette* touches on no matter of public interest. I cannot write books handling the topics of the day; it is of no use trying. Nor can I write a book for its moral. Nor can I take up a philanthropic scheme, though I honour philanthropy; and volun-

[1] George Smith was represented in *Villette* in the character of 'Dr John'. It has been suggested that Charlotte was, for a time, in love with her handsome publisher.

tarily and sincerely veil my face before such a mighty subject as that handled in Mrs. Beecher Stowe's work, *Uncle Tom's Cabin.* To manage these great matters rightly they must be long and practically studied – their bearings known intimately, and their evils felt genuinely; they must not be taken up as a business matter and a trading speculation. I doubt not Mrs. Stowe had felt the iron of slavery enter into her heart, from childhood upwards, long before she ever thought of writing books. The feeling throughout her work is sincere and not got up. Remember to be an honest critic of *Villette*, and tell Mr. Williams to be unsparing: not that I am likely to alter anything, but I want to know his impressions and yours.

116

CHARLOTTE BRONTË TO W.S. WILLIAMS

November 6th, 1852.

My Dear Sir,

I must not delay thanking you for your kind letter, with its candid and able commentary on *Villette*. With many of your strictures I concur. The third volume may, perhaps, do away with some of the objections; others still remain in force. I do not think the interest culminates anywhere to the degree you would wish. What climax there is does not come on till near the conclusion; and even then I doubt whether the regular novel-reader will consider the 'agony piled sufficiently high' (as the Americans say), or the colours dashed on to the canvas with the proper amount of daring. Still, I fear, they must be satisfied with what is offered; my palette affords no brighter tints; were I to attempt to deepen the reds, or burnish the yellows, I should but botch.

Unless I am mistaken the emotion of the book will be found to be kept throughout in tolerable subjection. As to the name of the heroine, I can hardly express what subtlety of thought made me decide upon giving her a cold name; but at first I called her 'Lucy Snowe' (spelt with an 'e'), which Snowe I afterwards changed to 'Frost'. Subsequently I rather regretted the change, and wished it 'Snowe' again. If not too late I should like the alteration to be made now throughout the MS. A *cold* name she must have; partly, perhaps, on the '*lucus a non lucendo*' principle – partly on that of the 'fitness of things', for she has about her an external coldness.

You say that she may be thought morbid and weak, unless the history of her life be more fully given. I consider that she *is* both morbid and weak at times; her character sets up no pretensions to unmixed strength, and anybody living her life would necessarily become morbid. It was no impetus of healthy feeling which urged her to the confessional, for instance; it was the semi-delirium of solitary grief and sickness. If, however, the book does not express all this, there must be a great fault somewhere. I might explain away a few other points, but it would be too much like drawing a picture and then writing underneath the name of the object intended to be represented. We know what sort of a pencil that is which needs an ally in the pen.

Thanking you again for the clearness and fulness with which you have responded to my request for a statement of impressions, I am, my dear sir, yours very sincerely,

C. Brontë

I trust the work will be seen in MS. by no one except Mr. Smith and yourself.

117

CHARLOTTE BRONTË TO ELLEN NUSSEY

Dec. 9th, 1852, Thursday Morning.

Dear Nell,

I got home safely at five o'clock yesterday afternoon, and, I am most thankful to say, found papa and all the rest well. I did my business satisfactorily in Leeds, the head-dress re-arranged as I wish; it is now a very different matter to the bushy, tasteless thing it was before.

On my arrival I found no proof-sheets, but a letter from Mr. Smith, which I would have enclosed, but so many words are scarcely legible, you would have no pleasure in reading it: he continues to make a mystery of his 'reason' – something in the third volume sticks confoundedly in his throat, and as to the 'female character' about which I asked, he responds crabbedly that, 'She is an odd, fascinating little puss', but affirms that he is 'not in love with her'. He tells me also that he will answer no more questions about *Villette*.

This morning I have a brief note from Mr. Williams intimating that he has 'not yet been permitted to read the 3rd vol.' Also there is a note from Mrs. Smith, very kind, I almost wish I could still look on that kindness just as I used to do: it was very pleasant to me once.

Write *immediately*, Dear Nell, and tell me how your mother is. Give my kindest regards to her and all at Brookroyd. Everybody was very good to me this last visit, I remember them with corresponding pleasure. Papa seems glad on the whole to hear you are not going to Yarmouth just yet; he thinks you should be cautious. – Yours faithfully,

C. Brontë

118

CHARLOTTE BRONTË TO ELLEN NUSSEY

December 15th, 1852.

Dear Nell,

I return Mrs. Upjohn's note which is highly characteristic, and not, I fear, of good omen for the comfort of your visit. There must be something wrong in herself as well as in her servants. I enclose another note which, taken in conjunction with the incident immediately preceding it, and with a long series of indications whose meaning I scarce ventured hitherto to interpret to myself, much less hint to any other, has left on my mind a feeling of deep concern. This note, you will see, is from Mr. Nicholls.[1]

I know not whether you have ever observed him specially when staying here, your perception is generally quick enough, *too* quick I have sometimes thought, yet as you never said anything, I restrained my own dim misgivings, which could not claim the sure guide of vision. What papa has seen or guessed I will not inquire though I may conjecture. He has minutely noticed all Mr. Nicholls' low spirits, all his threats of expatriation, all his symptoms of impaired health, noticed them with little sympathy and much in direct sarcasm. On Monday evening Mr. Nicholls was here to tea. I vaguely felt without clearly seeing, as without seeing, I have felt for some time, the meaning of his constant looks, and strange feverish restraint. After tea I withdrew to the dining-room as usual. As usual, Mr. Nicholls sat with papa till between eight and nine

[1] Arthur Bell Nicholls had been Curate at Haworth since 1844.

o'clock, I then heard him open the parlour door as if going. I expected the clash of the front-door. He stopped in the passage: he tapped: like lightning it flashed on me what was coming. He entered, he stood before me. What his words were you can guess; his manner, you can hardly realize, nor can I forget it. Shaking from head to foot, looking deadly pale, speaking low, vehemently yet with difficulty, he made me for the first time feel what it costs a man to declare affection where he doubts response.

The spectacle of one ordinarily so statue-like, thus trembling, stirred, and overcome, gave me a kind of strange shock. He spoke of sufferings he had borne for months, of sufferings he could endure no longer, and craved leave for some hope. I could only entreat him to leave me then and promise a reply on the morrow. I asked him if he had spoken to papa. He said, he dared not. I think I half led, half put him out of the room. When he was gone I immediately went to papa, and told him what had taken place. Agitation and anger disproportionate to the occasion ensued; if I had *loved* Mr. Nicholls and had heard such epithets applied to him as were used, it would have transported me past my patience; as it was, my blood boiled with a sense of injustice, but papa worked himself into a state not to be trifled with, the veins on his temples started up like whipcord, and his eyes became suddenly bloodshot. I made haste to promise that Mr. Nicholls should on the morrow have a distinct refusal.

I wrote yesterday and got this note. There is no need to add to this statement any comment. Papa's vehement antipathy to the bare thought of any one thinking of me as a wife, and Mr. Nicholl's distress, both give me pain. Attachment to Mr. Nicholls you are aware I never entertained, but the poignant pity inspired by his state on Monday evening, by the hurried revelation of his sufferings for many months, is something galling and irksome. That he cared something for me, and wanted me to care for him I have long suspected, but I did not know the degree or strength of his feelings. Dear Nell, good-bye. – Yours faithfully,

C. Brontë

I have letters from Sir J.K. Shuttleworth and Miss Martineau, but I cannot talk of them now.

119

CHARLOTTE BRONTË TO ELLEN NUSSEY

Haworth,
December 18th, '52.

Dear Nell,

You may well ask, How is it? for I am sure I don't know. This business would seem to me like a dream, did not my reason tell me it has long been brewing. It puzzles me to comprehend how and whence comes this turbulence of feeling.

You ask how papa demeans himself to Mr. Nicholls. I only wish you were here to see papa in his present mood: you would know something of him. He just treats him with a hardness not to be bent, and a contempt not to be propitiated. The two have had no interview as yet; all has been done by letter. Papa wrote, I must say, a most cruel note to Mr. Nicholls on Wednesday. In his state of mind and health (for the poor man is horrifying his landlady, Martha's mother, by entirely rejecting his meals) I felt that the blow must be parried, and I thought it right to accompany the pitiless despatch by a line to the effect that, while Mr. Nicholls must never expect me to reciprocate the feeling he had expressed, yet at the same time I wished to disclaim participation in sentiments calculated to give him pain; and I exhorted him to maintain his courage and spirits. On receiving the two letters, he set off from home. Yesterday came the enclosed brief epistle.

You must understand that a good share of papa's anger arises from the idea, not altogether groundless, that Mr. Nicholls has behaved with disingenuousness in so long concealing his aim, forging that Irish fiction, etc. I am afraid also that papa thinks a little too much about his want of money; he says that the match would be a degradation, that I should be throwing myself away, that he expects me, if I marry at all, to do very differently; in short, his manner of viewing the subject is, on the whole, far from being one in which I can sympathize. My own objections arise from a sense of incongruity and uncongeniality in feelings, tastes, principles.

How are you getting on, dear Nell, and how are all at Brookroyd? Remember me kindly to everybody. Yours, wishing devoutly that papa would resume his tranquility, and Mr. N. his beef and pudding,

C. Brontë

I am glad to say that the incipient inflammation in papa's eye is disappearing.

120

CHARLOTTE BRONTË TO ELLEN NUSSEY

Haworth,
April 6th, 1853.

Dear Ellen,

... My visit to Manchester is for the present put off by Mr. Morgan having written to say that since papa will not go to Buckingham to see him, he will come to Yorkshire to see papa; when, I don't yet know, and I trust in goodness he will not stay long, as papa really cannot bear putting out of his way. I must wait, however, till the infliction is over.

You ask about Mr. Nicholls. I hear he has got a curacy, but do not yet know where. I trust the news is true. He and papa never speak. He seems to pass a desolate life. He has allowed late circumstances so to act on him as to freeze up his manner and overcast his countenance not only to those immediately concerned but to every one. He sits drearily in his rooms. If Mr. Croxton or Mr. Grant, or any other clergyman calls to see, and as they think, to cheer him, he scarcely speaks. I find he tells them nothing, seeks no confidant, rebuffs all attempts to penetrate his mind. I own I respect him for this. He still lets Flossy go to his rooms and takes him to walk. He still goes over to see Mr. Sowden sometimes, and, poor fellow, that is all. He looks ill and miserable. I think and trust in Heaven that he will be better as soon as he gets away from Haworth. I pity him inexpressibly. We never meet nor speak, nor dare I look at him, silent pity is just all I can give him, and as he knows nothing about that, it does not comfort. He is now grown so gloomy and reserved, that nobody seems to like him, his fellow-curates shun trouble in that shape, the lower orders dislike it. Papa has a perfect antipathy to him, and he, I fear, to papa. Martha hates him. I think he might almost be *dying* and they would not speak a friendly word to or of him. How much of all this he deserves I can't tell, certainly he never was agreeable or amiable, and is less so now than ever, and alas! I do not know him well enough to be sure there is truth and true affection, or only rancour and corroding disappointment at the bottom of his chagrin. In this state of things I must be, and I am, *entirely passive*. I may be losing the purest gem, and to me far the most precious life can give – genuine attachment – or I may be escaping the yoke of a morose temper. In this doubt conscience will not suffer me to take one step in opposition to papa's will, blended as that will is with the most bitter and unreasonable prejudices. So I just leave the matter where we must leave all important matters.

Remember me kindly to all at Brookroyd, and believe me, yours faithfully,

C. Brontë

121

CHARLOTTE BRONTË TO ELLEN NUSSEY

Haworth,
May 27th, 1853.

Dear Ellen,

... You will want to know about the leave-taking; the whole matter is but a painful subject, but I must treat it briefly. The testimonial was presented in a public meeting. Mr. T. and Mr. Grant were there. Papa was not very well and I advised him to stay away, which he did. As to the last Sunday, it was a cruel struggle. Mr. Nicholls ought not to have had to take any duty.

He left Haworth this morning at 6 o'clock. Yesterday evening he called to render into papa's hands the deeds of the National School, and to say good-bye. They were busy cleaning, washing the paint, etc., in the dining-room, so he did not find me there. I would not go into the parlour to speak to him in papa's presence. He went out thinking he was not to see me, and indeed, till the very last moment, I thought it best not. But perceiving that he stayed long before going out at the gate, and remembering his long grief, I took courage and went out trembling and miserable. I found him leaning against the garden door in a paroxysm of anguish, sobbing as women never sob. Of course I went straight to him. Very few words were interchanged, those few barely articulate. Several things I should have liked to ask him were swept entirely from my memory. Poor fellow! But he wanted such hope and such encouragement as I could not give him. Still I trust he must know now that I am not cruelly blind and indifferent to his constancy and grief. For a few weeks he goes to the South of England, afterwards he takes a curacy somewhere in Yorkshire, but I don't know where.

Papa has been far from strong lately. I dare not mention Mr. Nicholl's name to him. He speaks of him quietly and without opprobrium to others, but to me he is implacable on the matter.

However, he is gone – gone – and there's an end of it. I see no chance of hearing a word about him in future, unless some stray shred of intelligence comes through Mr. Sowden or some other second-hand source. In all this it is not I who am to be pitied at all, and of course nobody pities me. They all think, in Haworth, that I have disdainfully refused him, etc. If pity would do Mr. Nicholls any good, he ought to have and I believe has it. They may abuse me if they will; whether they do or not I can't tell.

Write soon and say how your prospects proceed. I trust they will daily brighten. – Yours faithfully,

C. Brontë

122

CHARLOTTE BRONTË TO MRS. GASKELL

Haworth,
June 1st, 1853.

Dear Mrs. Gaskell,

June is come, and now I want to know if you can come on Thursday, the 9th inst.

Ever since I was at Manchester I have been anticipating your visit. Not that I attempt to justify myself in asking you; the place has no attractions, as I told you, here in this house. Papa too takes great interest in the matter. I only pray that the weather may be fine, and that a cold, by which I am now stupified, may be gone before the 9th, so that I may have no let and hindrance in taking you on to the moors – the sole, but, with one who loves nature as you do, not despicable, resource.

When you take leave of the domestic circle and turn your back on Plymouth Grove to come to Haworth, you must do it in the spirit which might sustain you in case you were setting out on a brief trip to the backwoods of America. Leaving behind your husband, children, and civilization, you must come out to barbarism, loneliness, and liberty. The change will perhaps do good, if not too prolonged. . . . Please, when you write, to mention by what train you will come, and at what hour you will arrive at Keighley; for I must take measures to have a conveyance waiting for you at the station; otherwise, as there is no cab-stand, you might be inconvenienced and hindered.

C. Brontë

123

CHARLOTTE BRONTË TO MRS. GASKELL

July 9th, 1853.

Thank you for your letter; it was as pleasant as a quiet chat, as welcome as spring showers, as reviving as a friend's visit; in short, it was very like a page of *Cranford*. . . . A thought strikes me. Do you, who have so many friends – so large a circle of acquaintance – find it easy, when you sit down to write, to isolate yourself from all those ties, and their sweet associations, so as to be your *own woman*, uninfluenced or swayed by the consciousness of how your work may affect other minds; what blame or what sympathy it may call forth? Does no luminous cloud ever come between you and the severe Truth, as you know it in your own secret and clear-seeing soul? In a word, are you never tempted to make your characters more amiable than the Life, by the inclination to assimilate your thoughts to the thoughts of those who always *feel* kindly, but sometimes fail to *see* justly? Don't answer the question; it is not intended to be answered. . . . Your account of Mrs. Stowe was stimulatingly interesting. I long to see you, to get you to say it, and many other things, all over again. My father continues better. I am better too; but to-day I have a headache again, which will hardly let me write coherently. . . . Yours very gratefully,

C. *Brontë*

124

CHARLOTTE BRONTË TO ELLEN NUSSEY

Haworth,
April 11th, 1854.

Dear Ellen,

Thank you for the collar; it is very pretty, and I will wear it for the sake of her who made and gave it.

Mr. Nicholls came on Monday, and was here all last week. Matters have progressed thus since July. He renewed his visit in September, but then matters so fell out that I saw little of him. He continued to write. The correspondence pressed on my mind. I grew very miserable in keeping it from papa. At last sheer pain made me gather courage to break it. I told all. It was very hard and rough work at the time, but the issue after a few days was that I obtained leave to continue the communication. Mr. Nicholls came in January; he was ten days in the neighbourhood. I saw much of him. I had stipulated with papa for opportunity to become better acquainted. I had it, and all I learnt inclined me to esteem and affection. Still papa was very, very hostile, bitterly unjust.

I told Mr. Nicholls the great obstacle that lay in his way. He has persevered. The result of this, his last visit, is, that papa's consent is gained, that his respect, I believe, is won, for Mr. Nicholls has in all things proved himself disinterested and forbearing. Certainly I must respect him, nor can I withhold from him more than mere cool respect. In fact, dear Ellen, I am engaged.

Mr. Nicholls, in the course of a few months, will return to the curacy of Haworth. I stipulated that I would not leave papa, and to papa himself I proposed a plan of residence which should maintain his seclusion and convenience uninvaded and in a pecuniary sense bring him gain instead of loss. What seemed at one time impossible is now arranged, and papa begins really to take pleasure in the prospect.

For myself, dear Ellen, while thankful to One who seems to have guided me through much difficulty, much and deep distress and perplexity of mind, I am still very calm, very inexpectant. What I taste of happiness is of the soberest order. I trust to love my husband. I am grateful for his tender love to me. I believe him to be an affectionate, a conscientious, a high-principled man; and if, with all this, I should yield to regrets, that fine talents, congenial tastes and thoughts are not added, it seems to me I should be most presumptuous and thankless.

Providence offers me this destiny. Doubtless then it is the best for me. Nor do I shrink from wishing those dear to me one not less happy.

It is possible that our marriage may take place in the course of the summer. Mr. Nicholls wishes it to be in July. He spoke of you with great kindness, and said he hoped you would be at our wedding. I said I thought of having no other bridesmaid. Did I say rightly? I mean the marriage to be literally as quiet as possible.

Do not mention these things just yet. I mean to write to Miss Wooler shortly. Good-bye. There is a strange half-sad feeling in making these announcements. The whole thing is something other than imagination paints it beforehand; cares, fears, come mixed inextricably with hopes. I trust yet to talk the matter over with you.

Often last week I wished for your presence, and said so to Mr. Nicholls, Arthur as I now call him, but he said it was the only time and place when he could not have wished to see you. Good-bye. – Yours affectionately,

C. Brontë

125

CHARLOTTE BRONTË TO ELLEN NUSSEY

Haworth,
August 9th, 1854.

Dear Ellen,

. . . Since I came home,[1] I have not had an unemployed moment; my life is changed indeed, to be wanted continually, to be constantly called for and occupied seems so strange: yet it is a marvellously good thing. As yet I don't quite understand how some wives grow so selfish. As far as my experience of matrimony goes, I think it tends to draw you out of and away from yourself.

We have had sundry callers this week. Yesterday, Mr. Sowden and another gentleman dined here, and Mr. and Mrs. Grant joined them at tea.

I do not think we shall go to Brookroyd soon, on papa's account. I do not wish again to leave home for a time, but I trust you will ere long come here.

I really like Mr. Sowden very well. He asked after you. Mr. Nicholls told him we expected you would be coming to stay with us in the course of three or four weeks, and that he should then invite him over again as he wished us to take sundry rather long walks, and as he should have his wife to look after, and she was trouble enough, it would be quite necessary to have a guardian for the other lady. Mr. Sowden seemed perfectly acquiescent.

Dear Nell, – During the last six weeks the colour of my thoughts is a good deal changed: I know more of the realities of life than I once did. I think many false ideas are propagated, perhaps unintentionally. I think those married women who indiscriminately urge their acquaintance to marry, much to blame. For my part, I can only say with deeper sincerity and fuller significance, what I always said in theory, 'Wait God's will'. Indeed, indeed, Nell, it is a

[1] Charlotte Brontë married Arthur Bell Nicholls on June 29th, 1854.

solemn and strange and perilous thing for a woman to become a wife. Man's lot is far, far different. Tell me when you think you can come. Papa is better, but not well. How is your mother? give my love to her, and Ann and Mr. Clapham, and Mercy, if she is good. – Yours faithfully,

C.B. Nicholls

Have I told you how much better Mr. Nicholls is? He looks quite strong and hale; he gained 12 lb. during the four weeks we were in Ireland. To see this improvement in him has been a main source of happiness to me, and to speak truth, a subject of wonder too.

126

CHARLOTTE BRONTË TO ELLEN NUSSEY

Haworth,
December 7th, 1854.

Dear Ellen,

I shall not get leave to go to Brookroyd before Christmas now, so do not expect me. For my own part I really should have no fear, and if it just depended on me, I should come; but these matters are not quite in my power now, another must be consulted, and where his wish and judgment have a decided bias to a particular course, I make no stir, but just adopt it. Arthur is sorry to disappoint both you and me, but it is his fixed wish that a few weeks should be allowed yet to elapse before we meet. Probably he is confirmed in this desire by my having a cold at present. I did not achieve the walk to the waterfall with impunity, though I changed my wet things immediately on returning home, yet I felt a chill afterwards, and the same night had sore throat and cold; however, I am better now, but not quite well.

. . . I am writing in haste. It is almost inexplicable to me that I seem so often hurried now, but the fact is, whenever Arthur is in, I must have occupations in which he can share, or which will not at least divert my attention from him; thus a multitude of little matters get put off till he goes out, and then I am quite busy. Good-bye, dear Ellen, I hope we shall meet soon. – Yours faithfully,

C.B. Nicholls

127

CHARLOTTE BRONTË TO ELLEN NUSSEY

Haworth,
January 19th, 1855.

Dear Ellen,

Since our return from Gawthorpe, we have had a Mr. Bell, one of Arthur's cousins, staying with us. It was a great pleasure: I wish you could have seen him and made his acquaintance: a true gentleman by nature and cultivation is not after all an everyday thing. . . .

I very much wish to come to Brookroyd, and I hope to be able to write with certainty and fix Wednesday the 31st January as the day: but the fact is, I am not sure whether I shall be well enough to leave home. At present I should be a most tedious visitor. My health has been really very good ever since my return from Ireland till about ten days ago, when the stomach seemed quite suddenly to lose its tone, indigestion and continual faint sickness have been my portion ever since. Don't conjecture, dear Nell, for it is too soon yet, though I certainly never before felt as I have done lately. I am rather mortified to lose my good looks and grow thin as I am doing, just when I thought of going to Brookroyd. . . . Dear Ellen, I want to see you, and I hope I shall see you well. My love to all. – Yours faithfully,

C.B. Nicholls

Thank Mr. Clapham for his hospitable wish, but it would be quite out of Arthur's power to stay more than one night or two at the most.

128

A.B. NICHOLLS TO ELLEN NUSSEY

Haworth,
February 1st, 1855.

Dear Miss Nussey,

Dr. MacTurk saw Charlotte on Tuesday. His opinion was that her illness would be of some duration, but that there was no immediate danger. I trust, therefore, that in a few weeks she will be well again.

We were very much concerned to hear of your mother's continued illness, both on your account and hers. Charlotte begs you will write a line soon to let her know how Mrs. Nussey gets on, and she is sure she can trust you to excuse her from answering until she is able. – Believe me, yours faithfully.

A.B. Nicholls

129

CHARLOTTE BRONTË TO ELLEN NUSSEY

February 21st, 1855.

My Dear Ellen,

I must write one line out of my weary bed. The news of Mercy's probable recovery came like a ray of joy to me. I am not going to talk about my sufferings, it would be useless and painful – I want to give you an assurance which I know will comfort you – and that is that I find in my husband the tenderest nurse, the kindest support – the best earthly comfort that ever woman had. His patience never fails, and it is tried by sad days and broken nights. Write and tell me about Mrs. Hewitt's case, how long she was ill and in what way. Papa, thank God! is better. Our poor old Tabby is *dead and buried.* Give my truest love to Miss Wooler. May God comfort and help you.

C.B. Nicholls

130

A.B. NICHOLLS TO ELLEN NUSSEY

Haworth,
March 31st, 1855.

Dear Miss Nussey,

Mr. Brontë's letter would prepare you for the sad intelligence I have to communicate. Our dear Charlotte is no more. She died last night of exhaustion. For the last two or three weeks we had become very uneasy about her, but it was not until Sunday evening that it became apparent that her sojourn with us was likely to be short. We intend to bury her on Wednesday morning. – Believe me, sincerely yours,

A.B. Nicholls

3

Emily Brontë: Her Life

Chapter One

Fact and Legend

Emily Brontë was born in 1818, on 30th July, and she died on 19th December, 1848. From first to last, there is no evidence that she laid any plans for the course of her life. She seems, above all, to have wished to avoid 'doing something about' her life, and when, from time to time, the obligation was put to her, to make some sort of career for herself, and so prepare for her future, she tried to meet these demands, and failed.

Indeed, Emily Brontë seems to have been determined that her life should come under the category of 'uneventful'; not because she was apathetic about life, but on the contrary, because she was intensely taken up with her own particular calling in life. Life, as she experienced it in her home, was meaningful. She bent all her efforts towards defining this meaning, by the direct methods of her literary work, and by indirect means, which included her household and family duties. Any time apart from this which she was persuaded to spend towards improving her lot, went against the grain. To the end, she caused very little to happen to herself by her own agency.

The result of this compressed, instinctive discipline, was the singular achievement for which we remember her name: her poems and her novel, *Wuthering Heights*. These are the principal facts in the life of Emily Brontë; so important as to place her character in the realm of legend.

All great genius attracts legend to itself. Legend is the common means of expressing the manifestation of genius in certain people, who cannot be described in ordinary terms. For this reason the legendary data which adhere to people of genius should be respected. One Brontë biographer claims to 'clear away the heaped rubbish of legend'. This is not the present writer's aim. Such legend is the repository of a vital aspect of truth; and ought not to be swept aside simply because it is not ascertainable; neither, of course, should it be taken as literal truth.

The literal facts about Emily Brontë we get from family correspondence and from the industry of subsequent researchers; there is little from Emily Brontë herself. The way in which these facts are presented – references to her, in letters and diaries – shows that, up to the time when she began to reveal her genius in her work, she was regarded by those most familiar with her, with the sympathy and understanding which near-relatives are wont to bestow on 'nervous' members of the family. Emily was not thought of as a genius until her work attracted attention; this is natural enough, for without her work she was merely a daughter in a clergyman's home, one whose special nature called for special consideration: Emily was shy, often to the point of rudeness, with strangers. ('How did Emily behave?' was her sister Charlotte's anxious question to a visitor who had returned from a walk with Emily.) Her relatives feared for her on the few occasions when Emily forced herself to leave her home for a few months. So far, she was loved and understood. During this first phase, Emily (who in the later, legendary light appears as a monolith of self-generated strength) is referred to simply with protective loyalty. Only strangers were patronizing; as late as Emily's twenty-fourth year, her master at the finishing school in Brussels, where she had spent a few uneasy months, wrote to her father that 'Miss Emily was learning the piano, receiving lessons from the best professor in Belgium, and she herself already had little pupils. She was losing whatever remained of ignorance, and also of what was worse – timidity.'

The facts to be gained from references to Emily Brontë in documents dating from her birth to the year 1846, are in significant contrast to the statements made about her as her worth became known, during the remaining three years of her life and after her death. More remarkable is the contrast between what was said at the time about Emily up to her twenty-eighth year, and what was put forward later concerning the same period, by people who remembered, now they came to think of it, that the author of *Wuthering Heights* had been remarkable for this or that quality.

So, after 1846, a new note appears, very gradually at first, in family references to Emily. This is apparent in her sister Charlotte's letters. Charlotte had always respected Emily; the new note is not simply a deepening of respect, although it contains an element of awe. Charlotte began, now, to see her sister as a *dramatic* being, and as Emily proceeded to her dramatic death, Charlotte was ever more taken up with this new image of her younger sister as a creature of concealed and terrible powers hacking her relentless way through a fatal consumption for which she would accept no alleviation. Emily took on the aspect of a legendary being.

All this was, of course, justified. Charlotte, in her anguished letters relating to Emily's last illness, invented nothing. Had this larger-looming Emily, in fact, existed all along?

In 1841, the youngest sister, Anne, who, like Charlotte, was then working as a governess away from home, had written 'Emily . . . is as busy as any of us, and in reality earns her food and raiment as much as we do'. In 1844, one of Charlotte's chance remarks about Emily when the sisters contemplated starting a school, was that 'Emily does not care much for teaching, but she would look after the housekeeping, and, although something of a recluse, she is too good-hearted not to do all she could for the well-being of children'. Such casual comments reveal nothing of the passionate lonely genius who, it seems, was revealed to her family in the last three years of her life.

It may be that Emily did not realize her own nature until she had produced *Wuthering Heights*. Perhaps she then became conscious of a new self-image, whose role she grimly pursued. This is speculative; but it is clear that, from contemporary sources we have two pictures of Emily Brontë. One, of a shy, quiet country girl, a girl who was useful in the house, and who had not shown any of her writings to her family since her childhood, when all the children had been prolific in writing. The later picture is more richly adorned. Everyone who had met the now famous woman, however briefly, contributed to the portrait of Emily Brontë the poet and novelist. M. Héger, the Brussels master who had once written to tell her father that she was losing her 'ignorance and . . . what was worse, timidity,' now pronounced on Emily in retrospect. 'She should have been a man – a great navigator' runs the celebrated passage. 'Her powerful reason would have deduced new spheres of discovery from the knowledge of the old; and her strong, imperious will would never have been daunted by opposition or difficulty; never have given way but with life.'

M. Héger had not seen Emily since the time when, nearly fifteen years before, he had assured her father of his hopes for her ignorance and timidity. It is difficult to reconcile his first opinion, which he no doubt modified to accommodate a father's pride, with the

Emily Brontë, portrait by Branwell Brontë, c. 1833
(*by courtesy of the National Portrait Gallery*)

'strong imperious will' and the 'powerful reason' he ascribed to Emily after her posthumous fame had caused him to think again. Still, these discrepant statements, like those made by her family before and after Emily had revealed herself, can be reconciled – they must be reconciled, because they represent impressions which we have every reason to believe were recorded in good faith.

It happens from time to time that we meet someone; we don't catch his name; we note he is shy, or hearty, or dull; perhaps he has some mannerisms which irritate us; or he may leave the vaguest impression on us; or we may put him down as 'unusual'. Some weeks later, we learn 'who he is': someone we have heard about; whose books we have read; or whose piano recitals, which we have never attended, are famous. Returning to our impression of the man, we change it, though we may never see him again. The irritating mannerisms are quite understandable, they are charming. If he was too jovial, he now seems to have been surprisingly friendly. Shy, he is now modest. The vagueness of his features in our memory is illuminated by our new knowledge. We remember some strong quality, as befits genius. The first impression is obscured, unless we happen to have described him in a diary or a letter, on our meeting with him. Anyone comparing this impression with the later reconstruction of it, would scarcely recognize the same man in each. Which is the more accurate portrayal, that of the real man whom we chanced to meet, or that of our reconstruction – the legendary figure, in other words? The second impression is the more real. The first merely prefigured the legend. But the legend alone is not enough; we need concrete as well as legendary impressions to bring us somewhere near a true picture of the man.

Emily Brontë's biographer faces a similar situation; but this is intensified by the fact that her earliest interpreters, those on whom we rely for most information, had known her in varying degrees of intimacy before they gained this new insight into her character. Her sister Charlotte was of course the best informed. Charlotte's friend, Ellen Nussey, was frequently in her company. M. Héger, a man of intelligence, had observed her daily throughout most of her ten-months' residence at his school. Was he insincere in his first assessment of Emily – concerning her timidity for instance? It is most unlikely; this was the accepted opinion of Emily at that time. Nor was the good man insincere in his oracular utterance, fifteen years later, as to her 'strong imperious will' among other heroic attributes – this legendary aspect of Emily had been current at least seven years by this time, initiated by Charlotte's introduction to *Wuthering Heights*.

It would be nothing new in Brontë biography to have opened this question merely to close it again by assuming that everything recorded of Emily Brontë by her contemporaries before they became aware of her talent, can be worked in with what was said afterwards, forming a composite picture. The two aspects, it is true, are to be reconciled. But the distinction between them exists to a remarkable degree. To assume simply that Emily Brontë's contemporaries were not aware of her deeper nature until they discovered it in her work, does not adequately reconcile the reserved, 'problem' girl with the impassioned superwoman subsequently described by Charlotte. This would not explain the nature and extent of the change in Emily's reputation, it would merely explain that there was a change.

A comparison with the case of her sister Charlotte may make this clear. Charlotte's success with *Jane Eyre*, her first published novel, was immediate; as it gradually became known, amongst their friends and neighbours that she was the author, there was a certain stir; a new aspect of Charlotte was observed, but the records do not suggest that anyone's previous impressions of Charlotte's character were suddenly put out of gear by this discovery. Causing some surprised comment at first, Charlotte Brontë nevertheless continued to be recognizable as her old self in the eyes of her acquaintances and intimates; her personal reputation never reached fever-heat. Whereas Charlotte's success called forth some respect, some disapproval, and some back-biting, Emily's book made no immediate impact, at first, outside her family circle. But gradually, as the author of *Wuthering Heights* was discovered in Emily, her reputation underwent a spectacular change; she became a mysterious force, a woman larger than life, increasing in stature after her death three years later.

Moreover the rhetoric of Charlotte in her biographical notes on Emily, and the rhetoric of M. Héger in his panegyric, can be cited as instinctive acknowledgements of their belief that Emily Brontë was no normal being. This was by no means due to literary discernment. Charlotte probably considered herself a better novelist than Emily; and justifiably so. M. Héger was traditional in taste; he would have been impressed but not satisfied with *Wuthering Heights*. It is clear, however, that some powerful element in the work moved them to employ a highly impassioned style to illuminate the character of the author. They used the language of legend as though this were Emily's natural due. Many modern biographical writings on Emily show a similar tendency (and though this is an implicit definition of her nature, it is not perhaps the most lucid method of approach).

From Charlotte's letters describing Emily's last illness and death, there is 'internal evidence' of a more than usually elevated prose style: an implicit sign, possibly, of Charlotte's revised conception of her sister some years before the public became curious about the person of Emily Brontë. The more direct evidence of this, however, lies in the substance of Charlotte's statements. Emily's incapacity to cope with the world had always evoked her sister's sympathy. In the last phase of Emily's life, Charlotte, who had hitherto expressed her fears for Emily, now expresses something very close to a fear of Emily. Accompanying the agony of mind which Charlotte experienced in watching her sister's brutal self-neglect, an objective and terrified fascination can be detected.

Emily Brontë was established as a legendary woman, first by those who had read her work, and next by people who had heard the legend. Villagers who remembered her, though seldom having spoken with her, obliged her first biographers by recounting this or that eccentricity. Legend-making is infectious. The Brontës' old servants added their reminiscences. Their stories are remarkably in keeping with the highly charged aura surrounding Emily's posthumous name. The making of legend is of course unconscious, and though the singularities attributed to Emily may not be accurate in detail, they are probably highly typical of her.

The purpose of this essay is not to discredit the accepted view of Emily Brontë, but to claim, first, that this conception is legendary in nature and so lends itself to diverse interpretations (theories about Emily Brontë are, perhaps, only exceeded in number by theories about Shakespeare). Next, it is intended to consider what was the essence of this legend, the essence which apparently lay concealed from Emily's closest intimates until the last years of her life. The method employed in the following pages is of analysis rather than synthesis, through which it is hoped to promote some fresh thoughts on the subject. The following essay is planned to reconstruct Emily Brontë's life-story exclusively from documents concurrent with the events. The posthumous records will be found to add little in the way of information, although, of course, they enrich any Brontë narrative.

Where Emily Brontë is concerned, the commonest fallacies held are those which attribute the qualities she acquired in the last three or four years of her life, to previous stages in her development. The result of this is that she seems to show no development. She is puzzle enough as it is, but invested with the right attributes at the wrong time it is no wonder that Mr Clement Shorter called her 'the sphinx of our modern literature'.

The tone of these 'afterthoughts' seems to follow Charlotte, whose special attitude after Emily's death prevents her from being a reliable witness to a progressive life-study of Emily. Charlotte, and Mrs Gaskell after her, and Miss Mary Robinson in turn, adopt some of Charlotte's fallacies, the principal being that which takes the last years of Emily's life to represent the whole. Emily was, as we will see, a more forceful proposition at the age of thirty than she was at nineteen. Yet they will have her a silent, morose, orgulous genius at a time when Emily was patently the most buoyant and accommodating member of the family.

For this reason, the following experiment has been undertaken, and for the same reason, of course, makes no claim to be a full or broad account of Emily's career. The narrow way is taken for the purpose of tracing Emily's development. This is supplemented by a general chapter considering some of the special qualities which distinguish Emily Brontë.

The method of interpretation should perhaps be mentioned. Attention is given to the impressions Emily Brontë made on the people she met, particularly during her stay in Brussels, so that by comparing the reactions of her acquaintance, it is possible to deduce something of Emily's state of mind, even though we have no direct references to her feelings. This oblique method of interpretation is not, of course, always called for.

Chapter Two

The Basic Story

The Brontë Parents

Emily Brontë was the fifth of six children – five girls and one boy. Patrick Brontë, her father, was Irish, a clergyman of the Church of England; her mother, Maria Branwell, was Cornish, of modest merchant stock.

Both were evangelically minded, touched by Methodist teaching. At the time of their marriage in 1822, however, the Methodists had been separated from the Established Church for some seventeen years, and while Maria Branwell's relatives appear to have become professing Methodists, her uncle, a Methodist minister at whose home she had met Patrick Brontë, later returned to the Church of England, to which she herself adhered after her marriage.

Patrick Brontë was the son of a poor Protestant farmer and a Catholic mother of County Down. He had earned the friendship of local patrons through whose influence he was able to enter St. John's College, Cambridge. The expenses were variously contributed to by his mother's own savings of seven pounds, an annual grant from benefactors who included William Wilberforce, and the leniency of the College itself. Patrick Brontë fulfilled their hopes, took his degree and was ordained. It is known that while at Cambridge he joined a Home Guard corps, formed to resist a possible French invasion.

Six years later, while holding his fourth curacy at Hartshead, near Dewsbury, he married Maria Branwell. In the previous year he had published his first book *Cottage Poems*, 'chiefly designed for the lower classes of society'; of which a sample:

Once she was gentle, fair and kind,
To no seducing schemes inclined,
Would blush to hear a smutty tale.

There was a second volume the next year. His children loyally carried with them to the grave their private opinion of their father's verse. He next published two prose tales, of similar merit, after which his literary activities are spasmodic.

The mother had no pretensions to authorship, and she did not see the publication of the one essay by her hand which remains to us. It is entitled 'The Advantages of Poverty in Religious Concerns', and in it the author reasserts the traditional blessings of poverty, adding that she is in a position to speak impartially, never having been impoverished herself; she maintains, however, that no respectable person need partake of the blessings of poverty, there being plenty of charitable institutions in England.

Emily Brontë's parents were in no way extraordinary people. The few surviving letters written by her mother to her father during their courtship, reveal an independent woman with a respect for the current proprieties. She considered Patrick Brontë sufficiently expansive to address him on one occasion as her 'Saucy Pat'. In his own letters, written after her death at Haworth Parsonage nine years later, we find a rhetorical style – he was consistently attracted to metaphors of tempest and thunder, combined with ingenuous optimism.

Early Environment

1820–1825

By the time the family moved finally to Haworth, where Patrick Brontë had obtained a perpetual incumbency, Emily was in her second year. Haworth, a village situated on a moorland steep in the West Riding of Yorkshire, was to be the Brontë's home until the last survivor, the father, died there some forty years later. In this gaunt house with a graveyard at the bottom of the garden, all but one of the Brontës died. Facing the broad unchanged moorland prospect, the parsonage still stands, the graveyard still lies. Their characteristics seem inseparably blended; the gravestones leaning awry like so many disused outhouses; and the house itself, a slab-like oblong memorial.

This, then, was the immediate physical environment in which Emily Brontë grew to awareness, with the other Brontë children – Maria, Elizabeth, Charlotte, and Branwell, her seniors; and her younger sister Anne. To these children, death was no hushed-up affair: its outward tokens resided next door, and could be visited through a gate in their own garden wall. The younger children especially – Emily and Anne who were still in babyhood when the family settled at Haworth – were therefore in the enviable position of growing up as conscious of death as they were of life. Whatever Emily Brontë's later preoccupations with the subject of death, the phenomenon itself caused her no bewilderment or wonder; she had never needed to exercise a conscious effort to accept the idea of death and so was free to consider its complex implications with an advanced simplicity which distinguished her attitude from that of contemporary writers.

Emily was cared for by young servant-women from the village during her mother's illness which began shortly after their removal to Haworth, ending with Mrs Brontë's death in September 1821.

In a letter written soon after her death, Patrick Brontë recorded the painful course of his wife's illness, during which time all the children contracted scarlet fever. After their recovery, Miss Branwell, a sister of Mrs Brontë, arrived from Penzance to take charge; and thereafter the young Brontës were in her care. Emily was now aged three.

There is little recorded of Aunt Branwell during her lifetime. So far as we are interested in her influence in the home, it can here be deduced rather from what this admirable woman refrained from doing, than from anything she did or said. We know that she was always referred to by the Brontës with restraint and respect, never with warmth, and on the other hand, never with fear or resentment. In fact, from the earliest references to Aunt Branwell in the children's writings and letters, it seems she was looked upon as 'part of the fittings'.

Miss Branwell was a Methodist, and with the method of Methodism, she organized the household, allotted duties and tasks to the children, and gave them elementary lessons, without any apparent pressure of her will. If there had been any suggestion of tyranny in Aunt Branwell's administration, we may be sure she would have put in a recognizable appearance in the Brontë sisters' novels. She was a woman of small independent means, accustomed to a mild Cornish climate and the sociable interchanges common to Methodists. Her residence, during the next twenty-odd years, in this harsh, isolated northern parish, with the responsibility of six children, was undertaken from a sense of duty. But her sense of duty must have been of an exceptional order. The highest testimony to Miss Branwell's conception of her duty lies in the prolific juvenile writings of Charlotte and her brother Branwell. This juvenilia shows evidence of the abundant freedom of spirit and the leisure to occupy themselves without hindrance, which all the children enjoyed under their Aunt's dominion. It is clear that Miss Branwell's sense of duty included a voluntary self-effacement. She neither imposed herself on the family as a monument of self-sacrifice, nor did she pose as a second mother. To highly advanced children like the Brontës, this was an enormous advantage. Their aunt's restrictions extended no farther than that required for a moderate domestic education. Beyond that they were at liberty to develop along their own lines. Miss Branwell made no emotional demands upon them, the artificiality of which they would easily have detected. Nor does it seem that she made any attempts to pry into their leisure activities. She must have known about the piles of notebooks filled with page after page of close script, of which a hundred-odd have survived. These bear no trace of censorship, nor of having been composed with a weather eye open in the adult direction. The Brontë Aunt, who has received little credit from commentators, gave the Brontës what they most needed, failing the presence of their mother: she represented the principle of practical order. Many years later, Charlotte, when touching her aunt for a loan, reminded her of her practical virtues: 'You always like to use your money to the best advantage; you are not fond of making shabby purchases; when you do confer a favour, it is often done in style. . . .'

As Miss Branwell was a Methodist, her religious influence in the household would certainly introduce a lyrical and fervent note into the Brontës' daily family worship. Differences in practice between Methodism and the Evangelical Anglicanism of their father were not great; the theological issues involved would hardly be apparent where the outward manifestations of these two forms of Christianity were so similar. We learn of no dichotomy between the religious teachings of the father and the aunt, neither of whom were contemplatives, neither of whom were doctrinaire, both of whom had been reared in a Wesleyan tradition.

Towards the beginning of Miss Branwell's stay at Haworth, Mr Brontë proposed marriage to a Miss Burder, a former love, whom he invited to share with him his '*small* but *sweet* little family' on whose 'endearing little ways' he expatiated. Miss Burder bethought her of the fact that she had been spurned by this same Mr Brontë. She did not accept. Her refusal was pronounced in letters vibrating with so much pent-up venom that it seems a mercy for the 'sweet little family' that they were spared her presence at Haworth. There were no further attempts to replace Miss Branwell, whose company Patrick Brontë does not seem to have relished greatly. He took to living in his study, for the most part, but we have the impression that they observed a companionable reserve, making an agreeable and placid household background for the children.

The family were not much involved in the social life of the district, but the spirit of Haworth was borne in to them by many agencies, and must be reckoned as part of the early Brontë environment. The household now included 'Tabby', a Haworth woman who served them up to the last weeks of Charlotte's life. With Tabby, the children enjoyed a warm kitchen-fireside communion, which is implied in their frequent references to her from childhood days onward. It was she, principally, who brought the lore of the countryside to life for them. From their father they heard something of local affairs, although he was most communicative on issues of national politics, a grasp of which the children quickly acquired; imaginatively, they transformed the famous military and parliamentary figures of the newspaper reports into Haworth-inhabiting heroes. Parliamentary debates, expounded by Papa, combined with the peculiar spirit of the population of local hills and wolds, to form new embodiments of fancy. Presently the Brontës were to 'establish' as they called it, their well-known day-dream epics, documented with intense industry. And from these sprang the Gondal dispensation, of which Emily and Anne were the exclusive proprietors. The Gondal invention served Emily as a motivating force for her poems, up to her last years. Gondal has its roots in the locality of Haworth; its nature and traditions were daily insinuated into Emily's infant understanding. She, alone of the Brontës, made use of the most primitive elements thus conveyed to her; the others were more socially and politically minded.

The village and neighbourhood were then recovering from the disruption in local conditions of life caused by the Industrial Revolution. As recently as 1812, unemployment and starvation had been followed by riots and the wrecking of machines in the neighbourhood. By now, the wool trade had passed from the cottages to the factories, but amongst the older people these memories persisted in a general anti-machine feeling. The new generation of mechanics were however, rising in hopeful numbers to seize all opportunities for the new adult-educational movements, embodied in the Mechanics' Institute. It was from the Mechanics' Institute Library at Keighley that the Brontë family borrowed books for their home reading years later.

Haworth had, in the mid-eighteenth century, enjoyed some fame as a sort of showpiece for the Evangelical Revival, spurred by the energy of its pastor, the Rev. William Grimshaw. He transformed the parish and its agricultural neighbourhood by means of thunderings and threats, and claimed to have raised the number of communicants at Haworth Church from twelve to twelve hundred. This militant worthy has been cited as having introduced Methodism to Haworth's Mechanics' Institute. This may well be; he welcomed the Wesleys as preachers in his church. He established a chapel for Methodists in the village, and in fact it was his practice to set up chapels throughout the countryside, so that country people had no excuse for defection. But it should be noted that his support of Methodism preceded the Methodist break with the Established Church. Thereafter, Grimshaw wrote to Charles Wesley, 'The Methodists are no longer members of the Church of England. They are as real a body of Dissenters from her as the Presbyterians, Baptists, Quakers, or any body of Independents. I hereby assure you that I disdain all further and future connection with them'.

Thus, his influence made Haworth a heated centre of a controversy between the Church and the Chapels which was continued during Mr Brontë's career. The combined religious note of Haworth, stemming from this Mr Grimshaw of fervent memory, was strongly evangelical with a puritan tendency. Independence and hard work seem to have been Haworth's prime virtues.

This was the world Emily had come to know by the time she was six years old. The house next door to the graveyard, an orderly, unnoticeable aunt, a Papa secluded in his study or absent on parish work intruding with occasional information about parliamentary feuds, Tabby in the kitchen representing the Haworth Idea in her dialect, her manners, her opinions and her gossipy narratives, a brother and three sisters active in imaginative speculations on all the above items, and one infant sister who was compliant with all suggestions as yet. At the age of six Emily went to school.

Emily's stay at the Clergy Daughters' School at Cowan Bridge was brief. Her two elder sisters, Maria and Elizabeth, contracted illnesses there of which they were brought home to die. Charlotte and Emily were withdrawn. The school was run on the bleak lines associated with nineteenth-century concepts of 'Charity' establishments. The experience left a burning resentment with Charlotte, but Emily has left no token of her impressions. The school record describes her thus: 'Emily Brontë. Entered Nov. 25, 1824. Aged 5 ¾. Reads very prettily and works a little. Left June 1, 1825. Subsequent career, governess.'

1826–1832

> 'Our plays were established; *Young Men*, June, 1826; *Our Fellows*, July 1827; *Islanders*, December 1827. These are our three great plays, that are not kept secret. Emily's and my best plays were established the 1st of December, 1827; The others March, 1828. Best plays mean secret plays; they are very nice ones. All our plays are very strange ones.'

Thus, Charlotte, in 1829; from henceforth she was to be the main family recorder. It is to Charlotte that we have to turn for most of our facts.

Of the 'great plays' established by the Brontë children about a year after the deaths of Maria and Elizabeth, we know a considerable amount. These were, as Charlotte stated, 'not kept secret'. The 'secret' plays were the best plays – those exclusive to herself and Emily, and concealed under so firm a pledge that no trace of them survives, other than this reference. We only know that they were 'very nice ones' and that they share with the not-secret plays, the quality of being 'strange ones'. In these latter, Emily too participated. In her newly assumed role of Brontë biographer, fourteen-year-old Charlotte recalled how, three years past, in 1827, their *Young Men's* play 'took its rise'.

> The *Young Men's* play took its rise from some wooden soldiers Branwell had; *Our Fellows* from Aesop's Fables; and the *Islanders* from several events which happened. I will sketch out the origin of our plays more explicitly if I can. First, *Young Men*. Papa bought Branwell some wooden soldiers at Leeds; when Papa came home it was night, and we were in bed, so next morning Branwell came to our door with a box of soldiers. Emily and I

jumped out of bed, and I snatched up one and exclaimed, 'This is the Duke of Wellington! This shall be the Duke!' When I had said this Emily likewise took one up and said it should be hers; when Anne came down, she said one should be hers. Mine was the prettiest of the whole, and the tallest, and the most perfect in every part. Emily's was a grave-looking fellow, and we called him 'Gravey.' Anne's was a queer little thing, much like herself, and we called him 'Waiting-boy'. Branwell chose his, and called him 'Buonaparte'.

It seems clear that the children did not only record these legendary sagas of their invention, they first enacted them. The stories were conceived and worked out in their playtime; the Brontës' childhood games were really drama in the making. Charlotte, as if perceiving instinctively that the physical scene which accompanied the inception of each play was itself meaningful, elaborates upon the domestic picture once more when she writes her introduction to their *Tales of the Islanders*, which appeared in miniature 'magazine' form.

June the 31st, 1829.

The play of the *Islanders* was formed in December, 1827, in the following manner. One night, about the time when the cold sleet and stormy fogs of November are succeeded by the snow-storms, and high piercing night-winds of confirmed winter, we were all sitting round the warm blazing kitchen fire, having just concluded a quarrel with Tabby concerning the propriety of lighting a candle, from which she came off victorious, no candle having been produced. A long pause succeeded, which was at last broken by Branwell saying, in a lazy manner, 'I don't know what to do.' This was echoed by Emily and Anne.

Tabby. 'Wha ya may go t'bed.'

Branwell. 'I'd rather do anything than that.'

Charlotte. 'Why are you so glum to-night, Tabby? Oh! Suppose we had each an island of our own.'

Branwell. 'If we had I would choose the Island of Man.'

Charlotte. 'And I would choose the Isle of Wight.'

Emily. 'The Isle of Arran for me.'

Anne. 'And mine should be Guernsey.'

We then chose who should be chief men in our islands. Branwell chose John Bull, Astley Cooper, and Leigh Hunt; Emily,

> Walter Scott, Mr. Lockhart, Johnny Lockhart; Anne, Michael Sadler, Lord Bentinck, Sir Henry Halford. I chose the Duke of Wellington and two sons. . . .

And from Charlotte again, we have a third picture of Haworth Parsonage and its inmates, accompanied by many casual curiosities of information which build up, as if by design for posterity, the real background to their fantastic activities. She tells us, in the *History of the Year 1829*,

> While I write this I am in the kitchen of the Parsonage, Haworth; Tabby, the servant, is washing up the breakfast things, and Anne, my youngest sister (Maria was my eldest), is kneeling on a chair, looking at some cakes which Tabby has been baking for us. Emily is in the parlour, brushing the carpet. Papa and Branwell are gone to Keighley. Aunt is upstairs in her room, and I am sitting by the table writing this in the kitchen. Keighley is a small town four miles from here. Papa and Branwell are gone for the newspaper, the *Leeds Intelligencer*, a most-excellent Tory newspaper, edited by Mr. Wood, and the proprietor, Mr. Henneman. We take two and see three newspapers a week. We take the *Leeds Intelligencer*, Tory, and the *Leeds Mercury*, Whig, edited by Mr. Baines, and his brother, son-in-law, and his two sons, Edward and Talbot. We see the *John Bull*; it is a high Tory, very violent. Mr. Driver lends us it, as likewise *Blackwood's Magazine*, the most able periodical there is. The Editor is Mr. Christopher North, an old man seventy-four years of age; the 1st of April is his birthday; his company are Timothy Tickler, Morgan O'Doherty, Macrabin Mordecai, Mullion, Warnell, and James Hogg, a man of most extraordinary genius, a Scottish shepherd. . . .

We see Emily, in the first picture, aged eight years, following the initiative of Branwell and Charlotte. Emily and six-year-old Anne were subordinates. Allowing for the fact that this account was written by Charlotte who would understandably portray herself in a leading light, it seems reasonable to conclude that Emily had not yet begun to make much impression on the family. Charlotte, besides being the eldest, was evidently the most precocious and leader-like of the Brontës; she had more power of endurance than Branwell, who was, at this time, respected equally with Charlotte as an elder by the two younger girls. When eventually Emily does begin slightly to assert her presence, it is never as a leader; she is seen in varying stages of separation from the rest of her family. From the episode of the toy soldiers we can deduce no more than that she preferred a 'grave-looking fellow' to any other among these wooden heroes.

By the next year, 1827, Emily has become co-equal with Charlotte in one respect: in the 'secret', or 'best' plays. That they were kept secret was possibly Emily's own provision, since at this time Charlotte appears eager to make known all her inventions to the other children. In December of the same year, in the scene which led to the inauguration of their play, *Islanders*, Emily is depicted still as following the lead of Charlotte and Branwell.

Their Tory heroes were derived from their father's enthusiasms. We learn from Charlotte's girlhood narrative how the children would gather round him while he read out the reports on occasions of important parliamentary debates. Branwell's choice of Leigh Hunt as one of his literary heroes was more recherché than Emily's Sir Walter Scott. Scott was, in fact, a constant favourite with the Brontës; next year they received a copy of his *Tales of a Grandfather*, inscribed 'to her dear little nephew and nieces' from Miss Branwell. *The Lay of the Last Minstrel* was amongst their father's books, to which the children had access. It was from these plays that the 'Angrian' sequence later took shape; as also the independent 'Gondal' narrative of Emily and Anne.

The last-quoted account by Charlotte offers a different picture of their home; this is an active morning scene, everyone is doing something. Of eleven-year-old Emily, we know only that she was brushing the carpet in the parlour. We see Emily during her childhood through an elder sister's eyes, where she is naturally given a secondary position. But it is clear from Charlotte's accounts that no one at this time considered Emily remarkable, and we may take it that her qualities were as yet not too distinct from those of this whole remarkable family.

Charlotte's absence at school – a Miss Wooler's establishment at Roe Head near Dewsbury – left Emily and Anne to develop a closer intimacy. Branwell, whose status as the only son and whose obvious cleverness had earned him some deference from the girls, was not inclined to co-operate with the two younger sisters. Gondal was founded about this time; Emily and Anne were regarded, at first, as a rebel faction of the official body which was centred at

'Glass Town', a scene of fabulous high-society activity. Gradually Gondal became accepted as an independent unit. And on Charlotte's return in the summer, Angria was initiated under the joint management of herself and Branwell, continuing on the more orthodox lines already set forth in the 'Glass Town' narrative.

Gondal (of which no early narratives survive) seems to have differed from Angria in its more legendary characteristics even at this early stage of its development. Angria is nearer to social fantasy, with direct or implicit reference, always to the world of contemporary politics. Angria was much more civilized. Gondal was a northern island territory in the North Pacific; there, the characters enacted their near-archetypal feuds, loyalties, loves, treacheries, slaughters, and what was worse, imprisonments. From the Gondal poems of Emily and Anne – those written when they were grown women – this mythological scene appears peopled with medieval characters nourishing primitive passions: a compound as of Scott and Homer. It may be that Gondal was an offshoot of those 'best' and 'secret' plays which, Charlotte tells us, she was sharing with Emily in 1827.

A list of Gondal place names is given by Anne; she jotted them down at the back of a geography book which the girls had presumably consulted for the purpose, if not of accuracy, of stirring up the imagination. The names recur in the surviving adult poems of Emily and Anne:

> Alexandia, a kingdom in Gaaldine.
> Almedore, a kingdom in Gaaldine.
> Elseraden, a kingdom in Gaaldine.
> Gaaldine, a large Island newly discovered in the South Pacific.
> Gondal, a large Island in the North Pacific.
> Regina, the capitol of Gondal.
> Ula, a kingdom in Gaaldine, governed by 4 Sovereigns.
> Zelona, a kingdom in Gaaldine.
> Zedora, a large Provence in Gaaldine, governed by a Viceroy.

Apart from the few months she spent at school as an infant, Emily's education had comprised her aunt's instruction in general and domestic rudiments, religious instruction from both her aunt and her father, self-instruction from her father's library, information gathered from her brother and sisters, and her personal observations. It was not a formal or in any way organized education, but it was not considered inadequate by current standards, nor can we possibly presume to judge otherwise. Charlotte, an avid thirster for knowledge, seems to have hankered after formal schooling; but from Emily, we get the opposite impression. We cannot say that her instinct in this matter was wrong. When Charlotte left Roe Head, she undertook the further instruction of Emily and Anne, aged 14 and 12 respectively. 'In the mornings from 9 o'clock to half-past 12, I instruct my sisters and draw, then we walk till dinner,' writes Charlotte to her schoolfellow Ellen Nussey. At about the same time, this sober routine was enlivened by the visits of a drawing master from Leeds, who encouraged the family's high hopes of Branwell as an artist; and of a music master from Keighley.

1833–1840

At Roe Head School Charlotte had formed her lifelong friendship with Ellen Nussey; Charlotte's letters to Ellen form the bulk source for biographical information. From these letters we obtain an enormous amount of useful facts; and also some sidelights on the characters of her brother and sisters, in employing which, we must try to judge from the context which of her statements represent an opinion or bias of Charlotte's own, and which stand for the view accepted by the whole family. The fact that she mentions Emily very infrequently amongst some hundreds of letters written during her sister's lifetime, does not necessarily mean that Emily appeared insignificant to those who knew her; but it does show that Emily had no *particular* significance within the family circle; otherwise, it would have been in keeping with Charlotte's dramatic nature to emphasize the fact.

With these reservations in mind, and remembering that Charlotte was always, to some extent, the spokesman of the family, we may find her references to Emily useful for the factual data they supply, or for the suggestions they supply towards a reconstruction of Emily Brontë in her earlier years. These considerations have been mentioned because it has often been the case with writers on Emily Brontë, that, faced with a lack of biographical documents by her own hand, and with a paucity of day-to-day comment upon her, they have seized upon every chance reference to make of it an event of luminous significance.

Ellen Nussey paid a visit to Haworth in the summer of 1833, the first of a series of visits of which she has left some interesting accounts, and which, since they were written long after Emily's death, are excluded from this narrative. If her opinion of Emily was expressed at the time, it is not recorded, but shortly after Ellen's departure Charlotte quotes Emily and Anne as saying 'they never saw anyone they liked so well as Miss Nussey'. This compliment seems quite sincere; indeed Emily and Anne hardly saw any new faces at all, and Ellen Nussey reveals herself always as an 'amiable' person, as her friends said of her. It is customary to describe Emily, even at this stage of her career, as a reserved, silent, scornful genius. An ordinary sociable girl like Ellen Nussey, it is assumed, would secretly appal Emily. There is no hint of such a situation in any of the correspondence between Charlotte and Ellen. Emily, at fifteen, is no morose misanthropist; she is normally capable of liking people, and she much liked Ellen; Charlotte was not given to expressing excessive flattery.

Anne and Emily continued to study under Charlotte's tutelage for the next two years. Meanwhile we have one autobiographical statement written in November 1834. It is set down in Emily's script, on behalf of herself and Anne.

> I fed Rainbow, Diamond, Snowflake, Jasper Pheasant (alias).
>
> This morning Branwell went down to Mr. Driver's and brought news that Sir Robert Peel was going to be invited to stand for Leeds. Anne and I have been peeling apples for Charlotte to make a pudding and for Aunt's . . . Charlotte said she made puddings perfectly and she . . . of quick but limited intellect. Tabby said just now Come Anne pilloputate (i.e., pill a potate). Aunt has come into the kitchen just now and said Where are your feet Ann Anne answered On the floor Aunt. Papa opened the parlour door and gave Branwell a letter saying Here Branwell read this and show it to your Aunt and Charlotte. The Gondals are discovering the interior of Gaaldine. Sally Mosely is washing in the back kitchin.
>
> It is past twelve o'clock Anne and I have not tided ourselves done our bed work, or done our lessons and we want to go out to play. We are going to have for dinner Boiled Beef, Turnips, potatoes and apple pudding. The kitchin is in a very untidy state. Anne and I have not our music lesson which consists of a *b major* Taby said on my putting a pen in her face Ya pitter pottering there instead of pilling a potate. I answered O dear, O dear I will

> derectly With that I get up, take a knife and begin pilling. Finished pilling the potatoes Papa going to walk Mr. Sunderland expected.
>
> Anne and I say I wonder what we shall be like and what we shall be and where we shall be if all goes well, in the year 1874 – in which year I shall be in my 57th year. Anne will be in her 55th year Branwell will be going on in his 58th year and Charlotte in her 59th year. Hoping we shall all be well at that time. We close our paper.
>
> Emily and Anne.

Anne's contribution to this production is a drawing of a lock of hair, described: 'A bit of Lady Juliet's hair done by Anne.'

What does this interesting document reveal? It has been much adapted for the purpose of revelation. We learn something about Emily's daily activities; we can infer something of her personal disposition towards the household; we can gather what some of her habits were, and also the degree of general tolerance which prevailed at Haworth. We also get an insight into Emily's power of expressing herself, in her seventeenth year: her mental equipment, her intelligence.

Taking the composition, first, as a means of assessing Emily's intellectual ability, it surely is not a remarkable composition for a girl of sixteen; and those who say it is, may possibly have in mind the 'great navigator' of M. Héger's posthumous description. In fact, it strikes the present writer as being rather backward in expression; and this, in view of the undoubted genius which Emily displayed at a later date, is an interesting discovery.

It is not only a matter of punctuation and spelling; there is a note of childishness running through the whole piece. It is in no way organized; not anything like so accomplished as are Charlotte's compositions (previously quoted) written at the age of thirteen. Emily's commentary on what is going on before her eyes is, of course, charming to all who enjoy close-up portrayals of the Brontë scene. Had it been set down purposely for the benefit of readers of Brontë biography, the thing would be almost too clever to be true; it has all the requisite 'atmosphere'. The narrative gives the same ingenuous illogical string of incidents, all in one breath, without any suggestion of a discriminative sense, that a lively child of ten might deliver. 'The Gondals are discovering the interior of Gaaldine. Sally Mosely is washing in the back kitchin.' Were these two items of equal value to Emily? Perhaps they were. Maybe it was as vital, to her mind, that Sally Mosely's wash-day should be celebrated, as the latest Gondal developments. On the other hand, we have heard of Gondal before, and will hear of it again, in Emily's scheme of things; Sally Mosely enjoys no further fame.

It is true that an advanced sense of mimicry emerges from her description of Tabby's dialect speech: this was a trick, also, of Charlotte, and the speculations concerning the far future date 1874 present signs of sophistication. On the whole, however, the piece is enjoyably juvenile; few schoolgirls of sixteen could ever have written anything so enjoyable or so childish. If this is so, it might have some bearing on the nature of genius; so far as Emily is concerned, we must observe, as no doubt had her family, that she was in many ways young for her years. But we must not forget that the very fact that she felt compelled to make even this voluntary record – one which possessed no function, like, for instance, a letter; one which for practical purposes was quite useless – in this she was old for her age, in common with the rest of the Brontës.

The information contained in this paper tells us much about the conditions in which the Brontës came to maturity. We get the impression of a warm slapdash harmony; a close intimacy between Emily and Anne. Tabby's invitations to lend a hand with the potatoes are repeatedly ignored. Aunt Branwell urges Anne to get up and do something; Anne cheeks back, but Aunt doesn't bother, she is already occupied elsewhere. Papa presents a letter to Branwell which is to be shared with Charlotte and Aunt, the Elders. The 'kitchin' is untidy, and so are Emily and Anne, whose daily duties are disclosed by the list of those not yet done. Nothing seems to have been 'done', in fact, except the feeding of their pet pheasant of four-fold 'alias'. Emily's attitude to everyone and everything concerned shows a genial satisfaction with life. It represents one day in an ocean of years; she may have been in uncommonly good spirits on this one day; on the other hand, this random piece might be taken, as is more likely, for an account of an average day in Emily Brontë's girlhood.

Charlotte, in a satirical Branwell-baiting story, gives his alleged opinions of his sisters at this time – 'miserable silly creatures not worth talking about. Charlotte's eighteen years old, a broad dumpy thing, whose head does not come higher than my elbow. Emily's sixteen, lean and scant, with a face about the size of a penny, and Anne is nothing, absolutely nothing'. Exaggerated, of course, for

Charlotte's purpose. Emily's leanness is in keeping with all accounts; it is Anne's being 'nothing' which deserves attention. This sentiment was a more or less lifelong conviction, not only of Branwell, but of Charlotte, who always tended to demote Anne's personality and talent. However, there is abundant evidence to show that Anne had a tenacious will and a good mind. She was far from being 'nothing' to Emily; in fact, she came closer to Emily than any other person ever did.

In July 1835, Charlotte announced, 'We are all about to divide, break up, separate. Emily is going to school, Branwell is going to London, and I am going to be a governess'. Charlotte was to return to Roe Head as a teacher, and there, too, Emily was entering as a pupil.

Neither cared for the idea, for Charlotte adds, 'Emily and I leave home on the 29th of this month; the idea of being together consoles us both somewhat'. Now that Branwell, off to London to enrol in the Royal Academy, seemed to be about to make his way in the world, the time had come for the girls to consider their future livelihood. The only suitable occupation open to them was teaching. Charlotte had had her schooling, she was equipped for the job. As for Emily, she would have to go to school first, in order to become a governess later. So it was planned. They left in July, and by November Emily was back at Haworth. Anne took her place at Roe Head. Branwell's hopes failed.

It was said after Emily's death, notably by Charlotte, and reaffirmed by Mrs Gaskell, that the trouble with Emily was homesickness. It is curious that no mention was made of Emily's distress at the time; it may be that Charlotte entertained some fears concerning her sister's future, which she would not reveal. How would Emily support herself when their father should die, and Haworth Parsonage be no longer their home? Some sort of systematic learning seemed necessary. But there was no further attempt to send Emily to school.

Her first extant poems date from the following year. She may possibly have destroyed her earlier pieces before she died; this is more likely than that they were destroyed by Charlotte or any other member of the household, as some suggest; both because Emily showed a strong proprietary interest in the disposition of her work, and because there is no evident reason why, had they destroyed anything at all, her executors should have chosen to destroy everything up to this particular year, and to preserve so much subsequent unfinished work. (Many of her poems are simply fragments put down as a poet's working notes.)

From 1836 forward we have, in her poems, the material for some insight into Emily Brontë's mind; and yet we have not. In the first place, some of the poems are composed for the specific requirements of the Gondal epic which was in constant process of elaboration by herself and Anne. It has been usual to assume that, from the first, Emily dominated Anne in the Gondal transactions. There is no evidence to support this. The only direct evidence of the attitude of Emily to Anne, and of Anne to Emily, comes in the secret papers they addressed to each other. These papers, as we shall see, do not suggest that Emily was the dominant party. That she was the superior poet is true. But in matters of collaboration, it is not always the superior partner who leads, organizes and directs the proceeding.

There seems to have been a mutual interchange between the two sisters on sufficiently loose a basis to allow each some freedom of individual expression. All the same, neither was entirely free; the demands of Gondal's development and action imposed on their Gondal work certain limits from which, as individual writers, they were free. So far as action was concerned, we do not know exactly what was Emily's contribution, and what Anne's, to the Gondal story. We only know which of the Gondal poems was produced individually by the sisters. The attitude and substance of these poems might have been pre-arranged by both partners.

Therefore it is impossible to assume, in Emily's Gondal pieces, any disposition of mind which would have a reliable bearing on her general outlook; it is true we may, from the point of view of literary criticism, declare that this or that poem is pantheistic in its philosophy, or mystical in tone. But we cannot, so far as the Gondal work is concerned, deduce that Emily was a pantheist or a mystic at the date of composition. If she had been the sole creator of Gondal, we would be able to reconstruct Emily's personal frame of mind much better. For even her 'personal' poems, from which she herself separated her Gondal pieces, are touched with Gondal heroics. The personal poems have, on the whole, nothing like the fullness of poetic *intention* which the Gondal productions convey. In fact, Emily appears at her most vital in the Gondal poems; we can truly judge these as her poems, but not as pure manifestations of her thought. The action of Gondal was the dominating factor, and this was devised only in part by herself, so far as we know.

Nor can we assume that each partner's contribution was made without previous consultation – that, in other words, the poems themselves dictated the pattern of Gondal events. It is unlikely that such a haphazard arrangement could have produced the organic results which even the fragmentary evidence of the extant poems discloses.

These are the particular dangers in adducing evidence from Emily Brontë's poems towards reconstructing her state of mind at any given time. Still less could one safely trace outward events of her life in them. For, apart from present considerations, few poets can be said to have experienced the physical or psychological events portrayed during the precise month or year in which a particular poem was composed. Years may go by before actual events emerge in a poem. No poem by Emily Brontë can possibly tell us whether in 1836 she was unhappy; in 1838, bitter; in 1840, transported with mystic joy. We cannot tell the date on which these emotions stirred within her; we only know the month and year on which her poems were completed (for she has recorded the dates); from this we can tell only that on those particular dates she was neither overwhelmed with despair nor in the transports of mystical rapture; she was absorbed in writing a poem about despair or rapture, as it may be. Such complete absorption in work is what most poets would describe as happiness whether it lasts a whole afternoon, several days, or half an hour. Only in the retrospect of her completed life's work, can we make deductions as to the philosophical bias of Emily Brontë's mind. We can then see the bent of her thought as it mastered the Gondal epic. For the present, we see her poems, month by month, in the contrary position of being in subjection to Gondal.

It is not proposed, therefore, to use Emily's poems as a biographical source. It is legitimate, however, to consider the implications of the fact of her poems' existence. This fact means that there were few periods in her life, especially from 1836 onwards, when she was not deeply engaged in her work. If her poems cause us to speculate that she had suffered greatly, had been frustrated in the most ardent longings of her spirit, had been many times melancholy, we do also know quite definitely that there were many and frequent intervals of happiness, on the occasions when she was practising her art. And since we can see the influence of other poets in her work, we must also recognize the fact that she had been happily reading these poets on many occasions. That she was seldom hilarious does not mean that she was often mournful.

Of course, some of her working hours yielded unsatisfactory results, as we know from the results themselves, and from an early hint contained in her comment, written underneath a poem: 'I am more terrifically and idiotically STUPID – than ever I was in the whole course of my incarnate existence. The above precious lines are the fruits of one hour's most agonizing labour between ½ past 6 and ½ past 7 in the evening of July – 1836.'

We may assume from this that she took her work seriously, as a vocation, something worth labouring at. She appears to have learned later not to force poems which showed signs of fruitlessness; not to try always to salvage something for her labours; instead, she simply left the poem unfinished.

Emily made no effort to gain public recognition. Branwell had been submitting his work, with more and more forcefulness, to *Blackwood's Magazine*. Charlotte sent a specimen of her prose to Southey, from whom she got a kind answer, advising her to forgo the career of letters. Emily's anxieties were not towards the publication but the perfecting of her work.

Charlotte was still teaching at Miss Wooler's school, now moved to Dewsbury Moor, when, in the October of 1837, she wrote, 'My sister Emily is gone into a situation as teacher in a large school of near forty pupils, near Halifax. I had had one letter from her since her departure; it gives an appalling account of her duties – hard labour from six in the morning until near eleven at night, with only one half-hour of exercise between.'

In later years it was said that Emily endured her teaching enterprise at Law Hill School for six months, and returned once more, homesick. As with her departure from Roe Head, there is complete silence in Charlotte's letters about Emily's further experiences at Law Hill, and her return. As nothing more is spoken of Emily until mid-1839, it has been suggested that she was at Law Hill for as long as eighteen months. The earliest authorities, however, agree on the period of six months, for the harrowing experience described by Emily, as Charlotte transmits it. Emily's first letter to Charlotte was probably her way of giving notice of her impending return. It may be that her duties were described with complete accuracy; or perhaps some excess of loathing of the work forced Emily to a poetic excess in order to hint her desire to be advised to leave. Either way, she deserves equal sympathy. 'Hard labour from six in the morning until near eleven at night' may be decoded into 'I am altogether unfit for this sort of work. I don't take to routine. I wish to get out of it' (especially remembering Emily's exaggerated phrase, 'agonizing labour' to describe an hour's difficulty with a poem). If it is true that Emily only had half an hour's exercise between rising and retiring, she must have written her poems in her daily half-hours; for during her first three months' stay there, she wrote fourteen poems, some of them her longest pieces; whereas, during the previous nine months of that year, at Haworth, she had written only twenty poems. Law Hill, therefore, increased Emily's incentive to write. This may imply that she was so miserable that she took her only escape in the practice of poetry. But it cannot be said to imply that she had less leisure there than she enjoyed at home. Poems so complete as those which Emily wrote at this period, are unlikely to have been composed in a half-hour's break in a seventeen-hour working day. And unless we prefer to enchant ourselves with a picture of Emily working at her poems far into the night, by the dim light of an ever-sinking tallow, at the top of a sleeping schoolhouse, we might, perhaps, take Emily's 'appalling account' with moderation.

She returned home, as she desired. The family perhaps understood that Emily was queer about going from home. It is unlikely that she herself felt any sense of personal failure; she applied herself to painting some of her pets. Her poems continued to absorb her, and began to develop into maturity during 1838. There is a possibility that Emily was content to play the queer sister, so long as she was left in peace. On the other hand any assumption of her eccentricity at this time is purely speculative, if we are to suspend full reliance on Charlotte's memory. At present, Charlotte's ambitions for the family do not seem to have troubled Emily, who did not share them.

In the spring of 1839 Charlotte and Anne took their first situations as private governesses, Charlotte having had some temporary frictions with her old employer, Miss Wooler. Anne expressed herself 'very well satisfied' with her employer in spite of difficulties in managing the children. Charlotte, however, discovered that working for a friendly headmistress of a girls' school, and being employed by a stranger in a private house, were very different propositions. She complained bitterly to Emily, in a letter addressing her as 'Dearest Lavinia', about the trials of her new life. 'I see now more clearly than I have ever done before that a private governess has no existence, is not considered as a living and rational being except as connected with the wearisome duties she has to fulfil' wrote Charlotte. Perhaps this was the very point Emily had made when she decided Law Hill was not for her; Charlotte was only now realizing the truth of the matter.

1840–1842

The arrival of a gay and charming curate, William Weightman, at Haworth, caused a flutter of high spirits amongst the girls. He was attentive to all, including Ellen Nussey on her visits to Haworth. Charlotte, with the authority of one who had already refused two clergymen in marriage, made much game of him. Amongst themselves, the girls referred to this young gallant as 'Miss Celia Amelia, sometimes merely 'Miss Weightman'. He despatched valentines to all of them, and made himself pleasant to other female hearts in the countryside as well. While on holiday, he would send large consignments of game to the parsonage. Only Anne seems to have taken him seriously; he was observed by Charlotte to be glancing and sighing in Anne's direction, one day in church. Emily's nickname 'The Major' was subsequently explained as having originated in a walk she took with Weightman and Ellen Nussey, when Emily walked protectively between the two. There is no question of Emily having need of protection from William Weightman, nor he from her. Although her work is constantly concerned with the subject of love, she had no realistic conception of it. We get no clue from her work that she ever experienced a love affair, far less that she ever entertained amorous feelings for a living person; love is a conceptual though passionate emotion in Emily Brontë's work. In contemporary reports, there is no indication of her falling in love with anyone; moreover, there is no sign that, merely lacking the opportunity of meeting men, she did not fall in love. She does not appear to have needed any object of amorous or sexual attention. That is not to say that she was without passion, but to say that passion in her was not focused towards attachments to her fellow men. In other words, she appears to have been a born celibate, about which condition, as it applies to Emily, fuller comment will be made in the latter part of this essay.

For Emily, alone with her aunt and father, housework and leisure to think and write were the daily fulfilments. Charlotte and Anne were rarely at Haworth during the next two years. Branwell had taken and lost a job as a tutor. While at Haworth he was not much in the house; he met his friends at the local inn. Presently, he left home again, having obtained a job as a clerk on the railroad. Charlotte and Anne changed their jobs but were little happier. 'We are all separated now', Charlotte informs one of her former suitors, Henry Nussey, 'and winning our bread amongst strangers as we can – my sister Anne is near York, my brother in a situation near Halifax, I am here (Rawdon, in the Leeds vicinity). Emily is the only one left at home, where her usefulness and willingness make her indispensible.'

If Emily made herself indispensable at home, this reveals not only her wisdom, but a true enjoyment of manual work in the familiar ease of her home. She was wise, because she safeguarded herself in this way from being uprooted. Both Charlotte and later, Anne, make a point of expressing Emily's household usefulness, as if to silence criticism, and to reassure themselves that Emily was not shirking at home while her sisters slaved for strangers.

Charlotte, Branwell and Anne all possessed, in some measure, a desire to get on in the world. Their literary work was, to them, but half-fulfilled if it remained unheard of outside the family. In 1840 Charlotte had submitted work to Wordsworth who had replied in a tone which provoked a saucy retort from her. Branwell had got so far in his endeavours as to have spent a day at Ambleside on the invitation of Hartley Coleridge. But these two Brontës were dissatisfied with any advice or response, however sanguine, however courteous, so long as it led nowhere in terms of publication. In reality, they submitted their work not for critical consideration, but for approval. Charlotte especially took no notice of any man of letters who advised her to stop writing; and she proved right.

Emily was not without ambition; if this had been so, her acquiescence in the common lot of clergymen's spinster daughters would have been more noticeable. She would have resigned herself to the necessity of taking a job as a governess. But her apparent listlessness, her willingness to be the useful stay-at-home, concealed a determined resistance to any attempt to make her useful elsewhere. This fact seems to have been tacitly assumed by her family. The cause of this strong preference for home life in Emily seems at first sight explicable in terms of Charlotte's posthumous statement to the effect that Emily was passionately attached to the moors around her home, and spent a great deal of her solitude in their familiar embrace; away from the moors, Emily pined; Haworth drew back the ailing homesick girl like a magnet. Whether this was wholly the case is a question which now becomes prominent. So far we have observed from the current data that Emily had been evidently dissatisfied with her life at Miss Wooler's school and at Law Hill school, and was now fairly satisfied with her life at Haworth.

It should be noted that Emily had been from home during her childhood on two previous occasions: once at Cowan Bridge where the school records suggest only that the authorities were pleased with her; there is no word from Charlotte, in all her later commentary on the Cowan Bridge episode, that her infant sister Emily was pining for home. Again, Emily had, at the age of ten, spent a holiday with Charlotte, Branwell and Anne, at the home of their great-uncle John Fennell. From there, Charlotte wrote home to tell of the drawings executed by all four children; there is no suggestion that Emily was pining.

It may be, then, that the irresistible call of the Haworth moorland did not affect Emily until she was past childhood. If this is so, we should expect to find stubborn resistance from Emily to a proposition put forward in July 1841, while Charlotte was home on vacation, which would entail leaving Haworth. 'There is a project hatching in this house', writes Charlotte to Ellen Nussey, 'which both Emily and I anxiously wish to discuss with you . . . Papa and aunt talk, by fits and starts, of our – *id est*, Emily, Anne, and myself – commencing a school.' Their aunt had offered to lend them the capital, to Charlotte's surprise. She goes on to discuss the many details of their plan. 'Aunt Branwell might go as far as £150; would it be possible to establish a respectable (not by any means a *showy*) school and to commence housekeeping with a capital of only that amount?' Then, the question of where the school should be. Charlotte had thought of the neighbourhood of Burlington as offering some scope for their project. 'This is, of course,' she added, 'a perfectly crude and random idea . . . We have no connections, no acquaintances there; it is far from here, etc. . . .'

We learn, then, that Emily was far from troubled about the prospect of leaving Haworth to start a school with her sisters. Charlotte says that like herself, Emily was 'anxious to discuss' the plan with Ellen. And from the arguments propounded in Charlotte's letter, we may assume that the project had been the subject of much discussion at the Parsonage, without any personal objections from Emily. But we also have Emily's own testimony of her reactions to this proposal. This comes in one of her 'birthday papers'.

There was an arrangement between Emily and Anne that each should write a personal reminiscence every few years on Emily's birthday; these papers were opened in a later year. Of these interesting compositions, only four remain – two by Emily and two by Anne. These were intentionally private communications; it is unlikely that anyone but the two sisters concerned was aware of this pleasant habit. Here is Emily's contribution for the year 1841.

A PAPER to be opened
when Anne is
25 years old,
or my next birthday after
if
all be well.
Emily Jane Brontë. July the 30th, 1841.

It is Friday evening, near 9 o'clock – wild rainy weather. I am seated in the dining-room, having just concluded tidying our desk boxes, writing this document. Papa is in the parlour – aunt upstairs in her room. She has been reading *Blackwood's Magazine* to papa. Victoria and Adelaide are ensconced in the peat-house. Keeper is in the kitchen – Hero in his cage. We are all stout and hearty, as I hope is the case with Charlotte, Branwell, and Anne, of whom the first is at John White, Esq., Upperwood House, Rawdon; the second is at Luddenden Foot; and the third is, I believe, at Scarborough, inditing perhaps a paper corresponding to this.

A scheme is at present in agitation for setting us up in a school of our own; as yet nothing is determined, but I hope and trust it may go on and prosper and answer our highest expectations. This day four years I wonder whether we shall still be dragging on in our present condition or established to our hearts' content. Time will show.

I guess that at the time appointed for the opening of this paper we i.e. Charlotte, Anne, and I, shall be all merrily seated in our own sitting-room in some pleasant flourishing seminary, having just gathered in for the midsummer lady-day. Our debts will be paid off, and we shall have cash in hand to a considerable amount. Papa, aunt, and Branwell will either have been or be coming to visit us. It will be a fine warm summer evening, very different from this bleak look-out, and Anne and I will perchance

> slip out into the garden for a few minutes to peruse our papers. I hope either this or something better will be the case.
>
> The *Gondaland* are at present in a threatening state, but there is no open rupture as yet. All the princes and princesses of the Royalty are at the Palace of Instruction. I have a good many books on hand, but I am sorry to say that as usual I make small progress with any. However, I have just made a new regularity paper! and I must *verb sap* to do great things. And now I close, sending from far an exhortation of courage, boys! courage, to exiled and harassed Anne, wishing she was here.

Emily was now twenty-three. She has had practice in prose as well as verse. Her 'paper', though not impressive in its style, is adequately framed. Had we no more than this to go by, Emily appears to be all right with the world. She is perfectly normal in tone, as she mentions each member of the family, their plans and prospects. It has not, indeed, so far been hinted in the current Brontë correspondence that Emily was anything but a normal, contented young woman. In addition, we know from the poems that she was highly gifted. Charlotte had no access to the poems as yet.

Emily had every reason for satisfaction, even for the buoyancy of spirit which her birthday note suggests. Her literary work has been making progress. Her verse prospers; the Gondal narrative continues; ('I have a good many books on hand . . .' is a reference to the Gondal 'volumes', also referred to, below, by Anne), the epic of Gondal is generally flourishing. The relationship of Emily Brontë to her work at this stage is not one of interwoven identity. There seems little similarity between the tragic mood of her recent poems, with their stress on themes of death, remorse, revenge, imprisonment, and the mood of personal well being which Emily conveys in her birthday note. The poems which took their place in the prose narrative of Gondal would be seen by Anne, as well as the birthday paper, and so it is not a question of Emily concealing the true state of her mind in her personal memorandum whilst revealing it in the poems. The most simple and obvious explanation of the striking contrast which exists between the tone of Emily's creative work, and that of her personal statement, is that her writings were, at this time, more objectively conceived than they appear to be. The Augusta, the Julius, the Douglas, and all the rest of Gondal's characters are not subjective variants on Emily Brontë herself because the biographical evidence shows otherwise; and also, for the reason already mentioned that the Gondal characters were not Emily's sole creation. And those poems which do not come into the Gondal category also apparently partake of poetic, not personal and actual, experience at this date. Poetic experience is, however, such that it may be prophetic; it may express a real tendency present in the poet's mind as one of many potentialities. Thus, Emily's lines written a few days before her birthday note,

> I see around me tombstones grey
> Stretching their shadows far away.
> Beneath the turf my footsteps tread
> Lie low and lone the silent dead;
> Beneath the turf, beneath the mould –
> Forever dark, forever cold,
> And my eyes cannot hold the tears
> That memory hoards from vanished years;
> For Time and Death and Mortal pain
> Gives wounds that will not heal again.
> Let me remember half the woe
> I've seen and heard and felt below,
> And Heaven itself, so pure and blest,
> Could never give my spirit rest. . . .

These lines may be said to prefigure a possible development in Emily Brontë's thought, but they do not furnish a picture of her mind to supplement that of her autobiographical birthday note. Both were written in July 1841; but the poem belongs to the realm of potential experience: it tells us only that in July 1841, Emily Brontë *had it in her* to suffer greatly from memories of horror; it does not tell us that she already bore those memories. The autobiographical fragment, on the other hand, expresses what we are concerned with at this point: Emily's state of mind in July 1841.

She was satisfied because she was fulfilling her innate will to write. Had the school project threatened her literary activity, we may suppose she would have resisted it. As she would be working together with her own accustomed kin, this fear did not present itself: they knew each other's ways. If she had suffered from a serious dread of being away from Haworth, she would not have embraced the scheme with the words 'I hope and trust it may go on and prosper and answer our highest expectations'. She acknowledged the fact that the present arrangement was unsatisfactory, with Charlotte and Anne miserably situated in private employment, herself with no provision for earning her living after their father's death. 'This day four years' she writes, anticipating the time when the paper should be opened, 'I wonder whether we shall still be dragging on in our present condition or established to our hearts' content.' She allows herself to speculate on the delightful possibilities, should the scheme come to fruition. She allows herself a guess: 'all merrily seated in our own sitting-room in some pleasant and flourishing seminary, having just gathered in for the mid-summer lady-day'.

As for the moors from which, it has been told, she could never tear herself away, Emily does not here repine them. Instead, she is concerned with something quite as important to a practitioner of the art of letters: cash. They would have paid off their debts and possess also a considerable sum in hand. Money meant leisure; freedom from the pressure of uncongenial work, freedom to pursue a vocation. It meant freedom for the sisters to sit merrily together in a pleasant room. She does not seem to realize that she is supposed to be passionately devoted to the Haworth scene; she is busy anticipating the luxuries in store, 'this day four years'. Will she not be homesick for the moors? We are not told that the thought occurred to her. 'It will be a fine warm summer evening,' she declares, 'very different from this bleak look-out. . . .' Emily adds her hope that 'this or something better will be the case'.

The spirit of the document is one of sensitive optimism. Everyone at home is 'stout and hearty' including herself; she has drawn up a new worksheet to get herself out of the difficulty of having too many fragments in hand; she has high hopes for getting work done; and she wishes only for the company of Anne.

This was true. Anne's paper is pitched on a more sober key. She writes from her employers' holiday residence in Scarborough, 'I dislike the situation and wish to change it for another'. Her hopes for the future were not therefore nourished by a present sense of well being, as with Emily. Anne records the school plan without enthusiasm:

> We are thinking of setting up a school of our own, but nothing definite is settled about it yet, and we do not know whether we shall be able to or not. I hope we shall. And I wonder what will

be our condition and how or where we shall all be on this day four years hence; at which time, if all be well, I shall be 25 years and 6 months old, Emily will be 27 years old, Branwell 28 years and 1 month, and Charlotte 29 years and a quarter. We are now all separate and not likely to meet again for many a weary week, but we are none of us ill that I know of, and all are doing something for our own livelihood except Emily, who, however, is as busy as any of us, and in reality earns her food and raiment as much as we do.

How little know we what we are
How less what we may be!

Four years ago I was at school. Since then I have been a governess at Blake Hill, left it, come to Thorp Green, and seen the sea and York Minster. Emily has been a teacher at Miss Patchet's school, and left it. Charlotte has left Miss Wooler's, been a governess at Mrs. Sidgwick's, left her, and gone to Mrs. White's. Branwell has given up painting, been a tutor in Cumberland, left it, and become a clerk on the railroad. Tabby has left us, Martha Brown has come in her place. We have got Keeper, got a sweet little cat and lost it, and also got a hawk. Got a wild goose which has flown away, and three tame ones, one of which has been killed. All these diversities, with many others, are things we did not expect or foresee in the July of 1837. What will the next four years bring forth? Providence only knows. But we ourselves have sustained very little alteration since that time. I have the same faults that I had then, only I have more wisdom and experience, and a little more self-possession than I then enjoyed. How will it be when we open this paper and the one Emily has written? I wonder whether the *Gondaland* will still be flourishing, and what will be their condition. I am now engaged in writing the fourth volume of *Solala Vernon's Life*. . . .

'How little know we what we are/How less what we may be!' had perhaps more relevance than she knew. Charlotte and Branwell both possessed a conscious conviction that they had great possibilities within them. Charlotte directed herself as best she could, to doing something to bring these possibilities to light. Branwell's talent was dissipated by eloquence; he entertained his friends with his wit, while Charlotte kept quiet, planned, and acted. Anne herself was Emily's closest friend, and in the general belief that she was overpowered by Emily, the possibility that Anne might have exerted some personal influence on her sister has been overlooked. Anne, who was the most realistic of the Brontës, did not seem to think of her own potential talent so long as there was little opportunity to exercise it. As we see, she continues with her Gondal volumes, but she wonders whether Gondaland will still be flourishing four years hence. She will not commit herself, like Emily, to guessing the future; nor like Charlotte, to putting plans in motion. But Anne was observant and reflective. She knew that many unforeseen things had occurred, and would occur. When at last she did get her independence, Anne was assiduous to act upon it; meantime she kept her aims within the limits of her present duty. Anne was a persuaded Christian: it was deliberate practice of her principles which prevented Anne from launching forth before her due time; she submitted to Charlotte's suggestions, and continued to do work she disliked while Charlotte experimented with life. These signs of Anne's strength of character have somehow earned her a reputation for weakness of purpose. It is, however, necessary to consider the obvious tenacity of will which kept Anne Brontë at the same tedious job for four years, during which time she started her first novel. She was not afraid to face the likelihood of the school plan coming to nothing, and indeed, of all their circumstances being altered. Anne, like Emily, had her reputation fixed for all time by the commentaries of her friends. 'Sweet gentle Anne' they said. Indeed she was gentle and sweet. But it does not follow that she was easily influenced in her opinions or actions; quite the opposite: she was the more released from obligations to concede matters of principle. Where her family was concerned, she acquiesced in Charlotte's plans; as youngest, she waited her turn; Emily she looked upon, for the present, as her fellow-fantastic, her playmate, and it may be that she detected possibilities of Emily's genius before Emily did herself. 'How little know we what we are. . . .'

Judging from Anne's work and the conduct of her life, it seems likely that she had, by now, tired of the Gondal legend. She was the least romantic of the Brontës. Anne had been in love, it is supposed with William Weightman, and possibly had by now given up hopes of him. She made the best of life as it was, nor would she relinquish her participation in the Gondal epic, since its continuance meant so much to Emily. From later indications, however, it is not improbable that Anne would have chosen to relinquish Gondal writing by this time.

At present, then, Emily accounts for herself in the light of a happy and normal woman who is following a natural bent for writing. The family were aware that only in certain circumstances was Emily happy and normal: perhaps no one, least of all Emily, was clear as to the precise nature of these circumstances. But it amounted to the practical result that Emily could not take a job. The proposal for setting up a school of their own had, however, met with Emily's pleasure. It was not, therefore, parting from Haworth which appalled Emily; nor was it exactly school life. What made certain situations intolerable to her seems to have been an instinctive antipathy towards applying her mind to an imposed system, within an environment governed by strangers. Presently Charlotte was in negotiations with Miss Wooler for taking over her school. The good lady showed hesitation. Charlotte did not wait, but plunged straightway into a new scheme. She would equip herself with a knowledge of French and German before setting up school. This would mean a period of study abroad. 'I longed to go to Brussels; but how could I get there?' she wrote, 'I wished for one, at least, of my sisters to share the advantage with me. I fixed on Emily. She deserved the reward, I knew. How could the point be managed? In extreme excitement I wrote a letter home, which carried the day.' A few days later, Charlotte addressed a letter to Emily: 'Dear E.J. – You are not to suppose that this note is written with a view to communicating any information on the subject we both have considerably at heart. . . .'

The plan had been agreed. The question now was only to find the school. Did Emily welcome the prospect of attending school as cheerfully as she had anticipated starting one? 'The subject we both have considerably at heart', writes Charlotte in a curious roundabout way, as if the plan were a secret, which, as we have seen, it was not. Maybe Charlotte phrased herself thus in order to sound Emily's true feelings in the matter. A little further on she puts in, 'Grieve not over Dewsbury Moor. You were cut out there to all intents and purposes, so in fact was Anne; Miss Wooler would hear of neither for the first half-year'. She continues:

'Anne seems omitted from the present plan but if all goes right I trust she will derive her full share of benefit from it in the end. I exhort all to hope. I believe in my heart this is acting for the best; my only fear is lest others should doubt and be dismayed. Before our half-year in Brussels is completed, you and I will have to seek

> employment abroad. It is not my intention to retrace my steps home till twelve months. . . .'

So Charlotte announces her intentions and lets it be known that doubt or dismay in others is her only fear. Charlotte was the great promoter of the Brontë sisters. She initiated their every encounter with the world during their lifetime, she stage-managed their posthumous reputations. Yet it is possible that without Charlotte's activities we might never have heard of the Brontës. It was she who started their books on the way to publishers; it was probably Charlotte who inspired Emily and Anne with the desire to write marketable books – novels. But for Charlotte, the younger sisters might have spent their talent on adding fabulous material to the sprawling Gondal saga. Charlotte's bossiness sometimes betrays a sort of desperation. She was desperately keen to achieve something in her life, she was desperately forceful when she greatly desired anything. So, in this matter, she declares not only her intentions, but her assumption that Emily's acquiescence is of course beyond doubt. Emily, however, regretted that negotiations with Miss Wooler over her school at Dewsbury Moor had come to an end; this had been the last hope for the project which had so delighted Emily. Charlotte does not appear to have considered whether Emily's disappointment over this might not indicate a disinclination to attend school in Brussels. 'You and I', states Charlotte, 'will have to seek employment abroad.' 'It is not my intention . . .' she continues, without enquiring Emily's intentions.

From Brussels, in May 1842, Charlotte reported their progress at Mme Héger's school. Charlotte herself was happy: 'My present life is so delightful, so congenial', she writes, 'to my own nature, compared with that of a governess. . . .' She even enjoyed the wrath of 'M. Héger, the husband of Madame . . . very choleric and irritable in temperament; a little black being . . .' And Emily? 'Emily and he don't draw well together at all. When he is very ferocious with me I cry; that sets all things straight. Emily works like a horse, and she has great difficulties to contend with, far greater than I have had.'

Emily had less knowledge of French than Charlotte; this was a drawback. Also, she had apparently little genuine interest in acquiring these educational advantages. Charlotte's interest came from the heart; she marvelled at herself being a schoolgirl at the age of twenty-six; she was able to enter into the spirit of the thing, and cry when appropriate. Also, she was a practised student. But Emily was in this situation from necessity; and she was not used to studying under the direction of professional teachers. She could not share Charlotte's pleasure, and at the same time, she had to work harder than her better informed sister. Emily so well applied herself to study that she was soon said by Charlotte to be 'making rapid progress in French, German, music and drawing'. 'Monsieur and Madame Héger', Charlotte adds, 'begin to recognise the valuable parts of her character, under her singularities.'

To the Hégers, the 'valuable parts' of Emily's character appear to have been her determined capacity for hard work, and her special ability in music. They were impressed by Charlotte's competence, and offered to take her as an English teacher, affording her opportunities for further study in French and German. They included Emily in this arrangement, offering to employ her 'some part of each day in teaching music to a certain number of the pupils'. Charlotte accepted this offer. Emily's singularities, now mentioned for the first time in Brontë correspondence, were possibly the outward signs of some inward reluctance to participate in the Brussels transaction.

Up to this time, Emily had not shown persistence in any activity which did not come naturally and easily to her. On this occasion, however, she made a considerable effort to give her mind to systematic instruction and study. The results were curious, so far as they are represented by allusions to Emily made by Charlotte and others. In the first place we find Emily not getting on with M. Héger. Less than a year ago, to judge by her birthday note, Emily had given the impression of being exceptionally agreeable by nature. This is the first time, indeed, that there is any hint of Emily being at odds with anyone.

A letter from Charlotte's former schoolfellow Mary Taylor, who was then in Brussels, informs Ellen Nussey of a meeting with Charlotte and Emily one evening, on which occasion Emily spoke only once or twice. Emily, in fact, was responding to unfavourable conditions in which she had reluctantly placed herself, with natural resentment. But further comments upon her at this time give us an aspect of Emily which shows she was not simply sulking because she could not have her own way.

We have to realize that those observations of Emily recorded by Charlotte approximate somewhat, if not exactly, to reality. We have cause to question Charlotte's information only where she gives it from memory. Charlotte's view of Emily at any given period during Emily's lifetime was informed by a lifelong experience of her sister in a variety of circumstances; she often, perhaps, misunderstood Emily; but Charlotte was in a position to interpret her sister's current reactions in the light of a general familiarity with her sister. But the impressions of comparative strangers have not undergone this interpretive process; and for that reason, they are both less true, and more telling, than are Charlotte's. Two people unfamiliar with Emily presently offered passing impressions of her at Brussels: Mary Taylor and M. Héger. As we shall see, the effect she had on them varies, but the common assumption is that she was difficult to get on with, not very likeable. Remarks to this effect are of insignificant value as definitions of Emily's true nature, but they are meaningful factors when we are concerned with the feelings which caused Emily to present herself in this light.

Meantime, Charlotte and Emily returned to Haworth in November 1842, summoned by the death of their aunt. William Weightman had died a few weeks before. The four Brontës were gathered in the Parsonage once more, with their father.

The sisters were provided, by their aunt's will, with a modest degree of independence. Her money was divided equally between Charlotte, Emily, Anne, and a fourth niece from her Cornwall family. Her personal belongings were variously distributed amongst the Brontës. One is tempted to wonder if their aunt had deliberated about the special suitability of the respective articles she named for each recipient. Charlotte had 'my Indian workbox'; Emily was specified for 'my workbox with a china top' and also 'my ivory fan'; to Branwell, her 'Japan dressing-box'; to Anne, 'my watch with all that belongs to it': practical treasures, amongst which the ivory fan bears a suggestion of feminine fancy. Maybe the fan had previously delighted Emily, or perhaps it was merely thrown in to make up for a workbox inferior to the one bestowed on Charlotte. Since Emily was later described as masculine in type, however, it may be worth noting this triviality; their aunt would, at any rate, hardly choose to bestow her fan on the sister least likely to appreciate it.

Early in October their father received a letter from M. Héger, urging him to send Charlotte and Emily back to Brussels. Their master praised them jointly and with Gallic courtesy for their industry and perseverance; he expressed sadness at the loss of pupils for whom he felt an affection almost paternal, sorrow that their education remained uncompleted. 'In a year', he proclaimed, with engaging confidence, 'each of your daughters would have been quite prepared for any eventuality of the future.' Then M. Héger commends them separately:

> Miss Emily was learning the piano, receiving lessons from the best professor in Belgium, and she herself already had little pupils. She was losing whatever remained of ignorance, and also of what was worse – timidity; Miss Charlotte was beginning to give lessons in French and to acquire that assurance, that aplomb so necessary to a teacher; only another year and the work would have been completed, and well completed. Then we should have been able, if convenient to you, to offer to your daughters, or at least to one of them, a position according to her taste. . . .

There is little doubt that M. Héger genuinely admired the sisters' determined application to the work they had gone to Brussels to do. He could not have been unaware that they had unusual gifts, and as he was a man with a real vocation for teaching – one who took an interest in comparative methods – he would have found such pupils stimulating.

His reservation in making a guarantee of employment to the sisters – 'or at least to one of them' – may be taken to imply the probable exclusion of Emily. (The rest of his sentence assures only one of the sisters, 'a position according to her taste, and that pleasant independence so difficult for a young person to find', which appears to imply that there was really no question of both being employed.) Charlotte, more accomplished than her sister, would naturally be preferred. But obviously he was not thinking of Emily merely in the comparative sense, as the sister who would be less useful for his school. He gives a definite impression of Emily, as he had first observed her: he had found a degree of ignorance and timidity in her; she was now losing this, he said.

In the academic sense, his impression of Emily's ignorance was perhaps justified; her timidity, too, may have been real enough. But it is curious that M. Héger should have introduced these somewhat disparaging terms in a letter which is otherwise brimming with tact. As we know from Charlotte's report, Emily did not get on with her master at first. It is probable, both from this and from an episode later revealed, that he disliked Emily. In his patriarchal style, he might well have made his comments purposely to put her in her place.

Emily was generally unpopular during her stay at Brussels (as even the posthumous reports of a family called Wheelwright can be seen to confirm). She had previously met Charlotte's friend, Mary Taylor, at Haworth. Mary Taylor, meeting Emily again in Brussels, had remarked on her lack of conversation. After Charlotte had returned, alone, to Brussels, Mary Taylor mentions Emily once more, in a letter to Ellen Nussey: 'I have heard from Charlotte since her arrival; she seems *content* at least, but fear her sister's absence will have a bad effect. When people have so little amusement they cannot afford to lose *any*'; from which sharp thrust, it is clear that Mary Taylor regarded Emily's social qualities with some contempt. She also displayed curiosity about Emily, about whom Ellen Nussey had evidently written. 'Tell me something about Emily Brontë,' Mary Taylor writes. 'I can't imagine how the newly acquired qualities can fit in, in the same head and heart that is occupied by the old ones. I imagine Emily turning over prints or "taking wine" with any stupid pup and preserving her temper and politeness!' We have to read into this some idea of what impression Ellen Nussey had gained of Emily since her return from Brussels. Ellen had paid a visit to Haworth before Charlotte's lone departure. Ellen had observed, at least, that Emily was changed. In the gossip of her letter Ellen had apparently suggested that Emily had acquired some Continental polish, humorously speculating, no doubt, that before long Emily would be keeping choice company. From Mary Taylor's reply we can see that at least she had a sense of Emily's intelligence.

The reactions of these people are of course immaterial except for the purpose of illuminating the question of how Brussels affected Emily. That she provoked a variety of new reactions shows either that a side of her nature which was hitherto not reported is now revealed, or that she underwent a noticeable change at Brussels. Most probably the true situation combines both alternatives. Charlotte refers to Emily's 'peculiarities' as if they were known to her correspondent. And then, the fact that she was so generally difficult to get on with at Brussels posits the probability that Brussels brought out these 'peculiarities' with unprecedented force. More important, however, is the nature and cause of this new aspect of Emily which emerges.

Her 'peculiarities', so far as we have seen, are normal ones, inherent in people with a strong sense of vocation. In her person Emily was amiable, hopeful and in vigorous spirits when she was pursuing her vocation along certain lines which excluded the discipline of formal scholarship. At Brussels, she got down to systematic study; she exerted her will towards acquiring knowledge; her amiability vanished, she was no longer friendly with the world; far from being able to control her distaste for the whole proceeding, she could not conceal it.

Emily Brontë may have been quite conscious of her reasons for this obvious horror of being 'educated', or some instinctive process may have moved her, of which she was unaware. The question arises, was she justified? The answer rests with her work, and may be elaborated by the critics of her work. It is, however, clear that the element of choice, at this time, existed for Emily: she was not incapable of response to that systematic ordering of her mind which she so definitely wished to reject. The 'ignorance and timidity' of M. Héger's attribution is misleading. Five essays are in existence, written in French by Emily Brontë under his direction.[1] Most of these are unlike anything else she is known to have produced, not only in genre, but in their rational content. They represent what are probably her first attempts to formulate her own philosophy, bringing her view of life to consciousness. Until this work had been forced upon her, the same philosophical attitudes which these essays make explicit, were concealed and implicit behind the imaginative fabric of her poems. These tenets more markedly inform *Wuthering Heights*. Her essay, 'King Harold on the Eve of the Battle of Hastings', for example, proclaims in fervent, undeniable tones, her delight in the concentrated power of the mighty romantic hero who is a species unto himself. Heathcliff of *Wuthering Heights* is the same thing in another guise, a fictional tributary to the rising cult of the superman. Not everyone who rejoices in *Wuthering Heights* would rejoice in the principles by which, in this brief and in many ways absurd essay, Emily takes her stand. Not everyone will care for her clear, unflinching presentation of Nature in its destructive cruelty, which she offers in her pieces, 'The Cat' and 'The Butterfly'. She reproduces in her creative work much of the thought which forms the theme of these essays. But the very act of creating a work of art is a kind of reparation for the most perverse theme. The nearer the work

[1] *Five Essays written in French by Emily Jane Brontë*, translated by Lorine White Nagel, University of Texas Press, 1948, from which following quotations are taken.

approaches perfection, the more has the principle of order prevailed against whatever chaos produced it.

Therefore it is not unlikely that Emily had a real fear of conscious enlightenment through study, because this would inevitably push her working hypotheses to their logical extremes. It is not unlikely that she feared the conclusions to which rational formulation would force her. Moreover, her intellect was capable of grasping the moral implications of her creative work; this is clear from her essays, in which her argument proceeds by induction; her proposition is contained in specific examples, upon which her generalizations follow.

It is not unlikely that Emily wished, consciously or otherwise, to avoid reaching conclusions, because they played a harsh moral searchlight upon the fruits of her untrained contemplative mind. She may have been justified; if she had entirely subjected her mind to training, and her work to moral censorship, there might have been no further fruits. Her attitude was, perhaps, self-protective. She was subject to her own poetic and inner discipline; all other discipline was foreign to her.

In her essay 'The Butterfly', there may be a hint of self-justification on this question, allegorically expressed. She describes a forest scene, and soliloquizing upon the 'natural order', finds not order but insanity: 'Life exists on a principle of destruction; every creature must be the relentless instrument of death to the others, or himself cease to live . . . the universe appeared to me a vast machine constructed only to bring forth evil. . . .' Then, 'like a censuring angel sent from heaven, there fluttered through the trees a butterfly with large wings of gleaming gold and purple . . . here is a symbol of the world to come – just as the ugly caterpillar is the beginning of the splendid butterfly, this globe is the embryo of a new heaven and a new earth whose meagrest beauty infinitely surpasses mortal imagination. . . .' She employs this traditional illustration towards its theological conclusion: 'God is the God of justice and mercy', suffering is seed for a divine harvest. Possibly, this essay has also a bearing upon her own desire to create harmony out of material which was, only too apparently, chaotic. But this is no more than a possibility; her concern here is not directly aesthetic.

1842–1848

Emily was not tempted to return to Brussels. Any pressing fears for her future had been removed by her aunt's small legacy. It is notable that within the first few weeks after her return from Brussels she gave Ellen Nussey the impression that she was changed into a more sociable being: quite the opposite impression to that formed by her acquaintances in Brussels. But this is understandable if, in her new-found release, her manner blossomed with unusual benevolence and grace. Most likely, she was particularly pleased with herself during the first weeks of freedom. Moods, up and down, were her 'peculiarities'.

Had she, then, acquired nothing from her nine months in Belgium? She seems to have deliberately rejected the whole experience. Brussels has no place in her writings.

But she was too intelligent to fail to appreciate the mental process which had been initiated there. She had been forced to organize her thought during that period; few people capable of deep and sustained thought can stop the process at will; it has its own attractions. There is no evidence that Emily was, at this period, engaged in philosophical speculation, but there are indications, in later years, that she had gradually become more of what is called a 'thinker'.

Emily was alone with her father at Haworth from the beginning of 1843. After the holidays Anne had returned to the Robinsons, her employers. Branwell had gone to join her as tutor to the Robinson boys. Charlotte was back in Brussels, being more or less in love with M. Héger.

'All appears to be going on reasonably well at home,' Charlotte wrote to Branwell in May, 'I grieve only that Emily is so solitary. . . .'

Emily does not appear to have grieved. She produced comparatively little verse, but we learn that the Gondal destinies, worked out mainly in prose, were to claim her attention for some years to come. When she was obliged, during May, to write to Ellen Nussey, she did not write the letter of a person suffering from loneliness, when we might expect a certain loquacity. She is cheerful and brief: it is the letter of a busy woman, and half-apologetic Emily adds, 'The holidays will be here in a week or two and then, if [Anne] be willing, I will get her to write you a proper letter, a feat that I have never performed – with love and good wishes. . . .' The ending is typical of the letters of authors at times when they are deeply occupied: a hint that further correspondence is not to be expected, an absent-minded 'Love and best wishes'.

Charlotte sent long letters to Emily bewailing her lot. Her second stay with the Hégers was turning out badly. Mme Héger, she was convinced, did not like her, which is not surprising in view of Charlotte's subsequent letters to M. Héger. The latter, Charlotte complained, was under the influence of the former. Emily knew nothing of Charlotte's passion for her master: 'I hope you are well and hearty. Walk out often on the moors'. Charlotte's advice may seem strange, considering Emily's proverbial craving for the moors, but Charlotte probably was aware that Emily was wont to sit long hours at her desk.

In October, Charlotte, in a fit of homesickness, inserted in her letter one of those Parsonage 'scenes' from which we learn so much of the daily life at Haworth.

> Dear E.J. – This is Sunday morning. They are at their idolatrous 'messe', and I am here – that is, in the *refectoire*. I should like uncommonly to be in the dining-room at home, or in the kitchen, or in the back kitchen. I should like even to be cutting up the hash, with the clerk and some register people at the other table, and you standing by, watching that I put enough flour, and not too much pepper, and, above all, that I save the best pieces of the leg of mutton for Tiger and Keeper, the first of which personages would be jumping about the dish and carving-knife, and the latter standing like a devouring flame on the kitchen floor. To complete the picture, Tabby blowing the fire, in order to boil the potatoes to a sort of vegetable glue! How divine are these recollections to me at this moment! . . . *You* call yourself idle! absurd! absurd! . . . Write to me again soon. Tell me whether Papa really wants me very much to come home, and whether you do likewise. I have an idea that I should be of no use there – a sort of aged person upon the parish. I pray, with heart and soul, that all may continue well at Haworth; above all in our grey, half-inhabited house. God bless the walls thereof! . . . Amen.

Charlotte returned to Haworth in January 1844. She could not bear inactivity; at once she organized the sisters into discussing a new school project. Their father could not be left alone. Haworth

Parsonage would be the schoolhouse. They had a circular printed advertising the Misses Brontës' Establishment. For months they wrote to the mothers of likely pupils, sent the circular far and wide, waited to hear the results of Ellen Nussey's endeavours on their behalf. Charlotte explained the plan in one of her letters to M. Héger: 'Emily', she informed him, 'does not care much for teaching, but she would look after the housekeeping, and, although something of a recluse, she is too good-hearted not to do all she could for the wellbeing of the children.' In other words, Emily had made it plain that so far as she was concerned there was nothing doing. She would look after the housekeeping, as usual, but she wanted her mind to herself. Charlotte reflected, no doubt, that, when it came to the bit, Emily was, after all, 'too good-hearted' not to do all she could for children. Emily was never put to the test. (Nor was the information volunteered years later by a former pupil of Emily's at Law Hill, thus refuted: Emily was alleged to have told her class she preferred her dog to themselves.) No mama of their acquaintance wanted to send her daughters across the bleak moorland to the lonely parsonage. Anne remained at the Robinsons. Charlotte paid periodic visits to Ellen Nussey. Emily saw to the housekeeping, her pets and her work.

In the middle of 1845, Branwell was dismissed from the Robinsons. He gave out a story which not one of the sisters doubted: he had fallen in love with Mrs Robinson, and she with him. Mr Robinson had discovered their secret, and threatened to shoot Branwell should he send so much as a message. Branwell became an object of wonder, pity, contempt, despair, and everything except mirth, to the household. The truth of the story is obscure; there were certainly many discrepancies between Branwell's tale and the facts which came to light after the Brontë children were dead. It may be that he had simply made a nuisance of himself by making unwelcome overtures to his employer's wife; perhaps she encouraged him a little at first, until he became too serious. Branwell, however, was a trifle mad. The story which depicted Mrs Robinson pining for him and he for her, true lovers separated by a cruel husband, consoled him for whatever his real misery was, whether hurt pride or simply boredom. His misery, however, was real; he drowned it daily at the local tavern. The sisters, awed, frightened, impressed, contemptuous, and a little thrilled, looked on and sighed when the creditors came to the door. Charlotte gave Ellen a running commentary on his condition, lamenting the unprotected upbringing of young men as compared with that of young ladies.

Anne had already decided not to return to the Robinsons after the holidays; she had not disclosed anything she knew of Branwell's affairs, which had probably prompted her decision. At the end of July, Anne and Emily composed two more birthday journals. Emily writes:

> Haworth, Thursday, July 30th, 1845.
>
> My birthday – showery, breezy, cool. I am twenty-seven years old to-day. This morning Anne and I opened the papers we wrote four years since, on my twenty-third birthday. This paper we intend, if all be well, to open on my thirtieth – three years hence, in 1848. Since the 1841 paper the following events have taken place. Our school scheme has been abandoned, and instead Charlotte and I went to Brussels on the 8th of February, 1842.
>
> Branwell left his place at Luddenden Foot. C. and I returned from Brussels, November 8th, 1842, in consequence of aunt's death.
>
> Branwell went to Thorp Green as a tutor, where Anne still continued, January 1843.
>
> Charlotte returned to Brussels the same month, and after staying a year, came back again on New Year's Day 1844.
>
> Anne left her situation at Thorp Green of her own accord, June 1845.
>
> Anne and I went our first long journey by ourselves together, leaving home on the 30th June, Monday, sleeping at York, returning to Keighley Tuesday evening, sleeping there and walking home on Wednesday morning. Though the weather was broken we enjoyed ourselves very much, except during a few hours at Bradford. And during our excursion we were, Ronald Macalgin, Henry Angora, Juliet Angusteena, Rosabella Esmaldan, Ella and Julian Egrement, Catharine Navarre, and Cordelia Fitzaphnold, escaping from the palaces of instruction to join the Royalists who are hard driven at present by the victorious Republicans. The Gondals still flourish bright as ever. I am at present writing a work on the First War. Anne has been writing some articles on this, and a book by Henry Sophona. We intend sticking firm by the rascals as long as they delight us, which I am glad to say they do at present. I should have mentioned that last summer the school scheme was revived in full vigour. We had

> prospectuses printed, despatched letters to all acquaintances imparting our plans, and did our little all; but it was found no go. Now I don't desire a school at all, and none of us have any great longing for it. We have cash enough for our present wants, with a prospect of accumulation. We are all in decent health, only that papa has a complaint in his eyes, and with the exception of B., who, I hope, will be better and do better hereafter. I am quite contented for myself: not as idle as formerly, altogether as hearty, and having learnt to make the most of the present and long for the future with the fidgetiness that I cannot do all I wish; seldom or ever troubled with nothing to do, and merely desiring that everybody could be as comfortable as myself and as undesponding, and then we should have a very tolerable world of it.
>
> By mistake I find we have opened the paper on the 31st instead of the 30th. Yesterday was much such a day as this, but the morning was divine.
>
> Tabby, who was gone in our last paper, is come back, and has lived with us two years and a half, and is in good health. Martha, who also departed, is here too. We have got Flossy; got and lost Tiger; lost the hawk Hero, which, with the geese, was given away, and is doubtless dead, for when I came back from Brussels I inquired on all hands and could hear nothing of him. Tiger died early last year. Keeper and Flossy are well, also the canary acquired four years since. We are now all at home, and likely to be there some time. Branwell went to Liverpool on Tuesday to stay a week. Tabby has just been teasing me to turn as formerly to 'Pilloputate'. Anne and I should have picked the black-currants if it had been fine and sunshiny. I must hurry off now to my turning and ironing. I have plenty of work on hands, and writing, and am altogether full of business. With best wishes for the whole house till 1848, July 30th, and as much longer as may be, – I conclude. Emily Brontë.

Gondal was still flourishing. Had they considered the possibility of winding up the affair? If so, they had decided that Gondal should continue as long as it delighted them. The two young women, aged twenty-seven and twenty-five, played at Gondal throughout their excursion to York. Emily thought this a better idea than the school scheme, the abandonment of which she is glad to announce. 'I don't desire a school at all', she declares. Why should they work when they were not in need? 'We have cash enough for our present wants, with a prospect of accumulation.' This picks up a motif in her previous paper: cash – this meant security, leisure, freedom to write, to keep up Gondal. She cannot understand why the rest of the family has a sense of dissatisfaction. 'I am quite contented for myself: not as idle as formerly, although as hearty.' Emily had, during Charlotte's absence abroad, written to tell of her 'idleness'. That had been, perhaps, a period of reflection. But there is the indication of things she had planned to achieve, as in her previous note. She knows now that she cannot do all that she wishes. But life, she suggests, would be more tolerable if everyone could be as unconcerned, 'as comfortable', 'as undesponding', as herself. Not everyone in the household had the temperament for taking life so easily.

During this year, all four Brontës happened to describe themselves in various documents. Anne, in her birthday note, admits to having had 'some very unpleasant and undreamt-of experience of human nature' during her stay at the Robinsons. 'E and I have a great deal of work to do. When shall we sensibly diminish it? . . . We have not yet finished our *Gondal Chronicles* that we began three and a half [years] ago. When will they be done?' Anne betrays some weariness with Gondal; she seems to have had enough of it, and may even have hinted as much to Emily. But Gondal delighted Emily. And, Anne writes, she was looking forward to hearing Emily's latest Gondal piece. But she is altogether weary in her note. Emily is 'hearty'? 'I for my part, cannot well be flatter or older in mind than I am now', declares Anne.

Three months later, Branwell describes himself in a letter to an old friend, 'I have lain during nine long weeks utterly shattered in body and broken down in mind. The probability of her becoming free to give me herself and estate never rose to drive away the prospect of her decline under her present grief. . . . Eleven continuous nights of sleepless horror reduced me to almost blindness. . . .'

And Charlotte, too, gives her self-portrait, in terms not dissimilar from her brother's. To M. Héger she confides, 'Day and night I find neither rest nor peace. If I sleep I am disturbed by tormenting dreams in which I see you, always severe, always grave, always incensed against me'.

Against these personal testimonies of the restless inner lives of Anne, Branwell and Charlotte, Emily alone is seen to be collected and even smug. No wonder she wishes they could be comfortable and undesponding like herself. Tormented by unquenchable passions or chilled with melancholy, the three sufferers must have found Emily infuriating at times, she was so contented.

In her birthday note, Emily refers to the 'prospects of accumulation' which apparently adhere to their cash. Emily had been left in charge of the investment of their aunt's legacies, and she considered she had done well by the family, having placed the money in railroad shares. Then came one of those national crises which are dotted all along the nineteenth century: a Panic. Charlotte wrote to Miss Wooler, 'I have been most anxious for us to sell our shares ere it be too late . . . I cannot, however, persuade my sisters to regard the affair precisely from my point of view.' Anne stood by Emily, apparently. Besides, Charlotte recalled that Emily had undertaken the business single-handed. 'I feel I would rather run the risk of loss than hurt Emily's feelings . . . I will let her manage still and take the consequences. . . . Disinterested and energetic she certainly is, and if she be not quite so tractable or open to conviction as I could wish, I must remember perfection is not the lot of humanity.'

This is the first occasion on which Charlotte is known to have hinted, even with qualifications, that Emily was difficult at times. Emily had been tractable enough to accompany Charlotte to Brussels. Since her return, however, she had taken her own line, first about the school, now about the railroad shares; they did not fail until after Emily was in her grave.

At this period Charlotte was pushing ahead with another project. A selection of the poems by the three sisters was to be printed at their own expense, under the pseudonyms, Currer, Ellis and Acton Bell. These poems appeared in July 1846. It is said that only two copies were sold. Few papers reviewed the book, but *The Athenaeum* of July 1846 printed a notice which places Emily's poems far above the others. This critic detected

> an inspiration, which may yet find an audience in the outer world. A fine quaint spirit has the latter [i.e. Emily], which may have things to speak that men will be glad to hear – and an evident power of wing that may reach heights not here attempted. . . . How musical he can be, and how lightly and easily the music falls from his heart and pen. . . . He is no copyist. There is not enough in this volume to judge him by – but, to our mind, an impression of originality is conveyed, beyond what his contribution to these pages embody.

This critic dismisses Charlotte and Anne briefly; he was a wise man, even though banal; he was original enough to spot Emily Brontë as soon as she appeared in print. She must have been enormously encouraged by this review.

The sisters had meantime written a novel apiece: *The Professor* by Charlotte, *Agnes Grey* by Anne, *Wuthering Heights* by Emily. While they wrote the books, Branwell was rapidly deteriorating, and so it is sometimes claimed that Emily and Anne drew upon their brother for 'copy', reproducing him in their novels. This seems unlikely; they actually saw too much of Branwell to use him effectively in this way. There was no mystery in Branwell to be worked out in their novels. Had they suspected the truth of his story, they might have found his very deception worth exploring. As it was, he could be neither a dissipated villain nor broken-hearted hero; he had no magnitude either way, for he was drunk half the time. 'A hopeless being', said Emily. That was pronounced on a day when he had given more trouble than usual. On the whole, they were not unsympathetic to their brother; even now, he invites pity. Only Charlotte was inclined to be hard on him; but then she had been hard on herself: she had stopped writing to M. Héger.

Wuthering Heights and *Agnes Grey* were accepted by a publisher, T.C. Newby, on a subsidy of £50 for the book, which contained both works. Emily and Anne were obviously keen, now, to get their work published, and entertained high enough hopes to feel justified in speculating this sum. Emily was perhaps especially hopeful, on the strength of *The Athenaeum*'s review. Charlotte had to write another novel before she found a publisher, Smith & Elder. This firm was so prompt with the publication of *Jane Eyre* that it came out some months before the novels of Emily and Anne appeared.

In the meantime, Branwell's old employer and enemy, Mr Robinson, died. Branwell gave out that Mrs Robinson's reason for failing to fly into his arms was that her husband's will left her totally unprovided for should she resume the least communication with Branwell.

The publishers of *Wuthering Heights* and *Agnes Grey* seemed in no hurry to fulfil their promise. Some proof sheets were received in August 1847, and their return was followed by another period of waiting. Meanwhile *Jane Eyre* by 'Currer Bell' was published, and was an immediate success. This encouraged the publisher of 'Ellis and Acton Bell' to bring out their long-delayed book, and to claim that Ellis and Acton were one and the same with Currer, author of *Jane Eyre*.

Their literary ventures were kept secret from their friends. 'Currer Bell''s fame was high; Charlotte was embarked on a new life of letter-writing. Her principal correspondent now was W.S. Williams, a reader for her publishers; she also began exchanging letters with well-known literary people who wrote to her. 'Currer Bell' was still her signature. The sisters had agreed to preserve their privacy; the Brontës of Haworth were not to be displayed to the world.

Between her birthday in the July of 1845 and the publication of *Wuthering Heights* in the December of 1847, we hear remarkably little about Emily. Between these dates, her poems had appeared in the sisters' joint volume, and she had written *Wuthering Heights* and a very few poems (that we know of). The novel had been completed in the first half of 1846. She wrote one long poem in September of that year, and thereafter apparently nothing until she started to redraft the same poem in May 1848. Almost two years are therefore unaccounted for by any of her writings. It has been suggested that she had started another novel, which she subsequently destroyed.

References to Emily are infrequent at this period. Charlotte's remark to Miss Wooler early in 1846, that Emily was 'not quite so tractable or open to conviction as I could wish', indicates that Emily's attitude to Charlotte, at least, had changed a little, since the time when she was merely the useful stay-at-home sister. This from Charlotte may be taken in conjunction with Emily's statement in her birthday paper, 'I am quite contented for myself . . . seldom or ever troubled with nothing to do, and merely desiring that everybody could be as comfortable as myself and as undesponding, and then we should have a very tolerable world of it'; Charlotte found her intractable, Emily found the whole family too fussy and querulous. Emily was then beginning to assert herself. Charlotte regretted the fact, but gave way. She was, perhaps, a little surprised that Emily, so amenable all her life, was now taking her own stand in some matters. And Charlotte had also been surprised by Emily's poems, which she never failed, in her letters to Mr Williams, to rate highly.

These circumstances may combine to account for a gradual change in Charlotte's tone in her references to Emily; and this becomes more pronounced as Emily entered the last years of her life. Charlotte is not always approving, but she respects Emily in a new way; her bewilderment grows into curiosity; later becomes awe, a recognition of Emily's literary power and of some newly awakened personal power. This, it could be argued, may signify a development in Charlotte's faculties of perception; it need not mean that Emily's personal development follows the course charted by Charlotte's reactions. But Charlotte does not betray any unforeseen facet of her own personality in her other relationships; her reactions to life at this stage do not lead us to suspect that Charlotte herself became more or less sympathetic or observant; her writing and her success exhilarated her, but this naturally aroused more self-interest than interest in her sisters. On the other hand, we know that Emily's personality in her last three years is not consistent with the personality she herself expressed in her 1845 birthday note. Still less is there constancy in the earlier and later delineations of Emily accepted by her family and their friends: Emily's earlier 'usefulness' in the house, her willingness to fall in with whatever was agreed by the family, are no longer the items which specially signify her character; instead, Charlotte unconsciously selects more subtle manifestations of Emily's personality, when writing of her; Emily has become more important. The legendary aspect begins to appear. As though speaking of some enigmatic celebrity, Charlotte writes in September 1847 to tell Ellen Nussey exactly with what facial expression Emily had received a gift. 'Emily is just now sitting on the floor of the bedroom where I am writing, looking at her apples. She smiled when I gave them and the collar to her as your presents, with an expression at once well satisfied and slightly surprised. . . .'

In October 1847, Emily is mentioned by Anne in the course of a dutiful letter to Ellen Nussey. Anne begins with the weather:

> Happily for all parties the east wind no longer prevails. During its continuance [Charlotte] complained of its influence as usual. I too suffered from it in some degree, as I always do, more or less; but this time, it brought me no reinforcement of colds and coughs which is what I dread the most. Emily considers it a very uninteresting wind, but it does not affect her nervous system.

Charlotte and Anne had a recurrent dread of the east wind; the Brontës had weak chests. Apparently, a bout of the east wind would get on their nerves. Not so Emily, who, to emphasize her unconcern, declared the very wind 'uninteresting'. Is this a foretaste of that lofty contempt for physical frailty towards which she was rapidly moving? But perhaps she meant simply that the east wind failed to evoke a response from her. Within three months, however, Anne reports that Emily has been down with influenza as a result of 'this cruel east wind'.

When Emily's novel was published, Charlotte was anxious for opinions on it. We do not have her friend Mr Williams' view, but we have Charlotte's reply:

> You are not far wrong in your judgment . . . Ellis has a strong, original mind, full of strange though sombre power. When he writes poetry that power speaks in language at once condensed, elaborated, and refined, but in prose it breaks forth in scenes which shock more than they attract. Ellis will improve, however, because he knows his defects.

Emily's defects, from this account, are the more violent scenes in *Wuthering Heights*, those which shocked Charlotte and many other readers, and which are, in fact, the scenes most typical of the book. 'He knows his defects'; does this mean that Emily had analysed her work? Possibly she had 'shocked' even herself with *Wuthering Heights*.

Charlotte almost certainly had read *Wuthering Heights* on its completion in the first half of 1846, if not during its composition; she had known of Emily's poems since the autumn of 1845. These helped to form the view of Emily's 'strong, original mind, full of strange though sombre power', but this is being implied only now, at the end of 1847. Charlotte's style when referring to Emily from this time onward automatically slips into rhetoric, which adds to the effect of awe. And that this was not due only to an increasing appreciation of Emily's work, but also to her daily observation of Emily herself, is most likely; if Emily had remained a constant factor, familiarity would have tended to accustom Charlotte to the genius her sister had displayed in her poems and novels; nor was there any new work of Emily's, so far as we know, to fill Charlotte with wonder. There now existed a real dichotomy between the present and the past impressions of Emily.

Where we do find constancy, and to a high degree, is in the development of Emily's poems, which converge towards *Wuthering*

Heights. It was submitted earlier, that the tone and character of the poems did not evidently absorb the concurrent experiences of her conscious life. The poems were not ultimately untrue to the character of Emily Brontë, but their themes were not progressively identical with her personal development. Not only did the poems represent features of her mind which she did not reveal to others, and which, indeed, were concealed from herself; those features were not then fully distinguishable. That the poems led up to *Wuthering Heights* does not mean they could not possibly have led to anything else, with an equally inevitable appearance.

In Emily Brontë's last years we see her personal behaviour approximating more closely to the character of her work; we recognize the author of *Wuthering Heights* and of the mystical poems in the manner in which she responded to her last illness. Previously, the Haworth Parsonage scenes depicted by herself and Charlotte, have not shown her as the living equivalent of the death-impassioned, earth-enamoured poems she was writing. The inescapable conclusion is that Emily had, in a short time, become conscious of the practical implications of her work; she had begun to realize principles which were dormant in her mind. This is not, of course, an unusual course of development in an artist; but the process of interpretation and reflection is normally gradual; otherwise, it can impede the practice of art. It has been observed that Emily seems to have wished instinctively to avoid this very process, in her repeated rejection of schooling.

The experience at Brussels did, in fact, exercise her capacity for philosophical reflection; she was forced, there, to reflect upon principles and ultimates, where before she had contemplated them. Or, rather, she forced herself. From all accounts, it was by a tremendous effort of will that Emily complied with Charlotte's conception of her duty. This was the first occasion, so far as we know, on which Emily had asserted her will with any degree of determination. There is nothing like the sustained exercise of will in meeting unpleasant demands to bring about an apparent change of character. In Emily this change was as swift as her effort was powerful, and it is apparent where she is observed to be asserting her personality increasingly from this time forward; and she directed this new-roused faculty towards defining, in terms of action, the principles which, in the years that followed, she came to recognize in her work. Emily Brontë is never so much a child of the Romantic Movement as in this. The Romantic poets tended to express in personal conduct the hypotheses underlying their creative writings. It was as if the principles involved in their work amounted to beliefs so passionately held, that it seemed necessary to prove them to others by putting them to the test of action. The result was not always satisfactory so far as the life of the poet was concerned.

In February 1848, Charlotte presented Mr Williams with the aspect of Emily which was next to emerge; her correspondent had suggested that the 'Bells' should visit London.

> Ellis, I imagine, would soon turn aside from the spectacle in disgust. I do not think he admits it as his creed that 'the proper study of mankind is man' – at least not the artificial man of cities. In some points I consider Ellis as somewhat of a theorist: now and then he broaches ideas which strike my sense as much more daring and original than practical; his reason may be in advance of mine, but certainly it often travels a different road. I should say Ellis will not be seen in his full strength till he is seen as an essayist.

For some reason, perhaps because she is trying to understand her own feelings, Charlotte is anxious to convey an impressive idea of Emily when she mentions her: Emily as a theorist holding 'ideas which strike my sense as much more daring and original than practical. . . .' Charlotte feared the practical issues of Emily's ideas, as she had every reason to do. In July, Charlotte and Anne went to London to prove that they were separate authors. Anne's publisher, T.C. Newby, had attempted to further his interests in America by claiming that *Wuthering Heights*, *Agnes Grey*, *Jane Eyre* and Anne's new novel, *The Tenant of Wildfell Hall*, were all the production of one author, Currer Bell. The two excited sisters turned up at the city offices of Smith & Elder, and though it had long been suspected that the 'Bells' were women, Charlotte's explanation, 'we are three sisters' was received with due surprise and pleasure. This admission was regarded differently by Emily, when they returned to Haworth after being subjected to rapid and exhausting hospitality by Charlotte's publisher. 'Permit me', writes Charlotte from the sober light of Haworth,

> to caution you not to speak of my sisters when you write to me. I mean, do not use the word in the plural. Ellis Bell will not endure

> to be alluded to under any other appellation than the *nom de plume*. I committed a grand error in betraying his identity to you and Mr. Smith. It was inadvertent – the words 'we are three sisters' escaped me before I was aware. I regretted the avowal the moment I had made it: I regret it bitterly now, for I find it is against every feeling and intention of Ellis Bell. . . .

In answer to his suggestion that they should see something of 'London society', she admits there would be great advantage in it, 'yet it is one that no power on earth could induce Ellis Bell, for instance, to avail himself of'.

Charlotte's next criticism of *Wuthering Heights* shows that she was uneasy about the moral significance of the character Heathcliff. She observes his 'naturally perverse, vindictive, and inexorable disposition': kindness might have made of him a human being, but under tyranny and ignorance he becomes a demon. 'The worst of it is', Charlotte continues, displaying her misgivings about the health of the book, 'some of his spirit seems breathed through the whole narrative in which he figures . . .' – which was an unconscious tribute to the author, none the less.

In September, Charlotte's publisher took over the book of poems from their previous publisher. Once more she eulogizes Emily's poems.

> They stirred my heart like the sound of a trumpet when I read them alone and in secret. . . . I was sternly rated at first for having taken an unwarrantable liberty. This I expected, for Ellis Bell is of no flexible or ordinary materials. But by dint of entreaty and reason I at last wrung out a reluctant consent to have the 'rhymes' as they were contemptuously termed, published. The author never alludes to them; or, when she does, it is with scorn. But I know no woman that ever lived ever wrote such poetry before. Condensed energy, clearness, finish – strange, strong pathos are their characteristics. . . .

There are phrases and words used here to describe Emily which have become almost keywords to a long line of comment upon her: 'of no flexible or ordinary materials'; 'contemptuously', 'with scorn'. Emily, contemptuous, scornful, inflexible, and made of superhuman material, has come down to us. The phrases date from this last year of Emily's life, when Charlotte was becoming ever more fervent in dramatizing her sister. Does this tendency in Charlotte, then, reflect something of how Emily appeared at the time?

We know Emily had been theorizing – delivering herself of ideas which, to Charlotte, were daring and original, but not practical. If Emily had worked out a philosophy from her own work, if she had evolved a system which was the logical equivalent of that in which her writings were placed, then Charlotte was right. It was not practical. If it were put into practice, in fact, it would be highly dangerous, for its principles were destructive.

Many factors already mentioned tend towards the conclusion that Emily had begun to dramatize in her own person the aspirations expressed in her work. If she saw herself in the end as the hero and cult of her own writings, we may expect to find more or less what we do find, a copy of her self-image, enlarged by the details her friends supplied after her death.

It is clear that Emily had gone sullen. She is described as inflexible, contemptuous and scornful of her own work, one who in her birthday notes had expressed herself in terms which suggest she was highly satisfied with her writing activities; far from being inflexible, she had appeared singularly accommodating. The human consummation of Gondal was the cult of the supreme hero: son of a special race; a being who recognized no law but that of Nature; one powerfully raised above the common destiny of man; in the world, a courageous stoic; in essence mystically united with Nature; amoral, ruthless. Such a being would partake of the extremes of passion, primitive action, and remain mystically remote in contemplation. In other words, he would be absurd.

Fortunately, Emily Brontë never got so far as this. She had envisaged one aspect of such a being in her short essay in French, 'King Harold on the Eve of the Battle of Hastings'.

> . . . a multitude of human emotions awaken in him, but they are exalted, sanctified, made almost divine. His courage is not temerity, nor is his pride arrogance. His anger is justified, his assurance is free from presumption. He has an inner conviction that by no mortal power will he be defeated. Death alone can gain victory over his arms. To her he is ready to yield, for Death's touch is to the hero what the striking off his chains is to the slave.

The reverse side of this paragon is Heathcliff in *Wuthering*

Heights, where Heathcliff's passions, instead of being 'exalted, sanctified, made almost divine', are degraded, accursed, made almost daemonic.

Emily's fatal illness, in her thirty-first year, accentuated any tendency she possessed to play out the part in her life. The illness itself, consumption, was inherent. It is not to be assumed that an early death was part of the heroics Emily had identified herself with, except so far as she would be bound to meet death in a manner appropriate to her role, whenever it should come her way. It may, of course, be argued that inherent consumption predisposed her to prepare for her death in this way, but this is a question which even those who understand the psychology of consumptives would perhaps be indefinite about. For the purposes of biographical accuracy, Emily's death was not willed by herself. She caught a cold at her brother's funeral, Branwell having submitted his tortured soul to more dissipation than the Brontë constitution could stand.

Charlotte records the bitter progress of Emily's last weeks, sometimes to Ellen Nussey, at other times to her publisher. To Ellen, at the end of October, she confided,

> Emily's cough and cold are very obstinate at present. I fear she has a pain in the chest, and I sometimes catch a shortness in her breathing, when she has moved at all quickly. She looks very, very thin and pale. Her reserved nature occasions me great uneasiness of mind. It is useless to question her; you get no answers. It is still more useless to recommend remedies; they are never adopted.

To W.S. Williams, a few days later:

> She is a real stoic in illness: she neither seeks nor will accept sympathy. To put any questions, to offer any aid, is to annoy; she will not yield a step before pain or sickness till forced; not one of her ordinary avocations will she voluntarily renounce. You must look on and see her do what she is obviously unfit to do, and not dare say a word – a painful necessity for those to whom her health and existence are as precious as the life in their veins.

Mr Williams recommended homeopathy. Charlotte handed Emily the letter 'taking care not to say a word in favour'. Emily's response was that 'Mr. Williams's intention was kind and good, but he was under a delusion: Homeopathy was only another form of quackery.' Not only would she not have quackery, she would not see any doctor; Charlotte repeats it again and again: 'She has refused medicine, rejected medical advice; no reasoning, no entreaty, has availed. . . .'

One day Charlotte read out a notice of *Wuthering Heights* from *The North American Review* to amuse Emily and Anne.

> As I sat between them at our quiet but now somewhat melancholy fireside, I studied the two ferocious authors. Ellis, the 'man of uncommon talents, but dogged, brutal, and morose', sat leaning back in his easy-chair, drawing his impeded breath as he best could, and looking, alas! piteously pale and wasted; it is not his wont to laugh, but he smiled, half-amused and half in scorn, as he listened.

To Ellen, on 23rd November:

> I told you Emily was ill, in my last letter. She has not rallied yet. She is *very* ill. I believe, if you were to see her, your impression would be that there is no hope. . . . Her pulse, the only time she allowed it to be felt, was found to beat 115 per minute. In this state she resolutely refuses to see a doctor; she will not give an explanation of her feelings, she will scarcely allow her illness to be alluded to. Our position is, and has been for some weeks, exquisitely painful. God only knows how all this is to terminate.

Charlotte had latterly felt an overwhelming love for Emily. In fact, it seems that the worse Emily treated her elder sister, the more did Charlotte love her. 'I think Emily seems the nearest thing to my heart in this world', she wrote.

Anne's relationship with Emily at this time is not known. The Gondal alliance had probably ended at the end of 1846. During 1847, as we know, Emily had written nothing which is left to us. Anne wrote only personal poems from 1847 onward. If it is true that Anne had wanted her release from Gondal, she may have taken advantage of her occupation with novels to bring it about. But Emily, too, may have tired of the game.

Anne was an orthodox Christian and a moralist: she would disapprove of Emily's manner of meeting her death, but she as well as Charlotte would suffer none the less from the torture of watching Emily die unalleviated. They had long prepared themselves to lose Branwell; the death of a sad, wrecked being is not so tragic, in the dramatic sense, as that of a proud and intelligent spirit. It was in the dramatic light that they saw Emily, for that was how she presented herself.

One wonders why Mr Brontë, the 'Papa' on whom the whole family looked as to a final authority, did not insist on Emily seeing a doctor. Did he too fear her? 'My father shakes his head', writes Charlotte tersely, 'and speaks of others of our family once similarly afflicted . . . who are now removed where hope and fear fluctuate no more. . . .'

Emily would not disclose anything of her motives. 'I *do* wish', Charlotte exclaims, 'I knew her state and feelings more clearly'. All she could do was to pester Emily to see a doctor. 'No poisoning doctor' was to come near her, said Emily. Desperately, Charlotte wrote out a careful description of the symptoms and sent them to a doctor recommended by her friend and publisher. The doctor sent some medicine 'which she would not take. Moments so dark as these I have never known. I pray for God's support to us all. . . .' This was written on Tuesday, 19th December.

To Ellen, December 23rd:

> Emily suffers no more from pain or weakness now. She will never suffer more in this world. She is gone, after a hard, short conflict. She died on *Tuesday*, the very day I wrote to you. I thought it very possible she might be with us still for weeks; and a few hours afterwards she was in eternity. Yes; there is no Emily in time or on earth now. Yesterday we put her poor, wasted, mortal frame quietly under the church pavement. We are very calm at present. Why should we be otherwise? The anguish of seeing her suffer is over; the spectacle of the pains of death is gone by, the funeral day is past. We feel she is at peace. No need now to tremble for the hard frost and the keen wind. Emily does not feel them. She died in a time of promise. We saw her taken from life in its prime. . . .

Anne also died of consumption, within five months, having taken much trouble to find a cure.

Charlotte lived another six years, the Rev Patrick Brontë another twelve.

Chapter Three

General

When all the afterthoughts, rumours, elaborations, legendary anecdotes and pure inventions which gradually clustered round Emily's posthumous reputation have been set aside, there still remains the recognizable outline of the Emily Brontë familiar to biography. This is not, however, the complete picture. The information which is so eagerly offered when anyone becomes posthumously famous is valuable, particularly where it gains wide credence. There seems to be an instinctive process of selection, whereby essential, if not literal truths attach themselves after a time to a reputation. So that the biographer who asserted of Emily in her earlier days that she showed pity and contempt for Anne cannot be ignored, only corrected. There is not a scrap of evidence to support the statement; there is much evidence to refute it. Still, the biographer comes in a long line of commentators who have said as much; thousands of people believe it. It is not literal truth, of course, but the statement carries an essential truth: it may be interpreted to mean, 'Emily had it in her to show contempt and pity for Anne. Anne had it in her to evoke pity and contempt'. It is part of a biographer's business to show what the subjects had it in them to do and be. But it is also necessary to show at what stage they notably did and were anything; it is necessary for the purpose of tracing the development of character.

What was of tremendous interest to everyone who wrote about Emily when she became the fashion, was her 'stoical' death; not only was this ennobled beyond all its most plain deserts, but from it were drawn adulatory conclusions which, to the less romantic temperament, distort her into a kind of daemonic monster. The first promoter of her reputation on this score, Charlotte more or less admitted she was obsessed by Emily's death, when she wrote to Ellen Nussey: 'I cannot forget Emily's death-day. It becomes a more fixed, a darker, a more frequently recurring idea in my mind than ever. It was very terrible. She was torn, conscious, panting, reluctant, though resolute, out of a happy life.' Charlotte was even further carried away in her memoir prefixing an edition of *Wuthering Heights* and *Agnes Grey*, but already we can detect more alliteration than accuracy. What does she mean, 'reluctant, though resolute'? We know Emily had been reluctant to ease her pain and to save her sisters' grief, we know she had been resolute to avoid medical care and to endure a somewhat spectacular illness with stoicism. But at the moment of her death, for what was she reluctant – life or death? She was, it seems, reluctant for death. 'Resolute' suggests that she forced herself to die, against her natural instincts; almost that she could live or die at will. This is a prevalent theme in Emily Brontë comment; the implication that Emily's illness and death were willed by herself is frequent. This, no doubt, is what she herself wished to believe; but it was not so. Emily Brontë succeeded on the whole in conveying to posterity the idea that she was superhuman.

It may be that Emily was, from 1847 onward, unbalanced in mind, and that this disaster fell more severely upon her during her last months. It does seem that she really believed herself to be superhuman, and in some way free to will or not to will death from a fatal disease. Of course it is said that consumption has an optimism of its own; but Emily does not give the impression of optimism. Her refusal of medical care, of any assistance, and her agonized attempts to move about as usual, show rather an effort to combat the fact of her illness: she appears to have felt that it only existed if she acknowledged it; if she ignored it, the infection would disappear. Nor does the manner of death convey the idea of death-wish: such a condition would not call forth those dramatic qualities which she displayed. She was the centre of attention during her illness; she attracted the silent horror of her sisters at her persistent refusal of any kind of help or alleviation; she knew they were aghast at this perverted martyrdom. These factors do not lend themselves to interpretation of a wish for death, but rather, a distorted wish for life – a wish to be observed as an autonomous, powerful sufferer.

As she was the author of this daily spectacle, we must conclude either that her mind was exceptionally tortured, or that it was exceptionally perverted. We have no grounds for thinking that Emily was a daemonic or vicious woman. She was latterly, it seems, 'possessed' – not with daemonic possession, but with delusions of her own powers, perhaps the early symptom of some more serious mental disease. This is not incompatible with the employment of rational powers; it was the more bewildering to the sisters as she did not speak of delusions; she enacted them. Branwell may perhaps have suffered from a similar calamity; in his case he wove stories around himself.

Charlotte, puzzled by Emily's conduct, seems to have tacitly accepted the situation as it was presented. Emily was more than human; she was some strange, rugged, monolithic mystic. In *Shirley*, Charlotte gives a somewhat nauseating example of what presumably she considered to be Emily's mysticism; Emily herself did it better, in verse. Did Anne, like Charlotte, take Emily seriously? Anne makes no direct comment, but since the character Shirley is cited as an accepted picture of Emily, it may not be out of place to refer to a poem by Anne. It should be said that Anne's verse, apart from her Gondal pieces, was unfeignedly autobiographical. And so when we read a poem by Anne we may assume she refers to some time or place or person within her present experience.

In the poem, which is dated August 1811 and entitled 'The Three Guides', Anne addresses three Spirits in turn, of Earth, of Pride, and of Faith. This is a strangely juxtaposed set of personifications; one wonders why Earth and Pride, a concrete and an abstract concept, should stand together as significant alternatives to Faith. But conventionally she rejects first the Spirit of Earth, then the Spirit of Pride, and finally accepts the Spirit of Faith. It is a very long poem, and a few stanzas must suffice to indicate the tone. The style so resembles Emily's, and is employed towards demolishing a theme so typical of Emily, that one cannot avoid the conclusion that Anne was guying Emily in more ways than one.

> Spirit of Pride! thy wings are strong,
>   Thine eyes like lightning shine;
> Ecstatic joys to thee belong,
>   And powers almost divine.
> But 'tis a false destructive blaze
>   Within those eyes I see;
> Turn hence their fascinating gaze;
>   I will not follow thee!
>
> ....

(Spirit of Pride replies)

Cling to the earth, poor grovelling worm;
'Tis not for thee to soar
Against the fury of the storm,
Amid the thunder's roar!
There's glory in that daring strife
Unknown, undreamt by thee;
There's speechless rapture in the life
Of those who follow me!

(The poet speaks)

Yes, I have seen thy votaries oft,
Upheld by thee their guide,
In strength and courage mount aloft
The steepy mountain-side;
I've seen them stand against the sky,
And gazing from below,
Beheld thy lightning in their eye,
Thy triumph on their brow.

Oh, I have felt what glory then,
What transport must be theirs!
So far above their fellow-men,
Above their toils and cares;
Inhaling Nature's purest breath,
Her riches round them spread,
The wide expanse of earth beneath,
Heaven's glories overhead!

But I have seen them helpless, dashed
Down to a bloody grave,
And still thy ruthless eye has flashed,
Thy strong hand did not save.
....

What shall they do when night grows black;
When angry storms arise?
Who now will lead them to the track
Thou taught'st them to despise:

It needs no elaborate method of detection to see Emily and her heroes in this. Anne, it is to be feared, disapproved strongly of Emily in the last two years of her life: she recognized her sister's remote brooding, her 'speechless rapture', her scorn, her assumption of 'powers almost divine' – she saw these attitudes together as 'a false destructive blaze', the self-consuming sin of pride. There is no other reason why Anne should choose this particular manifestation of pride, unless she had Emily in mind. It was certainly right along the lines of Emily's thought and, from what we see, her conduct. But Anne could not have lacked sympathy with her lifelong friend in her last illness. We learn of her 'silent grief' after Emily's death.

It is doubtful if there was much element of choice for Emily if she had become obsessed by the ideology of her work. Theorizing probably did her untold harm, as she had instinctively guessed when she did all she could to avoid having her mind organized in school life. She shows all the symptoms of such an obsession in her last months; Anne's earlier moralizing seems beside the point in so tragic an affair. Something corrosive had laid hold of Emily's being, and it seems most likely that if she had not died of consumption, she would have died mentally deranged. For she lacked the equilibrium of the pure mystic.

It might be worth noting that, if Anne's poem was an allegorical account of her experience of Emily in her later years, the 'pity and contempt' which Emily is wrongly said to have bestowed on Anne all her life, was amply forthcoming at the later date, towards the whole household.

Most of Emily's early biographers believed, with Charlotte, in Emily's self-styled superwomanism. It was enough for Charlotte and her successors to know Emily as a 'stoic', to be filled with admiration and awe. But while it is true that nobility of character may be an element in pure stoicism, it does not at all follow that stoicism, in its accepted sense of mere physical endurance, is in every circumstance noble. Anne's orthodox ethics would, of course, reject stoicism as a self-reliant rule of conduct, although in fact she herself displayed in her illness the virtues of 'Christian stoicism'. But even as a purely social ethic, it was as incorrect to ascribe to the stoicism demonstrated by Emily the nobility proper to the true stoical spirit, as it would be to call a man who tied himself to a stake, and himself lit the faggots, a martyr. Before any gesture or attitude can partake of glory, the circumstances are the decisive factor. Nobility is not the automatic attribute of stoicism. Was Emily Brontë's tormented and tormenting procession to the grave a noble death? It was not; neither was it an ignoble death, since, whichever way one looks at it, Emily Brontë was a woman distracted in her later days by a torturing self-image, a fantastic unattainable ideal. Her spirit suffered under this affliction infinitely more than did her body under disease.

Her former days were happy. She was the least neurotic of the sisters (it is sometimes said that neurotics are not the most likely to end insane). The impression given by Emily up to 1845 is that she held, understandably, an image of herself as a creative writer; and towards this image she continually struggled. She had not only genius, she had the will to write; and not only the will to write, the desire to profess creative writing – to follow a recognized vocation. That she concealed her work from Charlotte does not mean she did not intend to reveal any of her work to the world. Anne, for one, was privy at least to her Gondal writings. Emily seems to have been a severe critic of her own work, since she presumably destroyed the bulk of it. Her reluctance to produce her poems in 1845 may simply indicate that she did not consider her work ready for publication.

What is so striking about Emily in comparison with her sisters is her single-mindedness in connection with her writing. All her 'peculiarities' and prejudices and domestic considerations are explicable only if her work is placed in the centre of her existence. She would, in her birthday papers, grow lyrical over hard cash, because it meant leisure to write. She was unhappy when sent to school in her late teens, because the type of work she desired to do was not possible to a rationally trained mind. She revolted against her teaching job, because she was there, again, subject to a discipline alien to her work. She accepted the first plan for the Brontë school, because it was the easiest way to economize freedom, and hence to do her work in peace. The Brussels school she deliberately did not reject; but she revolted bitterly against her own acceptance of it, because her mind would be directed away from its proper path. Against the second plan for the 'Misses Brontës' Establishment', Emily did not even trouble to revolt, she simply declared she would not teach; she was financially independent, and did not see the need to employ herself other than with her writing and her household tasks. She suggested that she could not understand why the others did not feel the same. When Charlotte proclaimed Emily's devotion to the moors, there is no doubt this was true; of course she loved the moors, her dog, her sisters, her home; but she loved her work most.

The further question frequently arises, whether Emily was ever in love. Now, both Anne and Charlotte were, at various times, interested in men as potential husbands. Both fell in love; both pined for the return of love from the men concerned. Their feelings towards these men were not outside the normal conditions of love, with the exception of Charlotte's first passion for M. Héger, which differed from her more cautious attachment to her publisher, George Smith, in that she could not include within her aspirations, marriage with M. Héger. Otherwise, love as known to Anne and Charlotte included the elements of marriage, sex, companionship, children, womanly status and many others, combined as one emotion – love; and as one desire – to be loved in like manner.

Emily had no understanding of this at all. It was not because she had no experience of it: the mere potentiality for an experience makes for understanding; a lesser imagination than Emily's could have grasped the essentials of love between man and woman, given the potentiality. Emily had none. Her work reveals this lack of understanding, and in fact she substitutes for normal love, a different type of attachment which helps to give her writings their impressive distinction. So far as Emily herself is concerned, she appears to have been a born celibate. This is not to repeat what has elsewhere been suggested, that she was sexless, far less is it to suggest she was some kind of freak. It is questionable if there is such a phenomenon as a sexless human being; there are people of either sex and there are hermaphrodites. Emily was definitely of the female sex. A few people remembered, after her death, that she had masculine qualities, but this seems to be pure myth, built up from an overlying impression of *Wuthering Heights*. Her latter-day 'stoicism' possibly contributed to this idea, although in fact, her final gestures were more feminine than masculine.

One thing strikes one about Emily Brontë's relationship with people: she had no apparent desire for any company outside her family, and in particular, Anne. This may be evidence of her single-minded absorption in her work. But she did not therefore have any opportunity to realize her potentiality for the type of love she did understand, and which is apparent in her poems and in *Wuthering Heights*. It is a type of love peculiar to the natural celibate, and is a relationship which the current usage of the term

'Platonic' does not altogether describe. It is not a passionless friendship. It is a passionate and in many ways mystical union; and is described in early writings to the effect that the individuals are so closely united that they share as it were a single soul, without losing personal identity, not a common state, but not a freakish one. The partners were nearly always of the same sex, and that such a relationship presupposes celibacy (not merely continence) will make clear its great distinction from homosexuality. Such mystical intimacies were of course more frequent in the Middle Ages than they were in Emily's time. In the nineteenth century, the celibate man or woman was looked upon as one who had renounced the 'desires of the flesh'. The question whether the type of natural celibacy described above was conditioned by, or conditioned a desire for the relationship with which it is invariably associated, is probably unanswerable. The important factors are that such unions are not uncommon to earlier history, and that some people were celibates by special calling. Along with this is found a common desire for an Absolute in one sense or another.

From the evidence of the love relationships which Emily depicts in her work, it appears that this was the type of love she could understand. In *Wuthering Heights* of course, there is no conjoining Absolute to give us the sense that Cathy and Heathcliff are involved in any system more significant than each other. To that extent they appear as lost souls. Most likely, the only type of love Emily could have become personally engaged in, was that of a mystical union, but she was unlikely to find a soulmate at Haworth, indeed she did not look. Desire, either to possess or to be desired by another of such nature, is not the motive of this type of union. Desire for the Absolute, which Emily possessed in passionate quantity, is seen as the motive. In an earlier age, Emily Brontë would most possibly have thrived in a convent. (Charlotte compared her to a nun.) Emily was, perhaps, somewhat born out of time in this respect.

To a post-Freudian age, it is difficult to convey, without giving rise to scepticism, the nature of the type of celibate it is suggested Emily was, in the context of the term 'passion' which rightly adheres to her name. The most precise definition might be that she was a passionate celibate (and it should be clear that a frustrated spinster is not meant). So far as this affected her life, it is unlikely that Emily would have been an 'unfulfilled' woman. The later dissatisfaction and disintegration in her life arose from her shift of apprehension of the Absolute; she shifted it from an objective to a subjective position. She became her own Absolute; so that she would be forced to expend passion, adoration, worship, contemplation, on herself, a destructive process since sources of replenishment are not self-generated. Emily's inspiration would dry up; her whole being would be thrown into disorder. But formerly, she had all the forces of her 'passionate great genius', as Swinburne expresses it, to expend upon the universe at large, from which she also drew nourishment.

To the extent that she universalized every relationship between man and woman which she touched, she was unrealistic. But her genius was most positively manifest in its most distinctive forms, when she offered these universalized forms of love: 'I *am* Heathcliff' cries Cathy in *Wuthering Heights*. The proposition may not appeal to us for the reasons already described; the lovers are not really significant enough, they have not the magnitude to convince us that such a rare relationship is in any way justified; for they have no purpose beyond their mutual love to measure by. However, Cathy's is a definitive statement: the men and women in Emily's work are apt to meet each other on the grounds of a passionate mutual identity, which excludes sexual union. We are not told this, but it is a generally observed fact that Emily's men and women appear to be 'sexless'.

'She died in a time of promise', Charlotte said. Not exactly; the time of promise was past. But there had been a time of tremendous promise, so great that Emily's work represents a very small fulfilment of it. And this work is by no means negligible. Much of Emily's promise was in fact fulfilled. It is tempting to wonder if the promise might have been more richly fulfilled, and, what is more important, if Emily could have maintained her equilibrium, had she stood out against Charlotte and refused to go to school at Brussels. To fix on the Brussels episode as the one decisive factor in Emily's misfortunes may be unwise; it may be almost superstitious. It does not, however, seem to have been a very lucky move, and Charlotte, acting for the best all round, certainly did not see any connection between taking Emily to Brussels, and her helpless daily watch over her dying sister. And in the end, even had Emily's genius flowered for a longer period, there was still to be faced the early death common to the Brontë children, whom Emily had once said were 'all stout and hearty'.

Appendix

Emily Brontë's stay in Brussels presents one of the most puzzling aspects of her career. She was seen there in a new light, which is reflected in the remarks made by those with whom she came in contact. These have been considered in their context; but since Emily's encounter with M. Héger at Brussels has also seemed to the present writer to have marked a turning point in Emily Brontë's development, the following account by M. Héger might prove illuminating. This account was given by him to Mrs Gaskell some fifteen years after Emily's stay in Brussels. It compares strangely with the remarks he made on Emily at the actual time; but although he shows a new respect and admiration for the now famous novelist, there is also some moral censure which is new. In particular, we get a picture of Emily far from 'timid' as he at first described her, defiant and resentful towards his teaching methods; we see her speaking her mind. We cannot entirely rely upon M. Héger's testimony; moreover, against his first statement we must place the fact that he made it to her father, and would thus hardly enlarge upon her supposed shortcomings; against his second account, we must weigh the intervening fifteen years, during which period Emily's work had become known.

Although, therefore, the following report of what M. Héger said cannot be taken as direct evidence, the reference to Emily Brontë's open resistance to his methods of teaching can be seen to support the conclusions independently arrived at in the preceding essay.

> M. Héger, who had done little but observe, during the few first weeks of their residence in the Rue d'Isabelle, perceived that with their unusual characters, and extraordinary talents, a different mode must be adopted from that in which he generally taught French to English girls. He seems to have rated Emily's genius as

something even higher than Charlotte's; and her estimation of their relative powers was the same. Emily had a head for logic, and a capability of argument, unusual in a man, and rare indeed in a woman, according to M. Héger. Impairing the force of this gift, was her stubborn tenacity of will, which rendered her obtuse to all reasoning where her own wishes, or her own sense of right, was concerned. 'She should have been a man – a great navigator,' said M. Héger in speaking of her. 'Her powerful reason would have deduced new spheres of discovery from the knowledge of the old; and her strong, imperious will would never have been daunted by opposition or difficulty; never have given way but with life'. And yet, moreover, her faculty of imagination was such that, if she had written a history, her view of scenes and characters would have been so vivid, and so powerfully expressed, and supported by such a show of argument, that it would have dominated over the reader, whatever might have been his previous opinions, or his cooler perceptions of its truth. But she appeared egotistical and exacting compared to Charlotte, who was always unselfish (this is M. Héger's testimony); and in the anxiety of the elder to make her younger sister contented, she allowed her to exercise a kind of unconscious tyranny over her.

After consulting with his wife, M. Héger told them that he meant to dispense with the old method of grounding in grammar, vocabulary, etc., and to proceed on a new plan – something similar to what he had occasionally adopted with the elder among his French and Belgian pupils. He proposed to read to them some of the master-pieces of the most celebrated French authors (such as Casimir de la Vigne's poem on the "Death of Joan of Arc," parts of Bossuet, the admirable translation of the noble letter of St. Ignatius to the Roman Christians in the *Bibliothèque Choisie des Pères de l'Eglise*, etc.), and after having thus impressed the complete effect of the whole, to analyse the parts with them, pointing out in what such or such an author excelled, and where were the blemishes. He believed that he had to do with pupils capable, from their ready sympathy with the intellectual, the refined, the polished, or the noble, of catching the echo of a style, and so reproducing their own thoughts in a somewhat similar manner.

After explaining his plan to them, he awaited their reply. Emily spoke first; and said that she saw no good to be derived from it; and that, by adopting it, they should lose all originality of

> thought and expression. She would have entered into an argument on the subject, but for this, M. Héger had no time.[1]

If these are Emily's words, they support, too, the conclusion that Emily thought of herself consistently as a writer. A young woman training to be a governess would hardly have gone to such trouble to protect her 'originality of thought and expression' from outward discipline.

M.S.

[1] From E.C. Gaskell's *Life of Charlotte Brontë*, 1857.

4

Selected Poems of Emily Brontë

The scene of *Wuthering Heights*, including the original farmhouse
(*by courtesy of Walter Scott*)

Penistone Crags, the trysting place of Cathy and Heathcliff
(*by courtesy of Walter Scott*)

Introduction

A panegyric by Swinburne on Charlotte Brontë[1] devotes to minor attention to Emily, and a negotiation of some tortuous sentences will reward the reader with a statement so elementary that to draw attention to it might seem unnecessary, were it not that sometimes Emily Brontë's creative *genre* seems in danger of being misdefined. Extensive references to Emily Brontë as mystic, as poet of Christianity, as heretic, as heathen, as intellectual thinker, as psychical hermaphrodite, as emotional writer, have all been made in this century, with some justification. It has also been suggested, without justification, that she was a lesbian, and that she was an intellectual writer. (This latter definition is here rejected since a distinction must be made between her intellect and her mode of writing.) But emphasis on any one of these aspects of her mind or nature, however diverting, may prove misleading, for none presents her as a creative writer in her integrity.

Charlotte Brontë's rhetorical and praiseworthy posthumous note on her sister notwithstanding, it was Swinburne possibly, who most exactly located the essence of Emily Brontë, and strangely enough, it was he who expressed it in the most concise terms: 'There was a dark unconscious instinct as of primitive nature-worship in the passionate great genius of Emily Brontë.'

Swinburne here noted three of the most important factors in her work: her *instinctiveness*, of a 'dark unconscious' order; her pantheism and its particular type – that of *primitive* nature-worship; and her *passion*.

Emily Brontë's approach to life, to people, places and things, was manifest in her work in quite original, because in so instinctive a way. That is also true of her approach to the literature of her

[1] *A Note on Charlotte Brontë*, 1877.

past, for though it must be apparent that she was indebted to her reading of many poets earlier than and including Cowper, Burns, Wordsworth, Byron and Scott, she did not derive their various influences in any but an instinctive way. It would be surprising to find that she annotated, even mentally, the books she read; rather did she submit to the experience of her reading, allowing it to infiltrate, to become part of, her senses. Her instinct may be said to have acted as a filter through which the varied modes and feelings of the past achieved that purification necessary to her own poetic genius.

With the instinctive quality of her thought and expression, her pantheistic conception of life is closely associated. Her vision of nature was, as Swinburne wrote, a primitive one; her longing to become part of and one with the earth was not such that her intellect, more advanced, as is usually the case, than her instincts, could easily accede to.

O thy bright eyes must answer now,
When Reason, with a scornful brow,
Is mocking at my overthrow;
O thy sweet tongue must plead for me
And tell why I have chosen thee!
Stern Reason is to judgment come
Arrayed in all her forms of gloom:
Wilt thou my advocate be dumb?
No, radiant angel, speak and say
Why I did cast the world away;
Speak, God of Visions, plead for me,
And tell why I have chosen thee!

Thus she invoked her 'God of Visions', the nature-image that welded her being into unity; to this interrogation by her intellect, the only answer lies in her own definition of the possessing spirit, 'Thee, ever-present, phantom thing – My slave, my comrade and my king'. She did not find in nature, as did the Wordsworthians, a source merely of spiritual consolation or a philosophical springboard. Nor did she seek a moral lesson from nature, since her God of Visions represented a force which neither preached at nor indulged her, but simultaneously obeyed, befriended, challenged and enthralled. It was a conception of nature subject to no moral laws of the external world; it was a paradoxical, yet not chaotic concept, for the spirit of nature and its retinue, as conceived by her, observed their own peculiar *mores* operating on a transcendental plane. Her poetry was as much a product of the conflict between this and the outer world – of her sense of exile from her natural home, as was her obvious misanthropy.

'Emily Brontë's outlook is not immoral, but it is pre-moral', writes Lord David Cecil.[1] 'It concerns itself not with moral standards, but with those conditioning forces of life on which the naïve erections of the human mind that we call moral standards are built up.' So that, while she, alike with nature, was moved by and was faithful to a strange and unique system of being, this was not entirely unrelated to external modes of behaviour. It was, in fact, their primitive basis: her originality of ideas and expression derived truly from origins.

Emily Brontë's occupation of a world existing in a transcendental dimension may lead to the conclusion that she was a mystic. But if she is so defined, it must be added that she was a mystic of passion, for passion informs the tempo and feeling of all her creative writing. Yet, once more, this was not the passion of the outward world, but was the vital and prevailing attribute of Emily Brontë's exceptional view of life. In her can be seen, as Arthur Symons described it, 'the paradox of passion without sensuousness'. To interpret this passion that drives and directs her work as a reflection of her own or some other human being's objective experience, would be to misjudge the whole disposition of her thought. Arthur Symons might have reconciled his paradox had he considered how pre-human is her passion and her sensuousness; for the feelings and susceptibilities of Emily Brontë's creation are representative and archetypal rather than individual and specific as are human responses. It might be true to say that, had the events of her outward life evoked any great degree of emotional acknowledgment from her, the passion of her writings must have been of a much more chastened, less idealized, less emphasized order.

Emily Brontë died in 1848 in the thirty-first year of her life. The most gifted of a talented family, daughter of a clergyman, she received a good education according to current standards, tried school-teaching without success, and attended a finishing school in

[1] 'Emily Brontë and *Wuthering Heights*', in *Early Victorian Novelists*, 1934. Though written with special reference to *Wuthering Heights*, this work presents an insight into Emily Brontë's mind, invaluable to readers of her poetry.

Brussels for some months; she wrote a novel and a considerable number of poems, and caught a chill at her brother's funeral which led to her death of consumption at Haworth Parsonage, where she had spent most of her days. That is the factual record of her existence, of which little more is known.

But what of the thoughts, the spirit and temperament, the fierce and radiant genius that she embodied? Charlotte Brontë tells us,

> In Emily's nature the extremes of vigour and simplicity seemed to meet. Under an unsophisticated culture, inartificial tastes, and an unpretending outside, lay a secret power and fire that might have informed the brain and kindled the imagination of a hero; but she had no worldly wisdom; her powers were unadapted to the practical business of life. . . .

Charlotte was often deceived by her own eloquence, yet, despite the fact that her letters often speak of Emily as being contentedly engaged in the 'practical business of life' – in housework, for example, Charlotte's words describe most convincingly such a mind as created *Wuthering Heights*.

Most readers of Brontë biography will know of the extraordinary imaginative activity of the Brontë family in childhood. Charlotte, Branwell, Emily and Anne, deprived at an early age of their mother, governed by a competent, if somewhat chilly aunt, and by a father elsewhere preoccupied, were largely free to find amusement in their own populous imaginations. Thus they came first to invent a series of adventure tales in which all four participated, and then to commit these games to writing with such prolific industry that today those of Charlotte and Branwell, fill two large volumes of the *Shakespeare Head Brontë*. The two eldest children, Charlotte and Branwell, seem later to have formed a literary alliance, while Emily collaborated likewise with Anne. Though the legends, romances and poems of Angria – the fabulous territory conceived by Charlotte and Branwell – are fortunately extant, those of Gondal, the country of the two younger Brontës' devising, remain to us only in the adult poems of Emily and Anne. For, long after the childhood partnership of Charlotte and Branwell had ceased, Emily and Anne continued to people their dream world with heroic, exotic figures, with whose loves, wars and destinies they became so closely involved that, in fact, they played the Gondal game all their lives; and this close association between

Emily and Anne is one which many biographers have, in the present writer's opinion, underestimated. As we know from the messages they wrote to each other every four years in the ritualistic form of 'birthday papers', a strong sympathy existed between the two sisters: Anne, to whose lesser (though not inconsiderable) talent Emily provided a rich and vital stimulus, appears as Emily's confidante; Emily, as her younger sister's spiritual partisan.

Both Emily and Anne wrote poems that can be placed into the categories of 'Gondal' and 'personal'; the former do not, of course, describe their actual experiences. The isolated parsonage, exposed to the Yorkshire moorland, provided no such exhilaration, no such energetic scene of action such as their Gondal poems portray; rather did their home's bare setting supply a negative contribution to their work, in failing to distract. Emily's Gondal poems are among her finest. Derived not from outward but from inner experience, they are as personal to her as are her 'personal' poems. The Gondal characters, 'Julius Brenzaida', 'Alexander of Elbe', 'Augusta Geraldine Almeda', 'Rosina' and others, are caused to speak and act their parts, but Emily's own convictions, her judgments and all her tragic intimations, are implicit in their words and actions.

Throughout her poetry, the image of imprisonment and the vision of release by death prevail. Imprisonment she would equate with life; death represented her rehabilitation with nature. Death, for her, was not annihilation but a very positive force; not good, not evil, but at once the autonomous power whose victim she was, the submissive spirit whose victor.

There is a poem by Emily Brontë, as perfect a lyric as the nineteenth century produced, which seems strangely to have been ignored by anthologists. 'There let thy bleeding branch atone' has received little attention apart from being wrongly ascribed to Anne Brontë by an editor who later amended his sad fault. The import of this poem is not immediately recognizable since it belongs to the Gondal cycle whose framework can only be guessed. Nevertheless its atmospheric immediacy is undeniable; the diction is felicitous and pure; and its poetic idea – the association of a limb torn from a tree with the rough severance of an image from the memory – conveys the unusual degree of passion, embodied in traditional lyric formality, that makes this poem an outstanding one. The reason why such an important poem should have attracted scant notice is not, possibly, a matter of taste or opinion, but of the way in which Emily Brontë's critics have come to regard her; it is a question of what we are looking for, one that dictates what we shall find, and that affects the appreciation of all her work.

For in general, she is looked upon as a meteoric phenomenon, as a great romantic hermit, or as a profoundly individual heretic. Indeed, she was all these things. But for our own time, Emily Brontë is perhaps best seen as a part of the tradition of English poetry; and we shall not derive great advantage and pleasure from her work unless we notice and appreciate its traditional aspects.

Like Burns or Clare, Emily Brontë was an example of genius flourishing in isolation. It was this very physical and spiritual isolation that had a salutary effect on her writings: it was an isolation from the influences of contemporaneous social modes and from literary circles. But she was not isolated from literature; her solitary leisure was not spent entirely in day-dreaming and the composing of high fantasy, for Emily Brontë was a reader. While engaged in baking, we are told, she would have a book propped before her; she would enter a room full of people to snatch a book and retreat. The predominant characteristics of her poetry show how well she had assimilated her reading, and because the influence of Victorian literary criticism was never superimposed upon her, because her literary education was not drawn from current fashions, her assimilation of literature was instinctive, her natural discrimination and taste unadulterated. Like Burns or Clare, she is a poet in whom the tradition is manifest in an inevitable, because in so effortless, a way.

Now of *Wuthering Heights*, Lord David Cecil has justly written:

> So far from being the incoherent outpourings of an undisciplined imagination, it is the one perfect work of art amid all the vast and varied canvases of Victorian fiction.
>
> It seems odd that it should be so, considering the circumstances of its creation, considering that Emily Brontë's craftsmanship was self-taught, and that she evolved its principles unassisted by a common tradition.

There is no common tradition in which *Wuthering Heights* can be fixed, so far as the English novel is concerned. But does not the unique situation occur, in that Emily Brontë's novel is fed from traditional sources through the channels of her poetry? For, as many critics have observed, it is towards *Wuthering Heights* that her poems converge; they achieve fruition in that most poetic of structures.

It would be difficult to believe that the author of the lines,

> Is he upon some distant shore
> Or is he on the sea
> Or is the heart thou dost adore
> A faithless heart to thee?

or of 'Douglas's Ride', was not acquainted with the border ballads. Scott, whom we know to have been a favourite source of reading in the Brontë household, had done much, with his 'Minstrelsy of the Scottish Border', to revive during the first part of the nineteenth century the interest aroused earlier by Percy's '*Reliques*'.

Not only do Emily Brontë's prototypal warriors and defiant female figures comply with the ballad tradition, but her tempo and metres, her phraseology, her occasional brutal irony, testify to her knowledge of ballad formulae. 'Douglas's Ride', for all it owes to 'John Gilpin' and possibly 'Tam O' Shanter', is so technically and suggestively indebted to the earlier forms, even in its conventional fireside opening, that it is, in fact, an excellent piece of ballad pastiche. Many of her Gondal pieces acquire their ballad flavour less directly. 'And now the house-dog stretched once more' has something of Cowper's handling of the classical couplet, eminently suited to the narrative; while the Marmionesque sense of chivalry, the recognition of family loyalties which take precedence over private friendships in 'Come, the wind may never again', is reminiscent of Scott's tenor of thought.

But Emily Brontë's poems are not entirely of the bardic type. In sentiment, in form and in diction, they more often resemble Elizabethan and Jacobean lyrics: 'Fall, leaves, fall; die, flowers, away/ Lengthen night and shorten day.' The cadence echoes the seventeenth century, and only her acute auditory sensibility could have captured it. No later poet but Tennyson might have been capable of this lyric, though not of its final paradox, a fusion of the ballad influence with the lyric convention, and a strong metaphysical content: 'I shall smile when wreaths of snow/Blossom where the rose should grow.' The metaphysical lyric, in fact, achieved in Emily Brontë its most important development since Shelley.

There is also evidence in Emily Brontë's verse of the romantic naturalism of her own time: 'The violet's eye might shyly flash' suggests the precision of Wordsworth. And though there is scarcely a poem by her that does not bear an implicit tribute to other poets, these various influences are not transparent. They are blended with instinctive craftsmanship within the structure of her individual style; for Emily Brontë's own nobility of utterance, her manipulation of sounds, her percipient use of feminine endings, and her variable rhythms, direct and modulate all other elements.

It is her technical assimilation of influences that distinguishes her poetry, that endows it with the intensity, the emotional and somewhat ominous aura, which we associate with her as with no other poet: 'House to which the voice of life shall never more return/ Chambers roofless, desolate, where weeds and ivy grow.' Even in this earlier poem she achieved her characteristic tension with certainty and without conscious effort.

Many factors combine to condition the particular tendencies of a poet's style. In Emily Brontë we may well find some explanation of her strange, ebb-and-flow rhythms and her solemn, attenuated lines, in her own personality. For in these her pantheism is latent: her rhythms resemble the sweeping moorland and her language resounds with the storm and cataract.

Note: The poems are here arranged in chronological order. I have, for the most part, followed C.W. Hatfield's punctuation (in the use of which Emily Brontë was characteristically eccentric) as it appears in his edition of the poems from the manuscripts.

I do not, however, subscribe to Hatfield's suggestion that the last poem in this book was written by Charlotte Brontë and presented by her to the public as one of Emily's in order to 'help bring the public to a better understanding of Emily's work'. Apart from the extreme inadequacy of Hatfield's argument in favour of this theory, it is, I think, completely refuted by the internal evidence of the poem: Charlotte Brontë was not, as a poet, of that fibre which produced the lines, 'The earth that wakes one human heart to feeling/Can centre both the worlds of Heaven and Hell.'

Emily Brontë sometimes gave titles to her poems and at other times she did not. The principle followed in this selection is that where Emily Brontë has named a poem, her title is given; where she has not done so, the first line is given for a title. The poems headed 'A.G.A.', 'A.A.' and other initials belong to the Gondal cycle, the initials standing for various names of Gondal legendary characters.

M.S.

A Selection of Poems by *Emily Brontë*

I AM THE ONLY BEING WHOSE DOOM

I am the only being whose doom
No tongue would ask, no eye would mourn;
I never caused a thought of gloom,
A smile of joy, since I was born.

In secret pleasure, secret tears,
This changeful life has slipped away,
As friendless after eighteen years,
As lone as on my natal day.

There have been times I cannot hide,
There have been times when this was drear,
When my sad soul forgot its pride
And longed for one to love me here.

But those were in the early glow
Of feelings since subdued by care;
And they have died so long ago
I hardly now believe they were.

First melted off the hope of youth,
Then fancy's rainbow fast withdrew;
And then experience told me truth
In mortal bosoms never grew.

'Twas grief enough to think mankind
All hollow, servile, insincere;
But worse to trust to my own mind
And find the same corruption there.

THE SUN HAS SET, AND THE LONG GRASS NOW

The sun has set, and the long grass now
Waves drearily in the evening wind;
And the wild bird has flown from that old grey stone,
In some warm nook a couch to find.

In all the lonely landscape round
I see no sight and hear no sound,
Except the wind that far away
Comes sighing o'er the heathy sea.

A.G.A.

Sleep brings no joy to me,
Remembrance never dies;
My soul is given to misery
And lives in sighs.

Sleep brings no rest to me;
The shadows of the dead
My waking eyes may never see
Surround my bed.

Sleep brings no hope to me;
In soundest sleep they come,
And with their doleful imagery
Deepen the gloom.

Sleep brings no strength to me,
No power renewed to brave,
I only sail a wilder sea,
A darker wave.

Sleep brings no friend to me
To soothe and aid to bear;
They all gaze, oh, how scornfully,
And I despair.

Sleep brings no wish to knit
My harassed heart beneath;
My only wish is to forget
In the sleep of death.

I'M HAPPIEST WHEN MOST AWAY

I'm happiest when most away
I can bear my soul from its home of clay
On a windy night when the moon is bright
And the eye can wander through worlds of light –

When I am not and none beside –
No earth nor sea nor cloudless sky –
But only spirit wandering wide
Through infinite immensity.

ALL HUSHED AND STILL WITHIN THE HOUSE

All hushed and still within the house;
Without – all wind and driving rain;
But something whispers to my mind
Through rain and through the wailing wind,
    Never again.
Never again? Why not again?
Memory has power as real as thine.

A.G.A.

Why do I hate that lone green dell?
Buried in moors and mountains wild,
That is a spot I had loved too well
Had I but seen it when a child.

There are bones whitening there in the summer's heat,
But it is not for that, and none can tell;

None but one can the secret repeat
Why I hate that lone green dell.

Noble foe, I pardon thee
All thy cold and scornful pride,
For thou wast a priceless friend to me
When my sad heart had none beside.

And leaning on thy generous arm,
A breath of old times over me came;
The earth shone round with a long-lost charm;
Alas: I forgot I was not the same.

Before a day – an hour – passed by,
My spirit knew itself once more;
I saw the gilded vapours fly
And leave me as I was before.

OLD HALL OF ELBË

Old Hall of Elbë, ruined, lonely now;
House to which the voice of life shall never more return;
Chambers roofless, desolate, where weeds and ivy grow;
Windows through whose broken arches the night-winds
 sadly mourn;
Home of the departed, the long-departed dead.

A.A.

Fall, leaves, fall; die, flowers, away;
Lengthen night and shorten day;
Every leaf speaks bliss to me
Fluttering from the autumn tree.
I shall smile when wreaths of snow
Blossom where the rose should grow;
I shall sing when night's decay
Ushers in a drearier day.

DOUGLAS'S RIDE

Well, narrower draw the circle round,
And hush that organ's solemn sound;
And quench the lamp, and stir the fire
To rouse its flickering radiance higher;
Loop up the window's velvet veil
That we might hear the night-wind wail;
For wild those gusts, and well their chimes
Blend with a song of troubled times –

SONG

What rider up Gobelrin's glen
Has spurred his straining steed,
And fast and far from living men
Has pressed with maddening speed?

I saw his hoof-prints mark the rock
When swift he left the plain;
I heard deep down the echoing shock
Re-echo back again.

From cliff to cliff, through rock and heath,
That coal-black courser bounds;
Nor heeds the river pent beneath,
Nor marks how fierce it sounds.

With streaming hair and forehead bare
And mantle waving wide,
His master rides; the eagles there
Soar up on every side;

The goats fly by with timid cry,
Their realm so rashly won,
They pause – he still ascends on high;
They gaze – but he is gone.

O gallant horse, hold on thy course!
The road is tracked behind –

Spur, rider, spur, or vain thy force;
Death comes on every wind.

Roared thunder loud from that pitchy cloud?
From it the torrents flow;
Or woke the breeze in the swaying trees
That frown so dark below?

He breathes at last, when the valley is past;
He rests on the gray rock's brow –
What ails thee, steed? At thy master's need,
Wilt thou prove faithless now?

No; hardly checked, with ears erect,
The charger champed his rein,
Ere his quivering limbs, all foam beflecked,
Were off like light again.

Hark; through the pass, with threatening crash,
Comes on the increasing roar!
But what shall brave the deep, deep wave –
The deadly path before?

Their feet are dyed in a darker tide
Who dare those dangers drear;
Their breasts have burst through the battle's worst,
And why should they tremble here?

Strong hearts they bear, and aims as good,
To conquer or to fall;
They dash into the boiling flood,
They gain the rock's steep wall –

"Now, my bold men, this one pass more,
This narrow chasm of stone,
And Douglas, for our sovereign's gore,
Shall yield us back his own."

I hear their ever-nearing tread
Sound through the granite glen;

There is a tall pine overhead
Laid by the mountain men.

That dizzy bridge, which no horse could track,
Has choked the outlaw's way;
There, like a wild beast, he turns back,
And grimly stands at bay.

Why smiles he so, when far below
He sees the toiling chase?
The ponderous tree sways heavily
And totters from its place.

They raise their eyes, for the sunny skies
Are lost in sudden shade;
But Douglas neither shrinks nor flies –
He need not fly the dead.

A.G.A.

For him who struck thy foreign string,
I ween this heart hath ceased to care;
Then why dost thou such feelings bring
To my sad spirit, old guitar?

It is as if the warm sunlight
In some deep glen should lingering stay,
When clouds of tempest and of night
Had wrapt the parent orb away.

It is as if the glassy brook
Should image still its willow fair,
Though years ago the woodman's stroke
Laid low in dust their gleaming hair.

Even so, guitar, thy magic tone
Has moved the tear and waked the sigh,
Has bid the ancient torrent flow
Although its very source is dry!

SONG BY JULIUS BRENZAIDA TO G.S.

Geraldine, the moon is shining
With so soft, so bright a ray;
Seems it not that eve, declining,
Ushered in a fairer day?

While the wind is whispering only,
Far – across the water borne,
Let us in this silence lonely
Sit beneath the ancient thorn.

Wild the road, and rough and dreary;
Barren all the moorland round;
Rude the couch that rests us weary;
Mossy stone and heathy ground.

But when winter storms were meeting
In the moonless, midnight dome,
Did we heed the tempest's beating,
Howling round our spirits' home?

No; that tree with branches riven,
Whitening in the whirl of snow,
As it tossed against the heaven,
Sheltered happy hearts below –

And at Autumn's mild returning
Shall our feet forget the way?
And in Cynthia's silver morning,
Geraldine, wilt thou delay?

HOW STILL, HOW HAPPY!

How still, how happy! Those are words
That once would scarce agree together;
I loved the plashing of the surge,
The changing heaven, the breezy weather,

More than smooth seas and cloudless skies

And solemn, soothing, softened airs
That in the forest woke no sighs
And from the green spray shook no tears.

How still, how happy! Now I feel
Where silence dwells is sweeter far
Than laughing mirth's most joyous swell
However pure its raptures are.

Come, sit down on this sunny stone:
'Tis wintry light o'er flowerless moors –
But sit – for we are all alone
And clear expand heaven's breathless shores.

I could think in the withered grass
Spring's budding wreaths we might discern;
The violet's eye might shyly flash
And young leaves shoot among the fern.

It is but thought – full many a night
The snow shall clothe those hills afar
And storms shall add a drearier blight
And winds shall wage a wilder war,

Before the lark may herald in
Fresh foliage twined with blossoms fair
And summer days again begin
Their glory-haloed crown to wear.

Yet my heart loves December's smile
As much as July's golden beam;
Then let us sit and watch the while
The blue ice curdling on the stream.

LINES

The soft unclouded blue of air,
The earth as golden-green and fair
And bright as Eden's used to be:
That air and earth have rested me.

Laid on the grass I lapsed away,
Sank back again to childhood's day;
All harsh thoughts perished, memory mild
Subdued both grief and passion wild.

But did the sunshine even now
That bathed his stern and swarthy brow,
Oh, did it wake – I long to know –
One whisper, one sweet dream in him,
One lingering joy that years ago
Had faded – lost in distance dim?

That iron man was born like me,
And he was once an ardent boy:
He must have felt, in infancy,
The glory of a summer sky.

Though storms untold his mind have tossed,
He cannot utterly have lost
Remembrance of his early home –
So lost that not a gleam may come;

No vision of his mother's face
When she so fondly would set free
Her darling child from her embrace
To roam till eve at liberty:

Nor of his haunts, nor of the flowers
His tiny hand would grateful bear
Returning from the darkening bowers,
To weave into her glossy hair.

I saw the light breeze kiss his cheek,
His fingers' mid the roses twined;
I watched to mark one transient streak
Of pensive softness shade his mind.

The open window showed around
A glowing park and glorious sky,
And thick woods swelling with the sound
Of Nature's mingled harmony.

Silent he sat. That stormy breast
At length, I said, has deigned to rest;
At length above that spirit flows
That waveless ocean of repose.

Let me draw near: 'twill soothe to view
His dark eyes dimmed with holy dew;
Remorse even now may wake within,
And half unchain his soul from sin.

Perhaps this is the destined hour
When hell shall lose its fatal power
And heaven itself shall bend above
To hail the soul redeemed by love.

Unmarked I gazed; my idle thought
Passed with the ray whose shine it caught;
One glance revealed how little care
He felt for all the beauty there.

Oh, crime can make the heart grow old
Sooner than years of wearing woe;
Can turn the warmest bosom cold
As winter wind or polar snow.

A.G.A. TO THE BLUEBELL

Sacred watcher, wave thy bells!
Fair hill flower and woodland child!
Dear to me in deep green dells –
Dearest on the mountains wild.

Bluebell, even as all divine
I have seen my darling shine –
Bluebell, even as wan and frail
I have seen my darling fail –
Thou hast found a voice for me,
And soothing words are breathed by thee.

Thus they murmur, "Summer's sun

Warms me till my life is done.
Would I rather choose to die
Under winter's ruthless sky?

"Glad I bloom and calm I fade;
Weeping twilight dews my bed;
Mourner, mourner, dry thy tears –
Sorrow comes with lengthened years!"

AND NOW THE HOUSE-DOG STRETCHED ONCE MORE

And now the house-dog stretched once more
His limbs upon the glowing floor;
The children half resumed their play,
Though from the warm hearth scared away.
The good-wife left her spinning-wheel,
And spread with smiles the evening meal;
The shepherd placed a seat and pressed
To their poor fare his unknown guest.
And he unclasped his mantle now,
And raised the covering from his brow;
Said, "Voyagers by land and sea
Were seldom feasted daintily";
And checked his host by adding stern
He'd no refinement to unlearn.
A silence settled on the room;
The cheerful welcome sank to gloom;
But not those words, though cold and high,
So froze their hospitable joy.
No – there was something in his face,
Some nameless thing they could not trace,
And something in his voice's tone
Which turned their blood as chill as stone.
The ringlets of his long black hair
Fell o'er cheek most ghastly fair.
Youthful he seemed – but worn as they
Who spend too soon their youthful day.
When his glance drooped, 'twas hard to quell
Unbidden feelings' sudden swell;

And pity scarce her tears could hide,
So sweet that brow, with all its pride;
But when upraised his eye would dart
An icy shudder through the heart.
Compassion changed to horror then
And fear to meet that gaze again.
It was not hatred's tiger-glare,
Nor the wild anguish of despair;
It was not useless misery
Which mocks at friendship's sympathy.
No – lightning all unearthly shone
Deep in that dark eye's circling zone,
Such withering lightning as we deem
None but a spectre's look may beam;
And glad they were when he turned away
And wrapped him in his mantle grey,
Leant down his head upon his arm
And veiled from view their basilisk charm.

TO A.G.A.

"Thou standest in the greenwood now
The place, the hour the same –
And here the fresh leaves gleam and glow
And there, down in the lake below,
The tiny ripples flame.

"The breeze sings like a summer breeze
Should sing in summer skies
And tower-like rocks and tent-like trees
In mingled glory rise.

"But where is he today, today?"
"O question not with me."
"I will not, Lady; only say
Where may thy lover be?

"Is he upon some distant shore
Or is he on the sea
Or is the heart thou dost adore

A faithless heart to thee?"

"The heart I love, whate'er betide,
Is faithful as the grave,
And neither foreign lands divide
Nor yet the rolling wave."

"Then why should sorrow cloud that brow
And tears those eyes bedim?
Reply this once – is it that thou
Hast faithless been to him?"

"I gazed upon the cloudless moon
And loved her all the night
Till morning came and ardent noon,
Then I forgot her light –

"No – not forgot – eternally
Remains its memory dear;
But could the day seem dark to me
Because the night was fair?

"I well may mourn that only one
Can light my future sky
Even though by such a radiant sun
My moon of life must die."

SONG

O between distress and pleasure
Fond affection cannot be;
Wretched hearts in vain would treasure
Friendship's joys when others flee.

Well I know thine eye would never
Smile, while mine grieved, willingly;
Yet I know thine eye for ever
Could not weep in sympathy.

Let us part, the time is over
When I thought and felt like thee;
I will be an Ocean rover,
I will sail the desert sea.

Isles there are beyond its billow:
Lands where woe may wander free;
And, beloved, thy midnight pillow
Will be soft unwatched by me.

Not on each returning morrow,
When thy heart bounds ardently
Need'st thou then dissemble sorrow,
Marking my despondency.

Day by day some dreary token
Will forsake thy memory
Till at last all old links broken
I shall be a dream to thee.

LOVE AND FRIENDSHIP

Love is like the wild rose-briar,
Friendship like the holly-tree –
The holly is dark when the rose-briar blooms
But which will bloom most constantly?

The wild rose-briar is sweet in spring,
Its summer blossoms scent the air;
Yet wait till winter comes again
And who will call the wild-briar fair?

Then scorn the silly rose-wreath now
And deck thee with the holly's sheen,
That when December blights thy brow
He still may leave thy garland green.

F. DE SAMARA

WRITTEN IN THE GAALDINE PRISON CAVES TO A.G.A.

Thy sun is near meridian height,
And my sun sinks in endless night;
But if that night bring only sleep,
Then I shall rest, while thou wilt weep.

And say not that my early tomb
Will give me to a darker doom:
Shall these long, agonising years
Be punished by eternal tears?

No, *that* I feel can never be;
A God of *hate* could hardly bear
To watch, through all eternity,
His own creation's dread despair!

The pangs that wring my mortal breast
Must claim from Justice lasting rest;
Enough, that this departing breath
Will pass in anguish worse than death.

If I have sinned, long, long ago
That sin was purified by woe:
I've suffered on through night and day;
I've trod a dark and frightful way.

Earth's wilderness was round me spread;
Heaven's tempests beat my naked head;
I did not kneel: in vain would prayer
Have sought one gleam of mercy there!

How could I ask for pitying love,
When that grim concave frowned above,
Hoarding its lightnings to destroy
My only and my priceless joy?

They struck – and long may Eden shine
Ere I would call its glories mine:
All Heaven's undreamt felicity
Could never blot the past from me.

No, years may cloud and death may sever,
But what is done is done for ever;
And thou, false friend and treacherous guide,
Go, sate thy cruel heart with pride.

Go, load my memory with shame;
Speak but to curse my hated name;
My tortured limbs in dungeons bind,
And spare my life to kill my mind.

Leave me in chains and darkness now;
And when my very soul is worn,
When reason's light has left my brow
And madness cannot feel thy scorn,

Then come again – thou wilt not shrink;
I know thy soul is free from fear –
The last full cup of triumph drink,
Before the blank of death be there.

Thy raving, dying victim see,
Lost, cursed, degraded, all for thee!
Gaze on the wretch, recall to mind
His golden days left long behind.

Does memory sleep in Lethean rest?
Or wakes its whisper in thy breast?
O Memory, wake! let scenes return
That even her haughty heart must mourn!

Reveal, where o'er a lone green wood
The moon of summer pours,
Far down from Heaven, its silver flood,
On deep Elderno's shores.

There, lingering in the wild embrace
Youth's warm affections gave,
She sits and fondly seems to trace
His features in the wave.

And while on that reflected face
Her eyes intently dwell,
"Fernando, sing tonight", she says,
"The lays I love so well."

He smiles and sings, though every air
Betrays the faith of yesterday;
His soul is glad to cast for her
Virtue and faith and Heaven away.

Well, thou hast paid me back my love!
But if there be a God above
Whose arm is strong, whose word is true,
This hell shall wring thy spirit too!

FAR, FAR AWAY IS MIRTH WITHDRAWN

Far, far away is mirth withdrawn;
'Tis three long hours before the morn,
And I watch lonely, drearily:
So come, thou shade, commune with me.

Deserted one! thy corpse lies cold,
And mingled with a foreign mould.
Year after year the grass grows green
Above the dust where thou hast been.

I will not name thy blighted name
Tarnished by unforgotten shame;
Though not because my bosom torn
Joins the mad world in all its scorn.

Thy phantom face is dark with woe;
Tears have left ghastly traces there:
Those ceaseless tears! I wish their flow
Could quench thy wild despair.

They deluge my heart like the rain
On cursed Gomorrah's howling plain;
Yet when I hear thy foes deride
I must cling closely on thy side.

Our mutual foes – they will not rest
From trampling on thy buried breast;
Glutting their hatred with the doom
They picture thine, beyond the tomb.

But God is not like human-kind;
Man cannot read the Almighty mind;
Vengeance will never torture thee,
Nor hunt thy soul eternally.

Then do not in this night of grief,
This time of overwhelming fear,
O do not think that God can leave,
Forget, forsake, refuse to hear!

What have I dreamt? He lies asleep
With whom my heart would vainly weep:
He rests, and *I* endure the woe
That left his spirit long ago.

IF GRIEF FOR GRIEF CAN TOUCH THEE

If grief for grief can touch thee,
If answering woe for woe,
If any ruth can melt thee,
Come to me now!

I cannot be more lonely,
More drear I cannot be!
My worn heart throbs so wildly
'Twill break for thee.

And when the world despises,
When Heaven repels my prayer,
Will not mind angel comfort?
Mine idol hear?

Yes, by the tears I've poured,
By all my hours of pain,
O I shall surely win thee,
Beloved, again!

THERE LET THY BLEEDING BRANCH ATONE

There let thy bleeding branch atone
For every torturing tear:
Shall my young sins, my sins alone,
Be everlasting here?

Who bade thee keep that cursed name
A pledge for memory?
As if Oblivion ever came
To breathe its bliss on me;

As if, through all the 'wildering maze
Of mad hours left behind,
I once forgot the early days
That thou wouldst call to mind.

SHALL EARTH NO MORE INSPIRE THEE

Shall Earth no more inspire thee,
Thou lonely dreamer now?
Since passion may not fire thee
Shall Nature cease to bow?

Thy mind is ever moving
In regions dark to thee;
Recall its useless roving –
Come back and dwell with me.

I know my mountain-breezes
Enchant and soothe thee still –
I know my sunshine pleases
Despite thy wayward will.

When day with evening blending
Sinks from the summer sky,
I've seen thy spirit bending
In fond idolatry.

I've watched thee every hour;
I know my mighty sway,
I know my magic power
To drive thy griefs away.

Few hearts to mortals given
On earth so wildly pine;
Yet none would ask a Heaven
More like this Earth than thine.

Then let my winds caress thee;
Thy comrade let me be –
Since nought beside can bless thee,
Return and dwell with me.

AYE, THERE IT IS!

Aye, there it is! It wakes tonight
Sweet thoughts that will not die
And feeling's fires flash all as bright
As in the years gone by!

And I can tell by thy altered cheek
And by thy kindled gaze
And by the word thou scarce dost speak,
How wildly fancy plays.

Yes, I could swear that glorious wind
Has swept the world aside,
Has dashed its memory from thy mind
Like foam-bells from the tide –

And thou art now a spirit pouring
Thy presence into all –
The essence of the Tempest's roaring

And of the Tempest's fall –

A universal influence
From thine own influence free;
A principle of life intense
Lost to mortality.

Thus truly when that breast is cold
Thy prisoned soul shall rise,
The dungeon mingle with the mould –
The captive with the skies.

HOW CLEAR SHE SHINES!

How clear she shines! How quietly
I lie beneath her silver light
While Heaven and Earth are whispering me,
"Tomorrow wake, but dream tonight".

Yes, Fancy, come, my fairy love!
These throbbing temples, softly kiss,
And bend my lonely couch above
And bring me rest, and bring me bliss.

The world is going – Dark world, adieu!
Grim world, go hide thee till the day;
The heart thou canst not all subdue
Much still resist if thou delay!

Thy love I will not, will not share;
Thy hatred only wakes a smile;
Thy griefs may wound – thy wrongs may tear,
But O, thy lies shall ne'er beguile!

While gazing on the stars that glow
Above me in that stormless sea,
I long to hope that all the woe
Creation knows, is held in thee!

And this shall be my dream tonight –

I'll think the heaven of glorious spheres
Is rolling on its course of light
In endless bliss through endless years;

I'll think there's not one world above,
Far as these straining eyes can see,
Where Wisdom ever laughed at Love,
Or Virtue crouched to Infamy;

Where writhing 'neath the strokes of Fate,
The mangled wretch was forced to smile;
To match his patience 'gainst her hate,
His heart rebellious all the while.

Where Pleasure still will lead to wrong,
And helpless Reason warn in vain;
And Truth is weak and Treachery strong,
And Joy the shortest path to Pain;

And Peace, the lethargy of grief;
And Hope, a phantom of the soul;
And Life, a labour void and brief;
And Death, the despot of the whole!

A DAY DREAM

On a sunny brae alone I lay
One sunny afternoon;
It was the marriage-time of May
With her young lover, June.

From her Mother's heart seemed loath to part
That queen of bridal charms,
But her Father smiled on the fairest child
He ever held in his arms.

The trees did wave their plumy crests,
The glad birds carolled clear;
And I, of all the wedding guests,
Was only sullen there.

There was not one but wished to shun
My aspect void of cheer;
The very rocks grey, looking on,
Asked, "What do you do here?"

And I could utter no reply:
In sooth I did not know
Why I had brought a clouded eye
To greet the general glow.

So, resting on a heathy bank,
I took my heart to me,
And we together sadly sank
Into a reverie.

We thought, "When winter comes again
Where will these bright things be?
All vanished, like a vision vain,
An unreal mockery!

"The birds that now so blithely sing,
Through deserts frozen dry,
Poor spectres of the perished Spring
In famished troops will fly.

"And why should we be glad at all?
The leaf is hardly green,
Before a token of the fall
Is on its surface seen."

Now whether it were really so
I never could be sure;
But as, in fit of peevish woe,
I stretched me on the moor,

A thousand thousand glancing fires
Seemed kindling in the air;
A thousand thousand silvery lyres
Resounded far and near:

Methought the very breath I breathed

Was full of sparks divine,
And all my heather-couch was wreathed
By that celestial shine.

And while the wide Earth echoing rang
To their strange minstrelsy,
The little glittering spirits sang,
Or seemed to sing, to me:

"O mortal, mortal, let them die;
Let Time and Tears destroy,
That we may overflow the sky
With universal joy.

"Let Grief distract the sufferer's breast,
And Night obscure his way;
They hasten him to endless rest,
And everlasting day.

"To Thee the world is like a tomb,
A desert's naked shore;
To us, in unimagined bloom,
It brightens more and more.

"And could we lift the veil and give
One brief glimpse to thine eye
Thou would'st rejoice for those that live,
Because they live to die."

The music ceased – the noonday Dream
Like dream of night withdrew,
But Fancy still will sometimes deem
Her fond creation true.

MY COMFORTER

Well hast thou spoken – and yet not taught
A feeling strange or new;
Thou hast but raised a latent thought,
A cloud-closed beam of sunshine brought

To gleam in open view.

Deep down – concealed within my soul,
That light lies hid from men,
Yet glows unquenched – though shadows roll,
Its gentle ray can not control –
About the sullen den.

Was I not vexed, in these gloomy ways
To walk unlit so long?
Around me, wretches uttering praise,
Or howling o'er their hopeless days,
And each with Frenzy's tongue –

A Brotherhood of misery,
With smiles as sad as sighs;
Their madness daily maddening me,
And turning into agony
The Bliss before my eyes.

So stood I, in Heaven's glorious sun
And in the glare of Hell
My spirit drank a mingled tone
Of seraph's song and demon's moan –
What my soul bore my soul alone
Within its self may tell.

Like a soft air above a sea
Tossed by the tempest's stir –
A thaw-wind melting quietly
The snowdrift on some wintery lea;
No – what sweet thing can match with thee,
My thoughtful Comforter?

And yet a little longer speak,
Calm this resentful mood,
And while the savage heart grows meek,
For other token do not seek,
But let the tear upon my cheek
Evince my gratitude.

COME, WALK WITH ME

Come, walk with me;
There's only thee
To bless my spirit now;
We used to love on winter nights
To wander through the snow.

Can we not woo back old delights?
The clouds rush dark and wild;
They fleck with shade our mountain heights
The same as long ago,
And on the horizon rest at last
In looming masses piled;
While moonbeams flash and fly so fast
We scarce can say they smiled.

Come, walk with me – come, walk with me;
We were not once so few,
But Death has stolen our company
As sunshine steals the dew:
He took them one by one, and we
Are left the only two;
So closer would my feelings twine,
Because they have no stay but thine.

"Nay, call me not; it may not be;
Is human love so true?
Can Friendship's flower droop on for years
And then revive anew?
No, though the soil be wet with tears
How fair so'er it grew;
The vital sap once perishèd
Will never flow again;
And surer than that dwelling dread,
The narrow dungeon of the dead,
Time parts the hearts of men."

SONG

The linnet in the rocky dells,
The moor-lark in the air,
The bee among the heather-bells
That hide my lady fair:

The wild deer browse above her breast;
The wild birds raise their brood;
And they, her smiles of love caressed,
Have left her solitude!

I ween, that when the grave's dark wall
Did first her form retain
They thought their hearts could ne'er recall
The light of joy again.

They thought the tide of grief would flow
Unchecked through future years,
But where is all their anguish now,
And where are all their tears?

Well, let them fight for Honour's breath,
Or Pleasure's shade pursue –
The Dweller in the land of Death
Is changed and careless too.

And if their eyes should watch and weep
Till sorrow's source were dry
She would not, in her tranquil sleep,
Return a single sigh.

Blow, west-wind, by the lonely mound,
And murmur, summer streams,
There is no need of other sound
To soothe my Lady's dreams.

D.G.C. TO J.A.

Come, the wind may never again
Blow as now it blows for us
And the stars may never again shine as now they shine;
Long before October returns
Seas of blood will have parted us
And you must crush the love in your heart, and I, the love in mine!

For face to face will our kindred stand
And as they are so shall we be;
Forgetting how the same sweet earth has borne and nourished all –
One must fight for the people's power,
And one for the rights of Royalty,
And each be ready to give his life to work the other's fall.

The chance of war we cannot shun,
Nor would we shrink from our fathers' cause
Nor dread Death more because the hand that gives it may be dear;
We must bear to see Ambition rule
Over Love, with his iron laws;
Must yield our blood for a stranger's sake and refuse ourselves a tear!

So, the wind may never again
Blow as now it blows for us,
And the stars may never again shine as now they shine;
Next October, the cannon's roar
From hostile ranks may be urging us –
Me to strike for your life's blood, and you to strike for mine.

O THY BRIGHT EYES MUST ANSWER NOW

O thy bright eyes must answer now,
When Reason, with a scornful brow,
Is mocking at my overthrow;

O thy sweet tongue must plead for me
And tell why I have chosen thee!

Stern Reason is to judgment come
Arrayed in all her forms of gloom:
Wilt thou my advocate be dumb?
No, radiant angel, speak and say
Why I did cast the world away;

Why I have persevered to shun
The common paths that others run;
And on a strange road journeyed on
Heedless alike of Wealth and Power –
Of Glory's wreath and Pleasure's flower.

There once indeed seemed Beings divine
And they perchance heard vows of mine
And saw my offerings on their shrine –
But, careless gifts are seldom prized,
And mine were worthily despised;

So with a ready heart I swore
To seek their altar-stone no more
And gave my spirit to adore
Thee, ever present, phantom thing –
My slave, my comrade, and my King!

A slave because I rule thee still;
Incline thee to my changeful will
And make thy influence good or ill –
A comrade, for by day and night
Thou art my intimate delight –

My Darling Pain that wounds and sears
And wrings a blessing out from tears
By deadening me to real cares;
And yet, a king – though prudence well
Have taught thy subject to rebel.

And am I wrong, to worship where
Faith cannot doubt, nor Hope despair

Since my own soul can grant my prayer?
Speak, God of Visions, plead for me,
And tell why I have chosen thee!

THE PHILOSOPHER'S CONCLUSION

"Enough of Thought, Philosopher;
Too long hast thou been dreaming
Unlightened, in this chamber drear
While summer's sun is beaming –
Space-sweeping soul, what sad refrain
Concludes thy musings once again?

"O for the time when I shall sleep
Without identity,
And never care how rain may steep
Or snow may cover me!

"No promised Heaven, these wild Desires
Could all or half fulfil;
No threatened Hell, with quenchless fires,
Subdue this quenchless will!"

– So said I, and still say the same;
– Still to my Death will say –
Three Gods within this little frame
Are warring night and day.
Heaven could not hold them all, and yet
They all are held in me
And must be mine till I forget
My present entity.

O for the time when in my breast
Their struggles will be o'er;
O for the day when I shall rest
And never suffer more!

"I saw a Spirit standing, Man,
Where thou dost stand – an hour ago;
And round his feet, three rivers ran

Of equal depth and equal flow –

"A Golden Stream, and one like blood
And one like Sapphire, seemed to be,
But where they joined their triple flood
It tumbled in an inky sea.

"The Spirit bent his dazzling gaze
Down on that Ocean's gloomy night,
Then – kindling all with sudden blaze,
The glad deep sparkled wide and bright –
White as the sun, far, far more fair
Than their divided sources were!"

– And even for that Spirit, Seer,
I've watched and sought me lifetime long;
Sought him in Heaven, Hell, Earth and Air,
An endless search – and always wrong!

Had I but seen his glorious eye
Once light the clouds that 'wilder me,
I ne'er had raised this coward cry
To cease to think and cease to be –
I ne'er had called oblivion blest,
Not stretching eager hands to Death
Implored to change for lifeless rest
This sentient soul, this living breath.

O let me die, that power and will
Their cruel strife may close,
And vanquished Good, victorious Ill
Be lost in one repose.

R. ALCONA TO J. BRENZAIDA

Cold in the earth, and the deep snow piled above
thee!
Far, far removed, cold in the dreary grave!
Have I forgot, my Only Love, to love thee,
Severed at last by Time's all-wearing wave?

Now, when alone, do my thoughts no longer hover
Over the mountains on Angora's shore;
Resting their wings where heath and fern-leaves
cover
That noble heart for ever, ever more?

Cold in the earth, and fifteen wild Decembers
From those brown hills have melted into spring –
Faithful indeed is the spirit that remembers
After such years of change and suffering!

Sweet Love of youth, forgive if I forget thee
While the World's tide is bearing me along:
Sterner desires and darker hopes beset me,
Hopes which obscure but cannot do thee wrong.

No other Sun has lightened up my heaven;
No other Star has ever shone for me:
All my life's bliss from thy dear life was given –
All my life's bliss is in the grave with thee.

But when the days of golden dreams had perished
And even Despair was powerless to destroy,
Then did I learn how existence could be cherished,
Strengthened and fed without the aid of joy;

Then did I check the tears of useless passion,
Weaned my young soul from yearning after thine;
Sternly denied its burning wish to hasten
Down to that tomb already more than mine!

And even yet, I dare not let it languish,
Dare not indulge in Memory's rapturous pain;
Once drinking deep of that divinest anguish,
How could I seek the empty world again?

DEATH

Death, that struck when I was most confiding
In my certain Faith of Joy to be,

Strike again, Time's withered branch dividing
From the fresh root of Eternity!

Leaves, upon Time's branch, were growing
brightly
Full of sap and full of silver dew;
Birds, beneath its shelter, gathered nightly;
Daily, round its flowers, the wild bees flew.

Sorrow passed and plucked the golden blossom,
Guilt stripped off the foliage in its pride;
But within its parent's kindly bosom,
Flowed forever Life's restoring tide.

Little mourned I for the parted Gladness,
For the vacant nest and silent song;
Hope was there and laughed me out of sadness,
Whispering, "Winter will not linger long".

And behold, with tenfold increase blessing
Spring adorned the beauty-burdened spray;
Wind and rain and fervent heat caressing
Lavished glory on that second May.

High it rose; no winged grief could sweep it;
Sin was scared to distance with its shine:
Love and its own life had power to keep it
From all wrong, from every blight but thine!

Heartless Death, the young leaves droop and
languish!
Evening's gentle air may still restore –
No: the morning sunshine mocks my anguish –
Time for me must never blossom more!

Strike it down, that other boughs may flourish
Where that perished sapling used to be;
Thus, at least, its mouldering corpse will nourish
That from which it sprung – Eternity.

FROM
JULIAN M. AND A.G. ROCHELLE

Yet, tell them, Julian, all, I am not doomed to wear
Year after year in gloom and desolate despair;
A messenger of Hope comes every night to me,
And offers, for short life, eternal liberty.
He comes with western winds, with evening's
wandering airs,
With that clear dusk of heaven that brings the thickest
stars;
Winds take a pensive tone, and stars a tender fire,
And visions rise and change which kill me with desire –

Desire for nothing known in my maturer years
When joy grew mad with awe at counting future tears;
When, if my spirit's sky was full of flashes warm,
I knew not whence they came, from sun or thunder-
storm;

But first a hush of peace, a soundless calm descends;
The struggle of distress and fierce impatience ends;
Mute music soothes my breast – unuttered harmony
That I could never dream till earth was lost to me.

Then dawns the Invisible, the Unseen its truth reveals;
My outward sense is gone, my inward essence feels –
Its wings are almost free, its home, its harbour found;
Measuring the gulf it stoops and dares the final bound!

Oh dreadful is the check – intense the agony
When the ear begins to hear and the eye begins to see;
When the pulse begins to throb, the brain to think
again,
The soul to feel the flesh and the flesh to feel the chain!

Yet I would lose no sting, would wish no torture less;
The more that anguish racks the earlier it will bless;
And robed in fires of Hell, or bright with heavenly
shine,
If it but herald Death, the vision is divine!

NO COWARD SOUL IS MINE

No coward soul is mine
No trembler in the world's storm-troubled sphere
I see Heaven's glories shine
And Faith shines equal arming me from Fear.

O God within my breast,
Almighty ever-present Deity,
Life, that in me hast rest
As I Undying Life, have power in thee.

Vain are the thousand creeds
That move men's hearts, unutterably vain,
Worthless as withered weeds
Or idlest froth amid the boundless main

To waken doubt in one
Holding so fast by thy infinity
So surely anchored on
The steadfast rock of Immortality.

With wide-embracing love
Thy spirit animates eternal years,
Pervades and broods above,
Changes, sustains, dissolves, creates and rears.

Though Earth and moon were gone
And suns and universes ceased to be
And thou wert left alone
Every Existence would exist in thee.

There is not room for Death
Nor atom that his might could render void
Since thou art Being and Breath
And what thou art may never be destroyed.

OFTEN REBUKED, YET ALWAYS BACK RETURNING

Often rebuked, yet always back returning
To those first feelings that were born with me,
And leaving busy chase of wealth and learning
For idle dreams of things which cannot be:

Today, I will not seek the shadowy region;
Its unsustaining vastness waxes drear;
And visions rising, legion after legion,
Bring the unreal world too strangely near.

I'll walk, but not in old heroic traces,
And not in paths of high morality,
And not among the half-distinguished faces,
The clouded forms of long-past history.

I'll walk where my own nature would be leading:
It vexes me to choose another guide:
Where the grey flocks in ferny glens are feeding;
Where the wild wind blows on the mountain side.

What have those lonely mountains worth revealing?
More glory and more grief than I can tell:
The earth that wakes *one* human heart to feeling
Can centre both the worlds of Heaven and Hell.

5

At Emily Brontë's Grave Haworth, April 1961

A BBC TV RECORDING

For many years I was intensely occupied by Emily Brontë – almost haunted. What impressed me was the dramatic shape of her life. It's as if she had consciously laid out the plot of her life in a play called *Emily Brontë*. She might have been invented by Ibsen – a parson's daughter with a terrifying soul. And I was fascinated by her creative mind because it's so entirely alien to my own. She had a wide, sweeping vision of life. She dealt with primitive forces of life and death, and summed up her vision in one major novel, *Wuthering Heights*. My own creative instincts make for minor themes – I like to observe small sections of society in each novel, hoping they will eventually group themselves together like cells in a honeycomb. But novelists who present a total vision in one sweeping gesture delight me enormously. For years I have avoided Haworth because I'm always excited by places associated with great events. I felt this might affect my judgment. Perhaps I was right. A fortnight ago when I went to Haworth, I seemed to fall under a spell. I didn't fully realize until I came to Haworth Parsonage that Emily Brontë, more than any other novelist of her time, fed her genius on the chilly surroundings of the house where she lived and died of consumption at the age of thirty.

Life, death and eternity – these are Emily's great themes, and the scene is set brooding here on her doorstep. Rossetti said of Wuthering Heights 'the action is laid in Hell'.[1] I see what he means, and in a real sense all the harsh grandeur of the novel takes life from the

[1] Letter to William Allingham, 19 September 1854.

eye of Emily's imagination. She often wrote of graves and tombstones, but always in a large, dramatic way. She had a genius for lifting common images from the world around her and giving them vitality and magnitude. She was a woman with a vision of a dark, essential world hidden within the world of appearances. She calls the graveyard 'this dreary outlook'. Yet she was never happy away from home. About sixty thousand dead lie in this churchyard.

My first day here I tried to take a short-cut among the tombs, but I got lost in a sea of stones, and when I found the path it was an odd experience – a bit frightening in an enjoyable sort of way. It was at this point I realized I had left my London personality behind me.

I have always resisted the Brontë pilgrim idea. Thousands of people come here in the summer, so perhaps it's a good thing to pay a visit in the rain to Emily Brontë.

'Spinster of this parish'. To me the dead are just as much a part of a parish as the living. I think that was Emily Brontë's attitude to the dead too. She had a great sense of eternal life and a familiarity with death.

Sometimes I like to go for walks in graveyards. When I go off to the country and stay with friends, I usually try to find the local churchyard and go for a walk there. Sometimes I even write in a churchyard – one has a sense of communion with the dead as people who lived in the same environment as oneself, only at a different time. This graveyard at Haworth was one of the very first things that Emily Brontë ever saw. The view from her nursery window was of this graveyard and afterwards that nursery was her bedroom. And she saw this churchyard and the tombs and the everlasting moors beyond it. No wonder she had a sense of eternity.

In *Wuthering Heights* her two characters, Cathy and Heathcliff have a love that endures beyond the grave. That's how she ends the book.

I don't think Emily herself ever had a love affair or thought of marriage. None of the Brontë records suggest it and there aren't any legends, but she was a passionate woman. All her passion and all the intensity of emotion that was in her nature went into her writings and all her imaginative work. She had a domesticated side to her nature. She would prop a book up in front of her while ironing clothes. How she managed it I don't know. And she went on playing the Gondal game with Anne and recording it in her notebooks long after they were grown up. She enjoyed her home life and being generally full of business. Romantic-minded as she was, she was still a parson's daughter of the nineteenth century. But in her last illness she refused to see a doctor. She refused to die in bed. I don't approve of dying on a horsehair sofa when there is a bed handy, but this was Emily Brontë.

Her readers still thought that she was a man. The reviews grimly enlivened her last weeks:

> We are quite confident that the writer of Wuthering Heights wants but the practised skill to make a great artist. There is singular power in his portraiture of strong passion. He exhibits it as convulsing the whole frame of nature. We strongly recommend all our readers who love novelty to get this story for we can promise them that they have never read anything like it before.

'My sister Emily loved the moors', Charlotte said. Charlotte always took great pains to explain Emily to her readers. It was not the normal thing in the 1840s for a young woman to go traipsing about the countryside, although the habit was beginning to come into fashion. For the same reason Charlotte was almost apologetic about *Wuthering Heights*: 'To those who don't know the out-lying parts of the West Riding', she said, 'the novel must appear a rude and strange production.'

M.S.

6

My Favourite Villain: Heathcliff

BBC WOMAN'S HOUR, 12 OCTOBER 1960

Heathcliff of *Wuthering Heights* is quite the most fascinating villain I have encountered in fiction. He's an arch-villain – there's no doubt at all about his evil nature. And yet he is not repulsive; everything he does is on a scale larger than life; if he lies it is not a petty lie, it is the sort of lie that brings ruin on someone's head; if he steals, it is a whole family heritage that he steals – you couldn't imagine Heathcliff as a shoplifter. In a modern novel such a character would be depicted as at least partially mad. Emily Brontë succeeds in making him perfectly sane and utterly bad.

To me, most villains of nineteenth-century literature are slightly ridiculous, and I think that is because they are little, mean men. Heathcliff is a big bad man, he is never ridiculous, he is terrible, a real Prince of Darkness. He is not only the villain, he is the hero of the book in the grand Homeric sense.

The action, already noted, which according to Rosetti's famous comment is laid in Hell, is in fact laid very much in Yorkshire, in two remote mansions of the moors. It is a small rustic world in which the scene is set, a world of secluded landed gentry whose occupations are shooting and riding and farming. It is Heathcliff who dominates and colours the world of *Wuthering Heights* and who gives it all its fiendish magnitude. He carries hell about with him, so that one feels as the novel progresses, that the familiar moorlands have somehow become dislocated from their natural time and place; the inhabitants are outside of the ordinary law of the land: there are no magistrates to appeal to. An ordinary family quarrel becomes a blood feud; an ordinary love affair becomes a blood pact lasting beyond the grave.

Heathcliff comes on the scene as a foundling child – in Emily

Brontë's words, 'a little black-haired swarthy thing, as dark as if it came from the Devil', and from that moment he radiates an influence on all the other characters, at first attracting hatred and violence and then exerting them.

One thing I find curious is the fact that the mere physical action of the novel is not sufficient to explain Heathcliff's influence and power over the other characters. Sometimes he captures them physically, of course – Isabella Linton, the young Catherine, and even the solid Ellen Dean are at one point or another made prisoners behind locked doors at Wuthering Heights. But sooner or later they find some means of escape – and one has the impression that with their wits about them, they might have escaped sooner. Certainly, they walk very easily into the traps Heathcliff prepares for them. But it is obvious that in Heathcliff's presence, they haven't really got their wits about them. His real power goes far beyond that of property and physical possession: he is a kind of moral hypnotist, and it is in some deep hidden way that he is able to manoeuvre his victims. Even those who find his appearance repulsive, and who, like Edgar Linton, have every reason to detest him, unfailingly permit themselves to fall in with his huge plan for vengeance, they seem almost to collaborate unwillingly with him. And these are not weak characters. Ellen Dean, the housekeeper, and the older Catherine are each in their own way as strong and spirited as Heathcliff. And yet they find him finally irresistible.

Of course, it was brilliant of Emily Brontë to conceive Heathcliff's physical appearance in the way she did. The flesh-and-blood Heathcliff is tremendously endowed with male attractiveness of the dark brooding order. Even Mr Lockwood, whose reactions are so invariably sane and normal, reveals a definite admiration for him: 'He is a dark skinned gipsy, in aspect,' he reports, 'in dress, and manners a gentleman, that is, as much a gentleman as many a country squire: rather slovenly, perhaps, yet not looking amiss with his negligence, because he has an erect and handsome figure, and rather morose. . . .'

And we see the well-bred, dainty Isabella Linton simply throwing herself at him. 'Is Mr Heathcliff a man?' she asks after their marriage, 'If so, is he mad? And if not, is he a devil?' That he is, for the most part, a devil seems to be recognized only by two people in the novel, the older Catherine and Ellen Dean. Catherine puts up a fight before she accepts the destiny of this demon-lover. Ellen Dean's response is a peculiar mixture of homeliness and deep fear.

She has been Heathcliff's childhood nurse, and when she finds him on his deathbed she can hardly keep away from him, terrified as she is. 'I combed his black long hair from his forehead;' she says, 'I tried to close his eyes – to extinguish, if possible, that frightful, life-like gaze of exultation, before anyone else beheld it. They would not shut – they seemed to sneer at my attempts, and his parted lips, and sharp, white teeth sneered too!'

From first to last Heathcliff reveals this power of drawing strange, uncharacteristic passions out of the people of his environment; whenever he appears there is not only trouble, but wild agitation, frantic behaviour and violence. Emily Brontë's sister, Charlotte, wrote of *Wuthering Heights*, 'Whether it is right or advisable to create beings like Heathcliff, I do not know; I scarcely think it is.'

This seems to me an irrelevant statement, because the invention of a being so elemental as Heathcliff doesn't seem to come within the scope of things that are right or advisable. He is what he is: a giant character of high fiction. It is true that one is not likely to meet a full-scale Heathcliff in ordinary life, but that is because most of the Heathcliffs of the civilized world are subject to the restraints of society. In fact, I think we do occasionally come across the type of person Heathcliff represents – the obsessed spirit which infects everyone around it, the moral blackmailer, people of terrifying psychological influence; and of course, in ordinary life, one is best out of their way.

But Emily Brontë was not dealing with ordinary life and society. It is not the plain truth of realism, but the paradoxical truth of imaginative fiction which draws us to the immortal *Wuthering Heights* and its nightmare hero.

M.S.

Principal Works of the Brontës

Innumerable editions have appeared since their first publication (indicated in brackets) and are widely available. Other fragments and stories (generally from the Gondal group of juvenile writings) have been published in limited editions.

Novels

Charlotte Brontë
Jane Eyre (1847)
Shirley (1849)
Villette (1853)
The Professor (1857)

Emily Brontë
Wuthering Heights (1847)

Anne Brontë
Agnes Grey (1847)
The Tenant of Wildfell Hall (1848)

Poems

Charlotte, Emily and Anne Brontë (1846)